15001

1949

cutting gardens

cutting gardens

ANNE HALPIN
BETTY MACKEY

Principal photography by
DEREK FELL

A ROUNDTABLE PRESS BOOK

Simon & Schuster
NEW YORK LONDON TORONTO SYDNEY SINGAPORE TOKYO

SIMON & SCHUSTER
Simon & Schuster Building
Rockefeller Center
1230 Avenue of the Americas
New York, NY 10020

A ROUNDTABLE PRESS BOOK
Directors: Marsha Melnick, Susan E. Meyer
Project editor: Melissa Schwarz
Editorial assistant: Ross Horowitz
Design: Brian Sisco, Harakawa Sisco Inc
Gardens plans: Leah Lococo, Harakawa Sisco Inc
Color illustrations: Wendy Frost

PHOTO CREDITS
Unless otherwise noted below, all photographs are
copyright © Derek Fell

Still-life photography copyright © George Ross;
Cathryn Schwing, photo stylist (pages 38t, 40t, 42t,
45, 46t, 49, 50t, 53, 55, 57, 75, 78, 83, 85, 86)

Agricultural Research Service, USDA (page 144)
Monica Brandies (page 52)
Park Seed Co., Greenwood, SC (pages 95/Avena, 136/Talinum)
Joanna Reed (page 22)
Cynthia Woodyard (pages 44, 46b, 109/Foeniculum)

Printed and bound in Hong Kong

10 9 8 7 6 5 4 3 2 1

Library of Congress Cataloging-in-Publication Data

Halpin, Anne Moyer.
Cutting Gardens / Anne Halpin, Betty Mackey; principal photography by
Derek Fell.
            p.   cm.
   "A Roundtable Press Book,"
   Includes bibliographical references and index.
   ISBN 0-671-74441-0
   1. Flower gardening,   2. Cut flowers.   3. Flowers,   4. Flower
arrangement.   I. Mackey, Betty.   II. Title.
SB405.H33   1993
635.9'66--dc20
                                                    92-7562
                                                    CIP

TO JOHN —
A H

TO TOM —
B M

contents

introduction

For those of us who love to live with flowers, one of the most satisfying experiences is to go out into our gardens on a misty morning and cut dozens of our own fresh blossoms to bring indoors. The jewellike colors, heavenly scents, and myriad shapes and textures of fresh flowers brighten and freshen indoor rooms as nothing else can. A graceful arrangement in a carefully chosen container brings a touch of elegance to any room. And when the bouquet has come from one's own garden, it's like bringing a little piece of paradise indoors. ❧ *Cut flowers are not difficult to grow, and the range of flowers that can be grown for cutting is surprisingly diverse. There are cutting flowers for wet or dry soil, sun or shade. There are annuals, perennials, bulbs, herbs, and ornamental grasses suitable for cutting, as well as vines, shrubs, and even trees. Foliage is important, too. If you are new to gardening you can start with easy-to-grow blossoms such as marigolds and zinnias. More experienced growers can indulge in sublime but finicky favorites like delphiniums and phlox.* ❧ *This book offers instructions for designing, planting, and maintaining a cutting garden, as well as information on how to cut, condition, and arrange the flowers you grow. Whether you are a flower gardener interested in learning about how to create arrangements or a flower arranger who would like to grow your own blossoms, this book can help you get started.*

Tulips and grape hyacinths bring rich colors to spring bouquets.

CHAPTER ONE

planning a cutting garden

Masses of Siberian irises and shasta daisies keep company in this blue and white garden.

The first step toward achieving the cutting garden of your dreams is advance planning. Before you sow a single seed or buy the first plant, take time to consider carefully the kind of garden you want. Planning before you plant will pay off handsomely with more flowers, healthier plants, and a garden that you'll really love. You will also be able to avoid costly and frustrating mistakes. ❧ In this chapter you will find information on every aspect of the planning process. You'll learn how to choose the best location for the garden, and whether you want a garden that's strictly designed to produce flowers for cutting, or whether you want the garden to double as a display garden. ❧ Working with color is an essential part of the process of designing any flower garden. A basic understanding of color theory will make it easier for you to plan effective color schemes. Because you will be growing these flowers to cut and bring indoors, you will also need to think about colors that will work indoors as well as in the garden, and about the way the different flowers are used in arrangements. ❧ Many kinds of plants can supply material for cutting: annuals, perennials, bulbs, ornamental grasses, groundcovers, even trees and shrubs. But before you decide what to grow, it is important to assess the growing conditions on your property—soil, light and shade, moisture, temperature—and choose plants that will thrive in the conditions you have to offer.

What kind of garden for you?

A cutting garden can be whatever size and shape will work well in the space you have available. The most useful garden, from a flower arranger's point of view, is one whose main purpose is to produce flowers for cutting rather than display. But you can certainly cut bouquets from a display garden—and if your garden space is limited, you will want a garden that serves both needs. The garden plans in the next chapter feature gardens that contribute to the landscape as well as to the vase. The only caveat is that in a display garden you must snip individual flowers here and there throughout the garden to leave a balanced assortment of blossoms on the plants, whereas a production garden gives you the freedom to think only of your arrangements.

Cutting tulips of only one color, or a few of every color, will still leave a magnificent display in this garden.

A cutting garden that will double as a display garden can take any number of forms. You can create island beds of various shapes in the middle of a lawn, or plant informal beds that are round, elliptical, kidney-shaped, triangular, or any other shape that strikes your fancy. (If your house and grounds are formal in style, a square or rectangular shape will work best.) You can also plant cutting flowers in a border that divides different areas of your property or separates your property from your neighbor's.

If you have the luxury of enough space to plant a cutting garden that is strictly productive, put the garden in the backyard or some other out-of-the-way spot where it will not be the first sight to greet visitors. If you have a vegetable garden, it is easy to add a few rows of flowers. If you garden in raised beds, consider adding a bed or two primarily for cutting flowers.

In a production garden you can grow annuals from seed and harvest whatever is in bloom without worrying about the garden's appearance. You can plant mixed or leftover tulip bulbs without concern about garden design. Flowers whose foliage is not lovely at all times can be used here. If you like, you can cut flowers right down to the ground to get long stems for bouquets (though this kills or weakens the plants). But remember, a production garden does not have to be entirely out of sight; even with sections in early growth or just harvested, a neatly arranged, healthy, and abundant cutting garden is a charming sight. If you're concerned about aesthetics, plant tall flowers around the edges to hide regimented rows or blocks of plants inside. Even an edging of low-growing plants will create a sense of order.

A production garden can be any size or shape, as long as you can walk or reach into all parts to tend it. This type of garden may also be planted on borrowed space or in a community

The yellow achillea, pink foxglove, silvery lamb's-ears, and other flowers in this garden all thrive in a sunny location.

garden if you have no room at home, especially if you share your harvest. Just keep in mind that the farther from home the garden is located, the more work it will be to maintain it. Tools and supplies will have to be carried to the garden, and watering will be more complicated. You will be more likely to let weeding, watering, and other maintenance chores slide when you're not passing by the garden every day to notice what needs to be done. If you think putting the cutting garden out of sight will also keep it out of mind, forget planting a production garden and instead plan a cutting garden that will look good enough to be located close to the house.

A place for the garden

Most cutting flowers love the sun, so for the widest selection of flowers, plant your cutting garden in a place where it will receive at least six hours of unobstructed sunlight each day. If you don't have a place in full sun, don't despair; you can still grow flowers for cutting. You just have to choose them more carefully.

Consider the shade-tolerant flowers for cutting listed on page 14. Even these flowers like some sun, so pick the brightest location possible for your shady garden; try to find a spot that gets four hours of sun a day, or dappled shade all day.

The key to success in any garden is to choose plants that will flourish in the conditions you have to offer. Plant sun-lovers in full sun, shade-tolerant plants in a partially shaded location, plants that like plenty of moisture around their roots in damp, poorly drained soil, and plants that cannot tolerate "wet feet" in light soil with good drainage. Consider soil pH as well. Some plants, such as azaleas and rhododendrons, need acid soil in order to thrive; others, such as baby's breath, prefer soil that is slightly alkaline or neutral. (We recommend having your soil tested for pH and other qualities; see page 23.) Planting sun-loving flowers in the shade or moisture lovers in dry soil will make your garden much more difficult to maintain and far less rewarding. Strive to work with nature, not against it, when planning a cutting garden. The cultural needs of 200 cutting flowers are described in the Encyclopedia of Plants, starting on page 87.

Laying out the garden

When designing your cutting garden, remember that you will need easy access to all the plants in order to weed, water, fertilize, and harvest flowers. Plant the flowers in rows or blocks and leave space between the units. Mulching the walkways will help keep your shoes clean. As a rule of thumb, allow about 5 feet of row, or a block measuring at least 2 by 2½ feet, for each kind of flower you want to grow.

There are a number of factors to consider as you determine the placement of plants within your garden. To simplify maintenance, group plants according to their cultural requirements; for example, plant together flowers that need to be watered often. If you are growing several perennial flowers that are on the edge of their hardiness region in your garden, group them together in a cold frame in one corner of the garden in case winter protection is needed. (In case you are unfamiliar with the term, a cold frame is a bottomless, boxlike structure with a removable lid of glass or clear plastic, that provides a sheltered environment for plants in cold weather.) Remove the lid of the cold frame as soon as the weather is warm enough in spring, and leave it off until cold weather returns in late fall. If you are growing both annuals and perennials, plant all the annuals together for an easier fall cleanup.

To allow all the plants in the garden to receive the maximum possible amount of sunlight, put the tallest plants in the back, which is, ideally, to the north, so they will not cast shadows on shorter plants. Place the lowest growers in the front, on the south side of the garden, and medium-height plants in the middle.

Paying attention to plant heights is also important visually. Having a gradation of heights from lowest to tallest allows you to see all the plants when you stand outside the garden. It also

A stone wall makes a lovely backdrop for flowers of practically any color.
Planting the tallest plants at the back of the garden
and the shortest plants in the front provides the most effective display,
and enhances the illusion of depth and space.

creates an illusion of greater depth and space in the garden. The lowest plants create the foreground of the composition, the medium-height plants serve as the middle ground, and the tall plants—whether they are tall-growing herbaceous plants such as daylilies, or woody shrubs and trees—form the background.

In a border or bed that will be viewed primarily from one side, put the tallest plants at the back and the shortest plants in the front. In an island bed that will be seen from all sides, the shortest plants go around the outer edges and the tallest plants in the center.

Besides grouping plants by height, you may also find it convenient to group plants by color, particularly in a production garden. Plant rows or blocks of yellow, red, purple, pink, white, and other colors to make it easier to select flowers for arrangements.

Planning for seasonal bloom

To have a selection of flowers available for cutting throughout the outdoor growing season, plant flowers with different blooming times. You can grow bulbs for spring and a variety of perennials for spring, summer, and fall. Many annuals bloom continuously from late spring to early fall if you deadhead them (remove faded flowers) regularly to prevent the plants from setting seeds. Use annuals to fill in any gaps in bloom times. Your choice of cultivars can make a difference, too. For example, there are early, midseason, and late-blooming daffodils within the spring daffodil season and chrysanthemum cultivars that flower in midsummer, late summer, or autumn. For flowers with a limited bloom time, such as larkspur or sweet peas, which bloom for a few weeks in spring, you can stagger the plantings if you live where spring

The diminutive Iris reticulata *is easy to grow, and among the earliest flowers to bloom in spring.*

weather is cool; instead of sowing all the seeds at once, sow them in batches two to three weeks apart.

In most regions of the United States, spring brings primrose, crocus, forsythia, violet, hyacinth, flowering cherry, daffodil, and pansy, and later in the season alchemilla, tulip, lilac, bleeding heart, kerry bush, azalea, rhododendron, iris, sweet william, rose, peony, poppy, and mock orange, among many others, in a riot of crayon colors. Summer is ablaze with bright annuals, plus buddleia, monarda, lythrum, gladiolus, gaillardia, gazania, lobelia, hollyhock, more roses, campanula, astilbe, delphinium, and much more. Autumn arrives with many kinds of asters, dahlias at their peak, Japanese anemone, beauty berry, ornamental grasses, chrysanthemums, Nippon chrysanthemum or Montauk daisy, cimicifuga, boltonia, and the colorful leaves of maple and burning bush. Many annuals continue flowering into fall, and some roses will rebloom if cut back earlier in the season after they first flower. After the late fall frosts, winter show-offs include holly, ornamental grasses, conifers (try variegated pine in a winter wreath or bouquet!), evergreen ferns, and snowberry (*Symphoricarpus*), followed later by witch hazel, snowdrops, pieris, bergenia, and hellebore, which let us know that spring is around the corner.

What to grow

The choice of plants for a cutting garden is extensive, to say the least. You can choose among annuals, perennials, bulbs, vines, herbs, shrubs and trees, and even vegetables. You will, of course, want to include your favorite colors in the garden, while you also consider the decor of your home. What is the style of the architecture? Is your decor formal, contemporary, country? In which rooms would you like to see flowers? On which tables, windowsills, or hearths? What kinds of arrangements will be most appropriate, and what kinds of flowers will you need to create them? Do you want the flower colors to harmonize with or accent the room's decor? Take a leisurely walk through your home and make notes to refer to as you make up your plant list.

In addition to the colors of the flowers you will grow in the cutting garden, consider their form and texture and how you will use them in arrangements. To create interesting, well-composed arrangements, you will want to work with flowers of varying shapes, sizes, and textures. For example, spiky, vertical flowers like salvia and delphinium create upward movement in a floral composition. Round shapes can create the basic structure of a composition—be it triangular, square, round, or fan-shaped—and add mass and stability. Large, fluffy flower plumes like those of astilbe and ornamental grasses have a softening effect in an arrangement, while tiny flowers like baby's breath fill empty spots in the design and give it a finished look. Trailing vines add graceful lines that provide movement and activity. Large, unusual flower forms such as that of calla lilies can be featured in bold, sculptural designs to create a contemporary feel.

Think too about any special containers you plan to use to hold your flowers. You will want to grow the perfect flowers for them. Think about the freshness of daisies in a green glass vase, roses in a pewter bowl, sunflowers in an earthenware pitcher, peonies in Chinese porcelain, or lilacs in a brass spitoon.

Plan your cutting garden so that you have flowers for all of these uses. Each element is discussed in more detail in Chapter Four, Cutting and Arranging Flowers.

Annuals for a cutting garden

Annuals are plants that live their entire life in a single growing season; they bloom the same year they are planted, set seeds, and then die before the year ends. In all but frost-free gardens, tender biennials or perennials, such as geraniums and some salvias, are treated as annuals. These plants flower the first year from seeds or cuttings and are killed by frost in fall. Some hardy but short-lived perennials are also grown as annuals; some types of rudbeckia fit into this category.

Annuals are classified as tender or hardy. Hardy annuals can tolerate a bit of frost, but they usually dislike hot weather; tender annuals are killed by the lightest touch of frost but do well in heat. Sometimes the term *half-hardy annual* is used (especially in British gardening books) to refer to plants that are in between the hardy and tender types in cold tolerance.

✓ Hardy annuals such as candytuft, calendula, and baby's breath should be sown in early spring in most zones (but in late fall in warm climates). Plant other annuals after the danger of frost is past in spring.

Since most annuals for cutting range in height from 1 to 4 feet, they fit into the lower and middle visual levels of the garden. Annuals are great for providing a continuous stream of cut

This cutting garden of annuals includes tall, pink spider flowers, sunny marigolds, the small purple powderpuffs of ageratum, and brilliant red scarlet sage.

The bright reds and purples of these annuals are toned down by the deep green of the hedge behind them.
The garden includes impatiens, nicotiana, dahlias, and spider flowers.

flowers in rich colors for weeks or months from a small space in the garden, for the plants continue to bloom in their attempt to produce seeds before the season ends.

Larkspur, zinnia, China aster, tithonia, celosia, salvia, snapdragon, *Coreopsis tinctoria*, lisianthus, ageratum, cosmos, emilia, nigella, gaillardia, cleome, and Shirley poppy are just a few of the annuals that are valuable as cut flowers. Plant them to brighten and fill gaps in mixed borders with perennials and small shrubs or in beds by themselves. Most annuals can be grown from seed in about eight weeks, but some take longer. For the best cut flowers, choose long-stemmed standard or tall varieties whenever possible rather than dwarf bedding types.

Biennials for a cutting garden

Biennials provide a burst of frenzied bloom that is perfect for cutting gardens. After growing for one season, they pass the winter as neat, flat rosettes of leaves and then shoot up masses of flowers as the days become warmer and longer in their second spring. Sweet william, canterbury bells, and forget-me-nots are classic biennials. After flowering, biennials go to seed rapidly; they often self-sow, and self-sown seedlings are quick to germinate and will bloom the next year. Learn to recognize the seedlings of biennials in your garden. You can even create a self-sowing garden of biennials for cutting if you are able to weed it without removing the volunteer seedlings. Short-lived perennials such as foxglove, hesperis, and hollyhock are often grown as biennials, as are some of the hardiest annuals, including bachelor's button or cornflower, larkspur, and Shirley poppy. Most biennials fit into the lower and middle visual levels of a garden composition.

There is a lot of disagreement among garden writers about which plants are hardy annuals and which are biennials. That's because so many plants that grow quickly from seed during cool weather are somewhat flexible: If they don't have time to bloom and set seed their first year, they try to make it through winter to bloom the next year.

Biennials are especially easy to grow in unheated greenhouses and cold frames, as well as in warmer climates. In these sheltered conditions, plant them in autumn. Farther north, plant biennials in early summer.

This summer border of sun-loving perennials blooms in colors as warm as the season. Golden coreopsis and achillea are accented with red Flanders poppies and magenta rose campion.

Perennials for a cutting garden

Like garden clocks, herbaceous perennials, such as peonies and chrysanthemums, rebloom predictably at the same time each year. The tops die back to the ground in winter, but the plants return from the roots in the spring. Most perennials get larger and stronger each year, forming clumps as their roots spread and new stems grow. Many also self-sow and produce new plants from seed. When the plants begin to lose their vigor, they need to be dug and divided. The older parts of the plants are discarded, and the younger, vital parts are replanted. Because perennials are long-lived and tend to increase in number, it is wise to invest in superior varieties and cultivars.

Choose perennials for cutting that have strong stems that are neither too long nor too short, and that bloom prolifically either in a short burst or over a longer period. There are varieties at all

height levels, so these plants can fit into the foreground, the middle ground, or the background of the garden. Some perennial species, such as bearded iris, have been so extensively hybridized that they are available in a dizzying array of heights, sizes, and colors. Specialists grow entire gardens of irises, lilies, daylilies, chrysanthemums, and other extensively hybridized flowers.

There are perennial flowers for every season, starting with hellebore and primroses in late winter and early spring, and progressing through the season with pulmonaria, Iberis sempervirens, columbine, lily of the valley, and heuchera. As spring warms into summer, phlox, iris, peony, and poppies abound. Summer brings campanula, daylily, astilbe, lilies, liatris, heliopsis, coreopsis, and many more. Stars of the autumn cutting garden include boltonia, asters, and autumn chrysanthemums.

For many gardeners, a cutting garden just wouldn't be complete without perennials. Remember, though, that some perennials, such as peony and iris, bloom for only a few weeks, so the plants will not rebloom after the flowers are cut, although the foliage remains in the garden. If garden space is limited, these short-blooming plants may not be your best source of cut flowers.

Some perennials are hardier in winter than others, and there is tremendous variation in site preferences (wet, dry, sunny, shady) among the different types. Too much summer heat or insufficient cold in winter kills some kinds of perennials, especially in warm-climate gardens. But there are perennials suited to any climate and practically any location, no matter how difficult the growing conditions. Be sure to check the cultural requirements of all plants you are considering for your cutting garden, but be especially careful when choosing perennials since you will have them for a long time. The Encyclopedia of cutting flowers in this book provides information on each plant's environmental needs.

Bulbs for a cutting garden

Bulbs are valued in a cut flower garden for their jewellike colors and their ability to grow quickly and reliably. A true bulb contains an embryonic plant that is simply waiting for the right conditions to begin growing; they are almost foolproof, at least the first year you plant them. When you plant a daffodil bulb in the fall, your spring flower is already inside the bulb and will emerge as soon as the necessary moist, warm periods give it the signal.

Bulbs and bulblike plants are tender or hardy perennials that grow from enlarged rootlike structures that store food and are dormant for part of the year. While the form of a bulb looks distinct enough, some plants from corms, tubers, and rhizomes are sold along with other perennials in garden centers and catalogs, because their treatment in the garden is similar (bearded iris and daylilies are examples). Flowers from other corms, tubers, and rhizomes are generally sold and classed with bulbs (crocuses and dahlias fall into this category). They tend to be grouped with bulbs if they are easy to store in their dormant phase and can be sold bare-rooted, in soilless market packs.

Like other perennials, plants from bulbs and similar structures differ from one another in their preferred climate, soil, and exposure. Some bulbous plants (calla lilies and gladiolus, for example) from tropical regions are tender and will not stand frost; in all but warm climates they are grown as annuals or are dug and stored indoors over winter. Others (hyacinth, crocus, lilies, tulips, wood hyacinths, and most narcissus) are well adapted to cold climates but not to excessive heat.

Bulb plants come in a range of heights, from a few inches tall to eye level, but most fit into the lower and middle visual levels of the garden.

For cutting, bulbs that will be discarded after they flower once (some gardeners use tulips this way) can be planted closer together than the package directions indicate. But most hardy bulbs are exceptionally long-lived and easy to care for, so it pays to let them come back year after year.

Cutting flowers in your landscape

Trees and shrubs in your landscape can supply flowering branches, leaves, and berries to use in arrangements along with the flowers and foliage from your cutting garden. You will find a number of flowering woody plants covered in the Encyclopedia.

Wildflowers from fields, meadows, and woodlands (where you have obtained permission to pick, of course) can also add to the choice of materials for arranging.

Learn which of your existing landscape plants can contribute to indoor arrangements. Ivy, often used as a groundcover, also makes a graceful addition to bouquets. A mountain ash planted as a shade tree provides cuttable white flowers in spring and orange berries in fall. A vigorous climbing rose such as 'Madame Isaac Pereire' simultaneously screens an unwanted view and produces masses of fragrant blossoms for indoor bouquets. Azalea, rhododendron, hibiscus, magnolia, lilac, crabapple, cherry, pyracantha, and many other landscape favorites all yield lots of flowers for bouquets. These plants are also large enough to supply cutting

Not all cut flowers have to come from the garden. Field daisies and other wild plants can be lovely additions to informal bouquets.

materials without leaving conspicuous gaps in the garden. Branches from many shrubs and trees can also be cut and forced into early bloom indoors.

Climbing or trailing vines suited to cutting make delightful additions to arrangements. In addition to ivy, try vinca, thunbergia, honeysuckle, and jasmine. Herbs like dill, fennel, and mint can add texture and fragrance. Ornamental grasses, with their graceful leaves and fluffy or tasseled flower plumes, are also quite pretty in arrangements. And don't overlook diminutive ground-cover plants like lily of the valley and sweet violets; they are quite charming in small, intimate bouquets.

Assessing your growing conditions

The easiest way to a successful cutting garden is to choose flowers that will perform well in the growing conditions that exist in your garden. The first step in planning the garden is to consider carefully the environment you have to offer. You will need to think about temperature, soil, light, and moisture.

All plants thrive within a specific range of temperatures, according to the climate of their place of origin. When conditions become too hot or too cold for a plant, it will die. Plant hardiness is usually expressed in terms of the coldest temperature the plant can tolerate. Various maps have been devised to divide the United States into hardiness zones based on average minimum winter temperatures. The most widely used map is put out by the U.S. Department of Agriculture (USDA), and a newly revised version was published in 1990 (see page 144). Knowing your hardiness zone is helpful when you are ordering perennials, bulbs, and other plants from mail-order seed and nursery companies. Most gardening books also express hardiness in terms of zones, and we have used them for convenience in the Encyclopedia. If you are unsure which zone you live in, you can call your local

USDA County Extension office to obtain this information.

Be aware that hardiness zone maps are very general and cannot account for local conditions. You must think about the conditions right in and around your garden—the microclimates—as well as your zone when deciding which plants will survive in your garden. A garden located near a body of water, or in a place that is protected on the north side, will be warmer than most others in the same zone. A garden at the bottom of a hill, where cold air collects in pockets, or situated high on a windy slope will be colder than the average. Depending on your local conditions, you may be able to grow plants that are not generally considered hardy in your area, or you may not be able to grow some plants that work perfectly well for other gardeners in your zone.

Plants are also affected by the average maximum temperature, but there is no widely accepted classification system for heat-hardiness. We have tried to include this information in the Encyclopedia wherever possible.

The ideal garden soil for most cutting flowers drains well but also retains sufficient moisture for roots and is of good fertility and rich in organic matter. A good loam (soil that contains a mixture of sand, silt, and clay particles) has a crumbly texture and a rich, dark color—sort of similar to chocolate cake. It is naturally fertile and holds moisture well without becoming excessively sticky or wet. It is a good idea to test your soil for composition, pH, and nutrient and organic matter content. You can get a soil test through your local County Extension office or from a private soil-testing laboratory, or you can purchase a home test kit at a garden center.

Soil that is unusually high in sand appears pale and gritty. It loses water and fertilizer rapidly, and although it drains well, the overall growing environment it provides is poor and desertlike.

Cacti, succulents, and tough-leaved plants such as yucca are adapted to these harsh conditions and will thrive with little effort on your part. But unless you correct it, this type of soil will not support many kinds of flowers for bouquets. Silicone sands tend to be particularly infertile. Some sands are highly alkaline. To improve sandy soils, work in lots of organic matter and perhaps a bit of clay. To grow cut flowers in this type of soil, you can also add timed-release fertilizers that are not too rich in nitrogen and a water-holding polymer to retain more water for plants.

A site where the soil is rocky and quick to drain needs flowers that can tolerate dry conditions. See the list on page 25 for a selection of drought-tolerant plants.

Soils high in clay make life difficult for most plants as well, by excluding air and holding too much water. On the other hand, they are rich in trace elements and tend to be fertile. During droughts, the clay hardens and cracks into bricklike patches. Simply adding sand to clay soil does not help much: It creates cementlike soil instead. To loosen the texture of heavy clay soil, add garden gypsum or dolomitic limestone and plentiful amounts of humus, such as compost, leaf mold (compost made from shredded leaves), and peat moss, along with coarse builder's sand.

Soil ranges from acidic to alkaline or basic, measured on a pH scale from 0 (the most acidic) to 14.0 (the most alkaline); a measurement of 7.0 is considered neutral. Many cutting flowers and other garden plants grow best in soil with a mildly acid to neutral pH. Soils in northern areas with lots of moisture tend to be acidic, and rhododendrons and wildflowers native to such sites prefer an acid soil with a pH of about 5.0. South-western areas often have alkaline soils because of salts left behind during evaporation. Plants native to these regions tend to prefer pH ranges from 7.0 to 8.0. Many of the annuals that are so useful for cutting are not particular about pH unless it is unusually high or low. Unusual pH needs for specific plants are noted in the Encyclopedia. Although pH can be adjusted slightly, it is wisest to choose plants adapted to the pH you already have. You can raise pH with agricultural lime or lower it with the addition of

A cutting garden can thrive on the banks of a tiny stream when the flowers planted there can tolerate plenty of moisture. Astilbe, veronica, and hosta are some of the plants in this garden.

acid peat moss, aluminum sulfate, or ground sulfur. Changing pH is practical only if the change is not very great and if the area to be changed is not very large.

The amount of light your garden receives is another critical factor in determining which plants to grow. Count the hours of sun that fall on your garden site in summer after the trees have fully leafed out; in early spring, it is easy to under-estimate the amount of shade the trees will cast. Most flowers for cutting grow best with six or more hours of sunshine each day—either full sun or bright par-tial shade. In insufficient light, plants grow tall and leafy and then flop over if they are not staked securely. Good light helps your plants develop the strong stems needed for cut flowers. If the gar-den is to be near a slope or a building, a southern or western exposure with full sun is the most favorable for flowers in most regions. In hot, dry areas, how-ever, northern and eastern exposures may be better for many garden plants, because the added shade is beneficial in reducing stress.

Daylength affects plant growth, too, giving some flowers the signal that it is time to get ready to bloom as the days grow longer, and that it is time to prepare for winter as days grow shorter. The farther north you live, the more pronounced these changes are. In early summer, daylength reaches over twenty hours in parts of Canada, pulling garden flowers into an explosion of bloom. Although the outdoor growing season is short in the

North, gardeners in these cooler climates often do very well with annuals, which bloom like crazy in the longer days.

Plants vary in their need for moisture, but the majority of cutting-garden flowers prefer a moist but well-drained soil. If you live where rainfall is slight, you can help keep moisture in the soil by improving its water-holding capability with the addition of humus, and/or water-grabbing polymers, and a cover of mulch. When you must water, drip irrigation systems are best, because they use water most efficiently, delivering it directly to a plant's root zone. In many areas, water shortages are already common-place, and such shortages will become more widespread in coming years as our supply of unpolluted groundwater dwindles. All gardeners must be concerned about conserving water, even if there is no immediate problem in their area.

A less common but equally difficult problem is boggy soil that is too wet to support the growth of many plants. If your site is poorly drained, you can garden in raised beds and add sand and organic matter to improve the soil. Or you can create a bog garden of such plants as arum lilies, Louisiana iris, willows, royal fern, and Japanese primroses if they are hardy where you live.

DROUGHT-TOLERANT FLOWERS
FOR CUTTING

The following plants can all withstand dry soil to varying degrees. See the Encyclopedia beginning on page 87 for information on the moisture needs of these and other plants.

Achillea	*Euphorbia*
Armeria	*Gaillardia*
Artemisia	*Gazania*
Asclepias, butterfly weed	*Gypsophila*, baby's breath
Coreopsis	*Helianthus*, some sunflowers
Cosmos	*Helipterum*
Echinacea, purple coneflower	*Lavandula*, lavender
Echinops, globe thistle	*Linaria*
Eryngium, sea holly	Rugosa roses
Eschscholzia, California poppy	*Santolina*
Euonymus	*Tropaeolum*, nasturtium

Designing with color

Figuring out a color scheme can be the most enjoyable part of planning a flower garden. Color theory is complex and takes years of study to understand fully. But all of us have our own ideas about the kinds of colors we like to see together. In this section we will look at some basic color theory, but your own tastes will always be your best guide. In the end, the colors in your garden and your arrangements must please you. If the rules of conventional color theory don't satisfy you, break them!

Here are some issues to consider when you begin to think about color schemes for your cutting garden. First, do you prefer subtle, harmonious combinations of colors, or do you like bright, contrasting colors? What is the color scheme in your home? You will want to repeat or complement these colors in your garden to produce flowers that please you when you bring them in the house. Think about the colors of walls and furnishings in the rooms where you want to have floral arrangements, and plant flowers that match or harmonize with those colors, or that create a pleasing contrast. Choose colors for your cutting garden with your interior site in mind, just as you would choose fabrics or works of art for the same area. The Flower Color Guide on page 30 is a helpful planning tool.

One way to achieve a harmonious mix of colors is to grow several varieties of one type of flower—chrysanthemums, for example, or phlox, or Oriental poppies. Species and cultivars of a single flower may differ in color intensity and hue, but they will almost always harmonize with one another. Another way to create harmony is to grow different kinds of flowers in the same

Pink liatris, purple lavender, and pale yellow daylilies combine in a harmonious color scheme in this garden of sun-loving perennials.

color family. Try planting different shades of rose and pink, or of yellow and gold, for example.

If you are looking for striking color contrasts in arrangements and therefore in your garden, there are numerous ways to create them. Complementary colors, which we will discuss a bit later, create the sharpest contrast, and such color schemes can be too jarring for many tastes. Contrasting color schemes usually work best when the brightest, strongest color is used in small amounts as an accent, and the less intense color is spread over a large area to balance the brighter color. For example, if you want to plant deep purple salvia with bright golden coreopsis, plant a little coreopsis and lots of salvia surrounding it.

Indoors or out, the background color and quality of light set the stage for a floral display. Dark colors are best when seen from close up. If viewed from a distance or placed in deep shade, they tend to disappear. Pale, white, and bright colors on the other hand show well against dark backgrounds, such as paneled walls or evergreens. Pastels and white flowers can make shady areas appear lighter, gleaming against a dark background. Pastels are also especially effective in front of stone walls, gray rocks, and hedges and take on a special glow at dusk. But in strong, clear sunlight, pastels may look washed out.

In very sunny gardens and neutral-toned interiors strong, bright colors are more effective. Hot colors are subdued in strong sunlight, but they are not overpowered the way pastels and dark colors are. Brilliantly colored flowers can also be striking against dark foliage, or against a white wall. Dark-leaved plants make dramatic silhouettes against light, pale backgrounds such as light walls or sandy soil.

It also helps to remember that contrasting colors affect one another when planted close together in a garden or combined in a vase. For example, blue flowers cast a yellowish shadow on neighboring blossoms, and red flowers look orangy when they are next to white. Using white as a contrast color softens nearby colors.

It is best to avoid combining very pure contrasting colors. Pure blue and bright yellow, for example, look harsh next to each other. But when the blue is deepened toward violet and the yellow is soft and light, such as the yellow of *Coreopsis verticillata* 'Moonbeam', the combination is exquisite.

One other aspect of color to consider is its warmth or coolness. Warm colors (red, orange, yellow, pink) tend to come forward visually; that is, they appear closer than they actually are. Cool colors (blue, violet, green) recede and look farther away. To create an illusion of depth and space in a very small garden, plant warm-colored flowers in front of cool-colored ones. If your garden is large and is located near the house, the colors of the flowers closest to the house can echo the colors inside the adjacent room to create a visual link between house and garden. A bouquet in a window overlooking a garden of matching flowers is a lovely way to make the link even stronger.

Warm colors are stimulating and active, while cool colors are restful and quiet. For a serene, peaceful effect, plant a garden and create arrangements in blues and purples. For a cheerful but gentle feeling, choose flowers in warm shades of apricot, salmon, and pink, accented with red and purple. Shades that lie between warm and cool—yellow-green or red-violet—can combine the cheerfulness of warm colors with the calm of cool colors.

One final note on color temperature: Warm colors harmonize with one another (yellow-orange, orange, gold, red-orange, and scarlet), and so do cool colors (blue, blue-green, violet, and green). This factor can be important in multicolor gardens and arrangements because the warmth or coolness of a particular tint

can make or break the color scheme. For example, in a mix of pink and blue, which can be quite beautiful, a cool shade of pink will work best. On the other hand, in a mix of pink and red, it's best to use a warm pink.

Color schemes

There are many ways to combine colors in gardens and arrangements, but color schemes can be grouped into four basic types: monochromatic or single-color, analogous or related, contrasting, and polychromatic or mixed.

The simplest scheme for a garden or arrangement is monochromatic—built on a single color. Often a small amount of accent color is used as well. You might want to work with all white flowers, or all red, or all yellow. Single-color schemes work especially well in small gardens and in partial shade, where they impart a feeling of added space, openness, and brightness. Single-color gardens and arrangements need not be boring. You can vary the types of flowers; their heights, shapes, textures, and sizes; and the tones of the color (from bright to dark).

Gardens and arrangements built from related, or analogous, colors are quite harmonious, but they can also be dramatic. Think about a combination of flowers in blue, purple, lavender, and pink, or a range of sunny yellow, yellow-orange, and brilliant orange.

Complementary colors are opposite one another on the color wheel and provide the most striking contrasts. Orange and blue are complementary, as are yellow and violet, and red and green. These combinations can be quite intense, but you can soften them by adding some neutral tones, in a garden or a bouquet. White flowers and silvery foliage both tone down strong contrasts, and using lots of deep green foliage helps as well. Using soft shades of contrasting colors is also effective. In a combination of orange and blue, for instance, if the orange is a muted salmon or peach color, the combination will be gentle and quite beautiful.

As a rule, it is best to avoid putting very strong colors next to each other in an arrangement or in a small garden. A mix of magenta, orange, and purple would be jarring to most eyes.

The other type of color scheme is polychromatic, or mixed colors. A polychromatic garden or arrangement contains any combination of colors that appeals to you. Polychromatic schemes don't appeal to everyone, but they can be quite cheerful. Mixtures of bright pastels—small blossoms of peach, yellow, pink, and lavender, for instance—can look as festive as confetti.

Fragrant flowers

The alluring fragrance of flowers adds to the mystique of indoor bouquets, intensifying perception of their visual appearance. Most flowers and some kinds of foliage have scent, which is strongest while they are still in the garden or freshly picked. As you get to know the distinct personalities of different flowers, you'll know which scents are sweet, spicy, heavy, delicate, lemony, fruity, or heady. You can capture perfumed breezes in your garden by planting scented flowers such as lilies and roses near doorways and windows and within hedged or walled boundaries. The flowers listed at right are especially fragrant; some are always fragrant, some only at night, some during the day, and some only when brushed or touched.

SCENTED FLOWERS FOR CUTTING

Allium
Buddleia, butterfly bush
Calendula
Cheiranthus, wallflower
Clematis
Convallaria, lily of the valley
Dianthus
Freesia
Hamamelis, witch hazel
Heliotropium, heliotrope
Hesperis, dame's rocket
Hyacinthus, hyacinth
Iris, especially I. florentina
Lathyrus, sweet pea
Lavandula, lavender
Lilium, lily
Lobularia, sweet alyssum
Matthiola, stock
Monarda, beebalm
Muscari, grape hyacinth
Myosotis, forget-me-not
Narcissus
Nicotiana, flowering tobacco
Paeonia, peony
Philadelphus, mock orange
Phlox, many species
Polianthes, tuberose
Primula, primrose
Reseda, mignonette
Rosa, rose
Tropaeolum, nasturtium
Verbena
Viola odorata, sweet violet

FLOWER COLOR GUIDE

	white	cream	yellow	orange	peach	red	pink	violet	purple	blue	green	brown
Acanthus species, *(Acanthus)*	●											
Achillea species, *(Yarrow)*	●	●	●	●	●	●	●					
Agapanthus species, *(Lily-of-the-Nile)*	●								●	●		
Ageratum houstonianum, *(Floss Flower)*	●						●	●		●		
Alcea species, *(Hollyhock)*	●	●	●	●	●	●	●	●	●			●
Alchemilla species, *(Lady's Mantle)*			●									
Allium species, *(Flowering Onion)*	●	●	●	●	●	●	●	●	●			
Alstroemeria species, *(Lily of Peru)*	●	●	●	●	●	●	●					
Amaranthus species, *(Joseph's Coat)*			●		●	●	●		●		●	●
Ammi majus, *(Ammi)*	●											
Anaphalis species, *(Pearly Everlasting)*	●	●										
Anemone species, *(Anemone)*	●	●	●			●	●	●	●	●		
Anethum graveolens, *(Dill)*			●									
Anthemis tinctoria, *(Golden Marguerite)*			●									
Antirrhinum majalis, *(Snapdragon)*	●	●	●	●	●	●	●	●	●		●	●
Aquilegia species, *(Columbine)*	●	●	●	●	●	●	●	●	●	●		
Armeria species, *(Thrift)*	●					●	●					
Asclepias tuberosa, *(Milkweed)*	●	●	●	●	●	●						
Aster species *(includes Michaelmas Daisy)*	●		●		●	●	●	●	●	●		
Astilbe species, *(Astilbe)*	●	●			●	●	●					
Begonia species, *(Begonia)*	●	●	●	●	●	●	●					
Bellis perennis, *(English Daisy)*	●	●			●	●	●					
Bergenia species, *(Bergenia, Pig-squeak)*	●				●	●	●		●			
Brunnera macrophylla, *(Brunnera)*										●		

	white	cream	yellow	orange	peach	red	pink	violet	purple	blue	green	brown
Buddleia species, *(Butterfly Bush)*	●					●	●	●	●			
Calendula officinalis, *(Pot Marigold)*		●	●	●	●							
Callistephus chinensis, *(China Aster)*	●	●	●			●	●	●	●	●		
Camellia species, *(Camellia)*	●	●				●	●					
Campanula species, *(Bellflower)*	●	●						●	●	●		
Catananche caerulea, *(Cupid's Dart)*										●		
Celosia cristata, *(Cockscomb)*		●	●	●	●	●	●		●		●	●
Centaurea species, *(Cornflower)*	●	●				●	●	●	●	●		
Centranthus ruber, *(Jupiter's Beard)*						●	●					
Chaenomeles species, *(Flowering Quince)*	●				●	●	●					
Chieranthus chieri, *(Wallflower)*		●	●	●	●	●						
Chrysanthemum species, *(Feverfew, Daisy)*	●	●	●	●	●	●	●		●			
Chrysanthemum *(Parthenium)*	●	●										
Clarkia species, *(Godetia)*	●	●				●	●	●	●			
Clematis species, *(Clematis)*	●	●				●	●	●	●	●		
Cleome hasslerana, *(Spider Flower)*	●								●			
Consolida ambigua, *(Larkspur)*	●					●	●	●	●			
Convallaria majalis, *(Lily-of-the-Valley)*	●						●					
Coreopsis species, *(Coreopsis)*		●	●	●								●
Cornus species, *(Dogwood)*	●	●					●					
Corylus species, *(Hazel)*			●									
Cosmos sulfureus, *(Cosmos)*			●	●		●						
Cosmos tinctoria, *(Cosmos)*	●						●	●	●			
Crocus species, *(Crocus)*	●	●	●					●	●	●		●

Species	white	cream	yellow	orange	peach	red	pink	violet	purple	blue	green	brown
Cytisus scoparius, (Scotch Broom)			●									
Dahlia hybrids, (Dahlia)	○	●	●	●	●	●	●	●	●		●	
Delphinium species, (Delphinium)	○	●					●	●	●	●		
Deutzia gracilis, (Deutzia)	○						●					
Dianthus species, (Carnation, Pink)	○	●	●	●		●	●	●	●			
Dicentra species, (Bleeding Heart)	○	●				●	●					
Digitalis species, (Foxglove)	○	●	●		●	●	●	●	●			
Doronicum species, (Leopard's Bane)			●									
Echinacea purpurea, (Purple Coneflower)							●	●		●		
Echinops species, (Globe Thistle)										●		
Emilia javanica, (Tassel Flower)				●	●	●						
Eremurus species, (Foxtail Lily)	○	●	●	●								
Erica species, (Calluna, Heather, Heath)	○					●	●	●	●			
Eryngium species, (Sea Holly)	○									●		
Eschscholzia californica, (California poppy)	○	●	●	●	●	●	●					
Euphorbia species, (Poinsettia, Spurge)	○	●			●	●	●				●	
Eustoma species, (Prairie Gentian, Lisianthus)	○	●			●	●	●	●	●			
Filipendula species, (Meadowsweet)	○						●					
Foeniculum vulgare, (Fennel)			●									
Forsythia species, (Forsythia)	○		●									
Freesia species, hybrids, (Freesia)	○	●	●	●	●	●	●	●	●			
Fritillaria species, (Crown Imperial, Fritillary)	○	●	●	●		●	●		●			
Gaillardia species, (Blanket flower)		●	●	●		●			●			
Galanthus species, (Snowdrop)	○									●		

Species	white	cream	yellow	orange	peach	red	pink	violet	purple	blue	green	brown
Gazania species, (Gazania)	○	●	●	●	●	●	●					
Genista species, (Broom)			●									
Geranium species, (Geranium)	○					●	●	●	●	●		
Gerbera jamesonii, (Transvaal Daisy)	○	●	●	●		●	●					
Geum species, (Avens)			●	●		●						
Gladiolus hybrids, (Gladiolus)	○	●	●	●	●	●	●	●	●		●	●
Gomphrena globosa, (Globe Amaranth)		●		●		●	●	●	●			
Gypsophila species, (Babysbreath)	○						●					
Hamamelis species, (Witch Hazel)			●	●		●						
Helenium hybrids, (Sneezeweed)		●	●	●		●						●
Helianthus species, (Sunflower)	○	●	●	●		●						●
Helichrysum species, (Strawflower)	○	●	●	●	●	●	●		●			
Heliopsis helianthoides, (Heliopsis)			●									
Heliotropium peruvianum, (Heliotrope)	○								●	●		
Helipterum roseum, (Acroclinium)	○					●	●					
Helleborus species, (Hellebore)	○					●	●		●		●	●
Hemerocallis species, (Daylily)		●	●	●	●	●	●	●	●			
Hesperis matronalis, (Dame's Rocket)	○						●	●	●			
Heuchera species, (Coral Bells)	○	●				●	●				●	
Hosta species, (Funkia, Plantain Lily)	○							●				
Hyacinthoides hispanica, (Wood Hyacinth)	○							●	●	●		
Hyacinthus species, (Hyacinth)	○	●	●	●	●	●	●	●	●	●		
Hydrangea species, (Hortensia)						●	●	●	●	●	●	
Hypericum species, (Hypericum)			●									

Species	white	cream	yellow	orange	peach	red	pink	violet	purple	blue	green	brown
Iberis species, (Candytuft)	●				●	●	●	●				
Impatiens species, (Impatiens, balsam)	●			●	●	●	●	●	●			
Iris species, (Iris)	●	●	●	●	●	●	●	●	●	●		●
Kniphofia species, (Red-Hot Poker)			●	●		●						
Lantana camara, (Lantana)			●	●	●	●						
Lathyrus species, (Sweet pea)	●	●			●	●	●	●	●	●		●
Lavandula species, (Lavender)	●							●	●	●		
Lavatera species, (Mallow)	●					●	●		●			
Leucothoe species, (Leucothoe)	●	●										
Liatris species, (Gayfeather)	●						●	●	●			
Lilium species, (Lily)	●	●	●	●	●	●	●				●	●
Limonium species, (Statice)	●	●	●			●	●	●	●	●		
Linaria species, (Toadflax)	●	●	●	●	●	●	●		●			●
Lobelia species, (Cardinal Flower)	●					●	●	●	●	●		
Lobularia maritima, (Sweet Alyssum)	●					●	●		●			
Lunaria annua, (Honesty, Money Plant)	●							●	●			
Lupinus species, (Lupine)	●	●	●	●	●	●	●	●	●	●		
Lychnis species, (Lychnis, Viscaria)	●			●	●	●	●		●			
Lycoris species, (Spider Lily)						●						
Lysimachia species, (Loosestrife)	●	●										
Lythrum species, (Purple Loosestrife)							●	●	●			
Malus species, (Crab Apple)	●				●	●	●		●			
Matthiola species, (Stock)	●	●	●		●	●	●	●	●			
Mertensia virginica, (Virginia Bluebell)							●	●		●		
Molucella laevis, (Bells of Ireland)											●	
Monarda didyma, (Bergamot)	●				●	●	●	●	●			
Muscari species, (Grape hyacinth)	●									●		
Myosotis species, (Forget-Me-Not)	●						●			●		
Narcissus species, (Daffodil, Jonquil)	●	●	●	●								
Nicotiana alata, (Flowering Tobacco)	●					●	●	●	●		●	
Nigella damascena, (Love-in-a-Mist)	●						●	●	●	●		
Ornithogalum species, (Star-of-Bethlehem)	●									●		
Paeonia species, (Peony)	●	●	●			●	●		●			
Papaver species, (Poppy)	●	●	●	●	●	●	●	●	●	●		
Pelargonium specie, (Geranium)	●				●	●	●	●	●			
Penstemon species, (Penstemon)	●					●	●	●	●	●		
Perilla frutescens, (Perilla)	●								●	●		
Petunia cultivars, (Petunia)	●	●	●		●	●	●	●	●	●		
Philadelphus species, (Mock Orange)	●											
Phlox species, (Phlox)	●				●	●	●	●	●	●		
Physalis alkekengi, (Chinese Lantern)				●							●	
Physostegia virginiana, (False Dragonhead)	●						●	●				
Pieris species, (Andromeda)	●	●										
Platycodon grandiflorus, (Balloon Flower)	●								●	●		
Polemonium species, (Jacob's Ladder)	●						●		●	●		
Polianthes tuberosa, (Tuberose)	●											
Polygonatum species, (Solomon's Seal)		●									●	
Primula species, (Primrose)	●	●	●	●	●	●	●	●	●	●	●	●

Species	white	cream	yellow	orange	peach	red	pink	violet	purple	blue	green	brown
Prunus species, *(Almond, Peach, Cherry)*	○						●					
Pulmonaria species, *(Lungwort)*	○						●	●		●		
Ranunculus species, *(Buttercup)*	○		●	●	●	●	●					
Reseda odorata, *(Mignonette)*	○										●	
Rhododendron species, *(Azalea)*	○	●	●	●	●	●	●	●	●	●		
Rosa species, *(Rose)*	○	●	●	●	●	●	●		●			
Rudbeckia species, *(coneflower)*			●	●							●	●
Ruta graveolens, *(Rue)*			●									
Salpiglossis sinuata, *(Painted Tongue)*			●			●	●		●	●		●
Salvia species, *(Sage)*	○		●			●	●	●	●	●	●	
Santolina species, *(Lavender Cotton)*		●	●									
Scabiosa species, *(Pincushion Flower)*	○	●	●			●	●	●	●	●		
Schizanthus hybrids, *(Butterfly Flower)*	○		●			●	●	●	●			
Scilla species, *(Squill)*	○						●	●	●	●		
Sedum spectabile, *(Stonecrop)*						●	●				●	
Silene species, *(Viscaria, Catchfly)*	○					●	●	●	●	●		
Solidago species, *(Goldenrod)*			●									
Spiraea species, *(Spirea)*	○					●	●	●				
Stokesia laevis, *(Stoke's Aster)*	○							●		●		
Syringa species, *(Lilac)*	○							●	●			
Tagetes species, *(Marigold)*			●	●	●	●						●
Talinum paniculatum, *(Jewels of Opar)*							●					
Thalictrum species, *(Meadow Rue)*	○		●					●	●			
Tithonia rotundifolia, *(Mexican Sunflower)*				●	●	●						
Torenia fournieri, *(Wishbone Flower)*	○			●			●	●		●		
Trachymene coerulea, *(Blue Lace, Didiscus)*										●		
Trollius species, *(Globe Flower)*		●	●	●								
Tropaeolum majus, *(Nasturtium)*		●	●	●	●	●	●					
Tulipa species, *(Tulip)*	○	●	●	●	●	●	●		●			
Verbena species, *(Verbena)*	○					●	●	●	●	●		
Veronica species, *(Veronica)*	○						●	●	●	●		
Viburnum species, *(Viburnum)*	○							●				
Vinca species, *(Periwinkle vine)*	○						●	●		●		
Viola species, *(includes Violet, Pansy, Viola)*	○	●	●	●	●	●	●	●	●	●		●
Zantedeschia species, *(Calla lily)*	○	●	●	●	●		●				●	
Zinnia elegans, *(Zinnia)*	○	●	●	●	●	●	●		●		●	

cutting garden plans

To inspire your garden planning, the following pages contain ten plans for different kinds of cutting gardens. All of these gardens are intended to serve as display gardens as well as sources of flowers for cutting, and they will look beautiful in any part of the landscape where growing conditions are suitable. ❧ We have tried to provide a variety of different shapes, sizes, and styles in these plans. You will find ideas for gardens or perennials, annuals, and combinations of the two; for a garden made up entirely of bulbs; and for specialty gardens that feature two classic favorite cutting flowers: roses and lilies. There is also a garden for a shady location; a low-maintenance garden that mixes easy-care late-summer and autumn perennials with ornamental grasses; a garden with a patriotic color scheme of red, white, and blue; and for art lovers, a garden inspired by Monet's famous gardens at Giverny. ❧ These plans are based on the gardens shown in the photographs that accompany them, but they are not exact duplicates of the gardens in the photos. In some cases we have added a plant or two that are not found in the original garden. In other cases we have reproduced only a portion of the garden in the photograph in order to keep to a size that is more reasonable for most homeowners. The plans are not for gardens on the grand scale. ❧ Along with each plan, we have included a photograph of an arrangement to give you ideas of what is possible

This sunny garden of bright primary colors combines two species of Salvia, the familiar scarlet type and a blue-violet variety, both grown as annuals, with rich golden coreopsis.

Every year is different in the garden and a garden of annuals like this one may never look quite the same twice, even if you follow the same plan every year.

with the kinds of flowers grown in each garden. We hope these arrangements will spark your own creativity.

If you want to copy a plan exactly as it appears in the book, consult the plant list that accompanies each plan. But always keep in mind that plants perform differently at different times and in different situations. Their behavior is significantly influenced by growing conditions, the combination of soil, light, and moisture in a particular garden. Climate also plays a role: the day length and temperature range where you live can encourage or hinder a plant's performance. Remember, too, that every year is different, and your flowers may bloom earlier or later, more abundantly or less profusely, depending on annual weather conditions and the age of the plants themselves. Perennials need a year or two to settle in and begin to expand their root systems. And when they become old and crowded, their flowers will decline in quality and quantity. For the best bloom, older perennial plants need to be divided and replanted in spring or fall to maintain their vigor, as described in Chapter Three.

If your garden does not look exactly like the one in the photograph, allow for individual variations, and give it some time, too. If you find that you are still not satisfied at the end of the first growing season, add some more plants next year to fill in any

gaps. If your space is limited, you may wish to use only a part of the garden plan, or to adjust the size of the garden.

The dimensions of these gardens can be adjusted to fit the space you have available. Here's how to do it. First, use lime, string, or a garden hose to lay out the outline of the garden in the location you have chosen before you do any digging or order any plants. Then mark the approximate shape of each clump of plants shown on the plan. Next, figure out how many plants you will need.

To estimate how many plants to buy, first calculate how many square feet the garden—or each clump of plants—will cover. To find the area of a circular garden or clump, multiply the radius (the distance from the center to the outer edge) by itself, and then multiply by pi (approximately 3.14). For an oval garden or clump, measure from the center to one of the nearest edges and to one of the farthest edges, add the distances together, and divide by 2, to get an average radius. Multiply this number by itself and then multiply the total by pi. For a rectangular garden, simply multiply the length by the width. To convert square feet to square inches, multiply by 144. Next, figure out how many square inches each plant will need, by multiplying the spacing distance between plants (see the Encyclopedia beginning on page 87) by itself. Then divide the number of square inches covered by each plant into the number of square inches in each clump or section of the garden to find the approximate number of plants you will need to fill the space. Now you are ready to prepare your shopping list of plants. If you will be ordering by mail, it's best to get your order in early, to be sure you get all the plants you want. Nurseries sometimes run out of the most popular plants, and sometimes stocks are lower than usual because of crop failures.

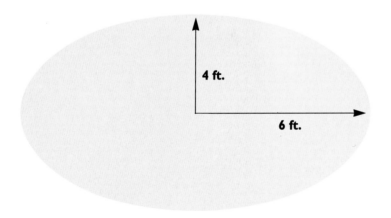

4 ft.

6 ft.

To calculate the area of an oval garden, for example, 8 feet wide by 12 feet long, measure the short radius, (4 feet) and the long radius (6 feet) and add them together (4 + 6 =10). Divide by 2 to get the average radius (10 ÷ 2 = 5) or 5 feet. Multiply the average radius by itself (5 x 5 = 25), then by pi (25 x 3.14) to get the total area in square feet, or 78½ square feet. If you want to plant a bed of chrysanthemums, which should be spaced 1 foot apart, divide the total area of the bed by 1 foot to calculate the total number of plants you will need.

A SPRING BULB GARDEN

This garden of bulbs (except for the perennial leopard's bane) is easy to care for and provides plenty of flowers to cut in spring. The garden in the photo contains late-blooming hybrid tulips in clear, bright colors. Darwin and Single Late hybrids are good choices for the red, white, and yellow flowers. Some examples are 'Ivory Floradale' (white); 'Golden Delicious', 'Mrs. John T. Scheepers', or 'Jewel of Spring' (yellow); and 'Parade', 'Dover', or 'Black Forest' (red). The deep pink tulips in the left rear are a lily-flowered type.

If pastels are more to your liking, substitute cultivars in soft pink, peach, and pale yellow, or creamy ivory. Or for a different look, plant daffodils and narcissus in place of some or all of the tulips. The tiny flowers on the right side of the photo are foamflower, but better choices for cutting would be grape hyacinth or forget-me-nots.

The plan is based on a garden measuring roughly 12 by 8 feet. The garden in the photograph was planted around three large evergreens (which provide a handsome backdrop for the flowers) and a boulder in the foreground. If your site lacks such features, simply extend the plant groups to fill the space you have available.

The tulips, doronicum, and fritillaria in this garden are set off by the deep green of the conifers behind them.

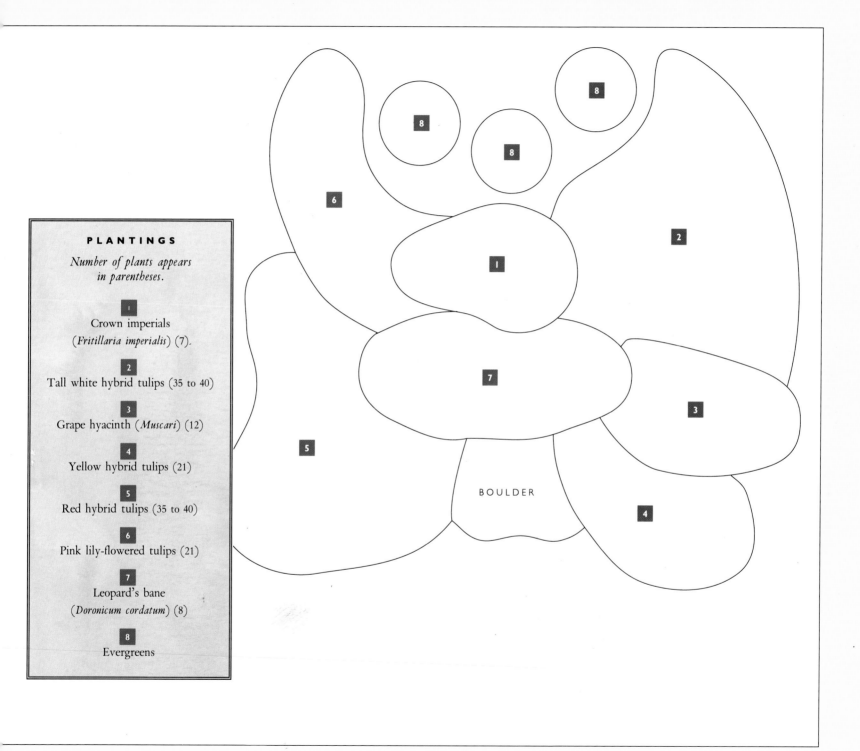

PLANTINGS

Number of plants appears in parentheses.

1
Crown imperials
(*Fritillaria imperialis*) (7).

2
Tall white hybrid tulips (35 to 40)

3
Grape hyacinth (*Muscari*) (12)

4
Yellow hybrid tulips (21)

5
Red hybrid tulips (35 to 40)

6
Pink lily-flowered tulips (21)

7
Leopard's bane
(*Doronicum cordatum*) (8)

8
Evergreens

BOULDER

A PATRIOTIC THEME GARDEN

This garden of elegant perennials expresses an all-American color scheme: deep blues and violets, rich red, and shimmering white. Foxgloves add a purple note, and hybrid delphiniums can be planted in a range of heavenly blue shades. The plants are arranged in a crescent that is 4 to 5 feet wide at the center, and 18 to 20 feet from end to end. The bed is narrow enough to allow easy access from either side for cutting flowers and for weeding, watering, and other maintenance chores.

To show off the garden at its best, plant it as an island in the lawn. A location in full sun is a must. In most places, the flowers will be at their peak in June.

A crescent-shaped border like this one can be executed on a relatively small scale, as shown in the plan, or as a grand, sweeping edging for a large lawn.

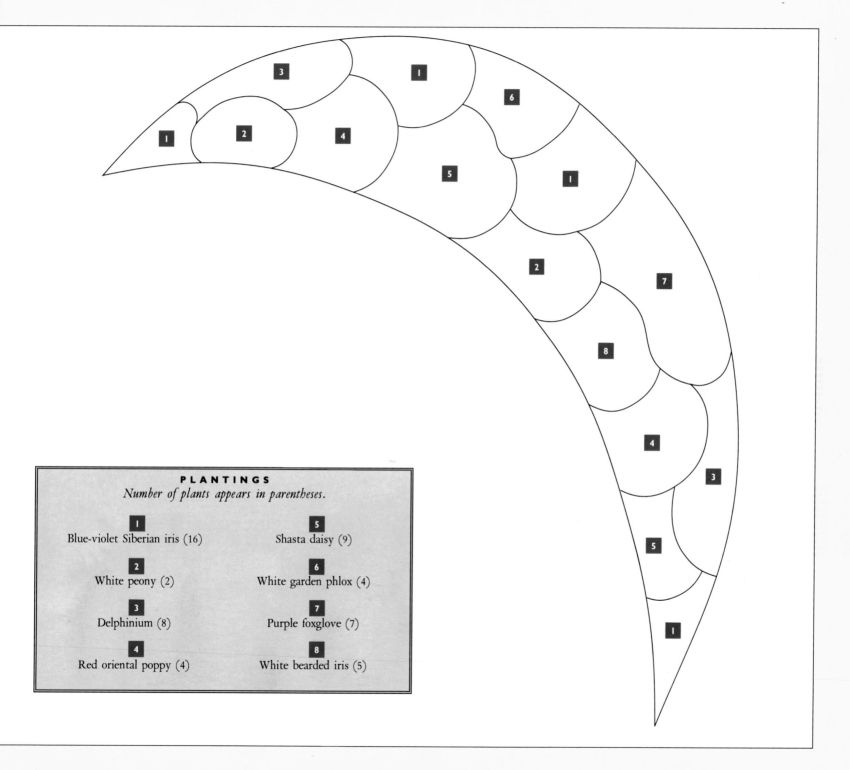

PLANTINGS
Number of plants appears in parentheses.

1
Blue-violet Siberian iris (16)

5
Shasta daisy (9)

2
White peony (2)

6
White garden phlox (4)

3
Delphinium (8)

7
Purple foxglove (7)

4
Red oriental poppy (4)

8
White bearded iris (5)

A GARDEN OF ANNUALS

Photographer Derek Fell's cutting garden, shown in the photo, is neatly laid out in rectangular beds of annuals. Mulched paths provide access to both sides of each bed, so it's easy to get in to cut flowers. The plan is based on beds measuring 3 by 6 feet. You can make the beds longer or shorter than the ones shown in the photo, depending on the amount of space you have available. You can also have more or fewer beds.

At the back of Derek's garden, pole beans grow on netting to form a leafy screen, and also to help supply the kitchen. To adhere more strictly to the cutting garden theme, you could plant ivy or honeysuckle to use in arrangements, instead of the beans. A few fruit trees along the edge of the garden provide branches of flowers to cut in spring.

The purple and white salvia shown in the photograph are variants of the familiar scarlet sage, *Salvia splendens*, which you can substitute if you like brilliant red color. You can also substitute mealycup sage, *S. farinacea*, especially the cultivar 'Victoria', which has spikes of rich, violet-blue flowers and is grown as an annual in many gardens.

This garden of rectangular beds of annuals is easy to maintain; the mulched paths provide ready access to all the flowers, and keep the garden neat.

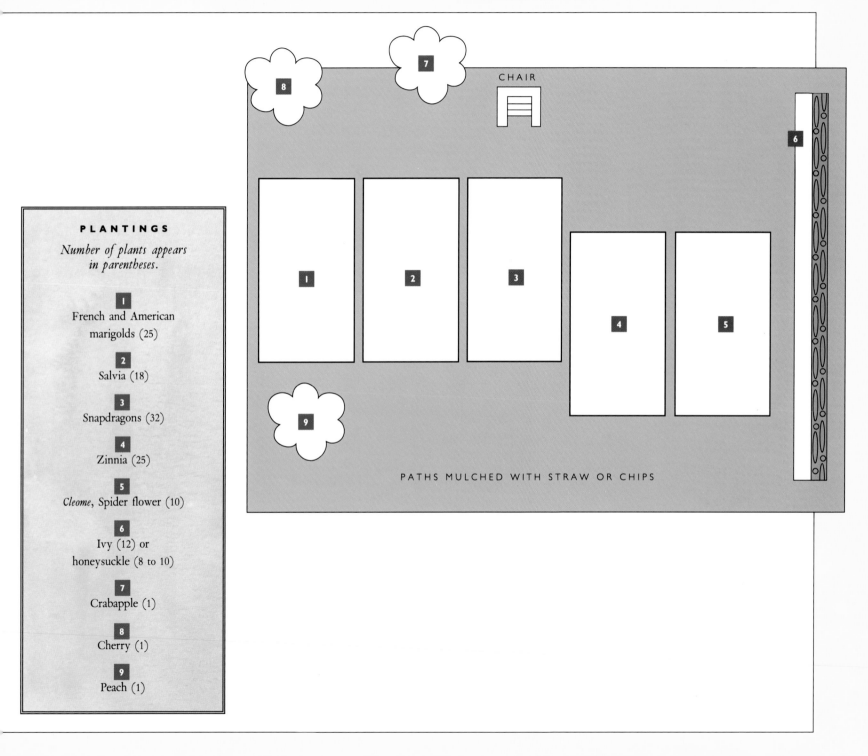

PLANTINGS

Number of plants appears in parentheses.

1
French and American marigolds (25)

2
Salvia (18)

3
Snapdragons (32)

4
Zinnia (25)

5
Cleome, Spider flower (10)

6
Ivy (12) or honeysuckle (8 to 10)

7
Crabapple (1)

8
Cherry (1)

9
Peach (1)

CHAIR

PATHS MULCHED WITH STRAW OR CHIPS

A LOW-MAINTENANCE GARDEN

Here's a plan for a garden of perennials and ornamental grasses that will start blooming in summer and continue to provide material for arrangements well into fall. The purple and gold colors of the flowers look autumny, too. The lacey, silvery foliage of the artemisia (the cultivar shown in the photograph is 'Powis Castle') adds sparkle to the garden and to floral arrangements.

The look of this garden is contemporary and casual, and the plants require little in the way of maintenance. The deep purple chrysanthemums will need to be divided every couple of years for the best bloom, but you could substitute a dwarf variety of aster that needs less frequent division. The plan is based on a garden that is about 10 feet long and 8 feet from front to back.

Ornamental grasses add a special quality to this garden. Their graceful leaves and tall flower plumes sway and rustle in the breeze and can be left standing in the garden all winter, when they dry to warm shades of tan and beige. The eulalia grass cultivar used in this garden, 'Gracillimus', is especially handsome, although it does grow quite large, as does the feather reed grass. If you prefer smaller grasses, try substituting *Lagurus* (hare's tail grass) or *Panicum* (switch grass). The flower heads of the grasses can be used in arrangements either fresh or dried.

The graceful seedheads of ornamental grasses contribute a soft, informal note to either fresh or dried arrangements.

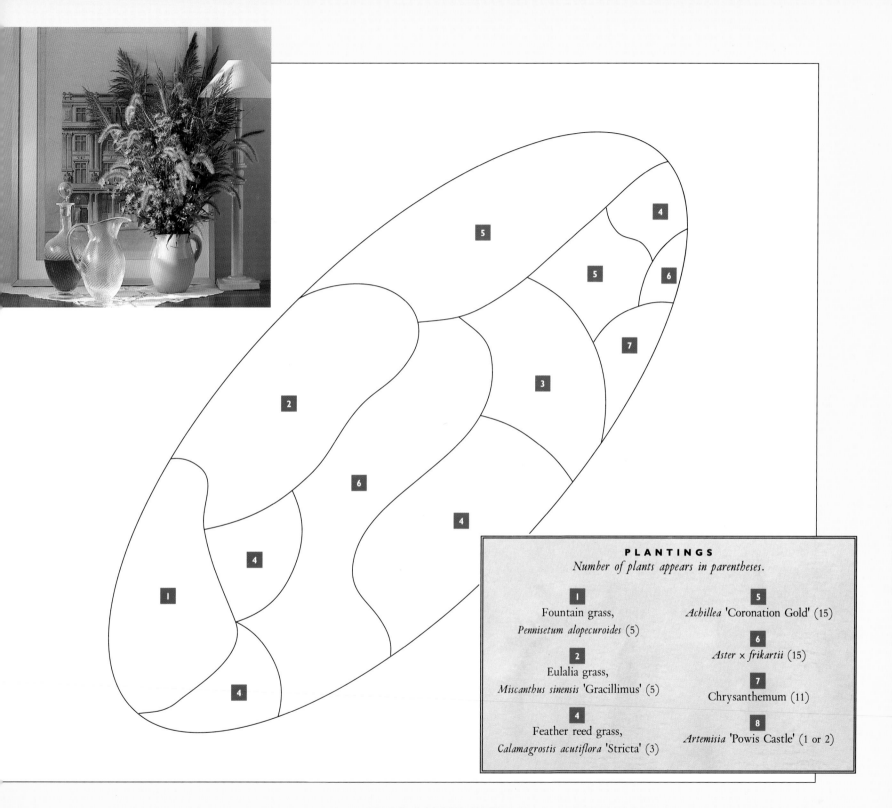

PLANTINGS

Number of plants appears in parentheses.

1
Fountain grass,
Pennisetum alopecuroides (5)

2
Eulalia grass,
Miscanthus sinensis 'Gracillimus' (5)

4
Feather reed grass,
Calamagrostis acutiflora 'Stricta' (3)

5
Achillea 'Coronation Gold' (15)

6
Aster × *frikartii* (15)

7
Chrysanthemum (11)

8
Artemisia 'Powis Castle' (1 or 2)

A PARTIAL SHADE GARDEN

If your property is shady, you can still grow flowers for cutting. This garden for partial shade contrasts feathery astilbe in pink, red, and gleaming white against the rich green foliage of ferns and a groundcover. The plan is based on a garden of roughly 15 by 20 feet.

A path of brick or flagstones winds through the garden to allow easy access to all the plants. The deep green foliage of three conifers provides a soothing, neutral backdrop for the flowers. This garden features mostly white and light-colored flowers, which help light up the dark green foliage.

In addition to the plants in this garden, other good plants for a cutting garden in partial shade include hosta (for flowers and foliage), columbine, brunnera, forget-me-nots, Jacob's ladder, primula, and Virginia bluebells. The ferns shown in the photo are ostrich fern, but toothed wood fern or florist's fern (*Dryopteris dilatata*, formerly *D. spinulosa*) would be a very good choice. Good groundcovers for shade include European wild ginger (shown in the photo), wishbone flower, and lily of the valley, all of which are good for cutting.

The white, pink, and deep red astilbes seem to glow in the subdued light of this partially shaded garden.

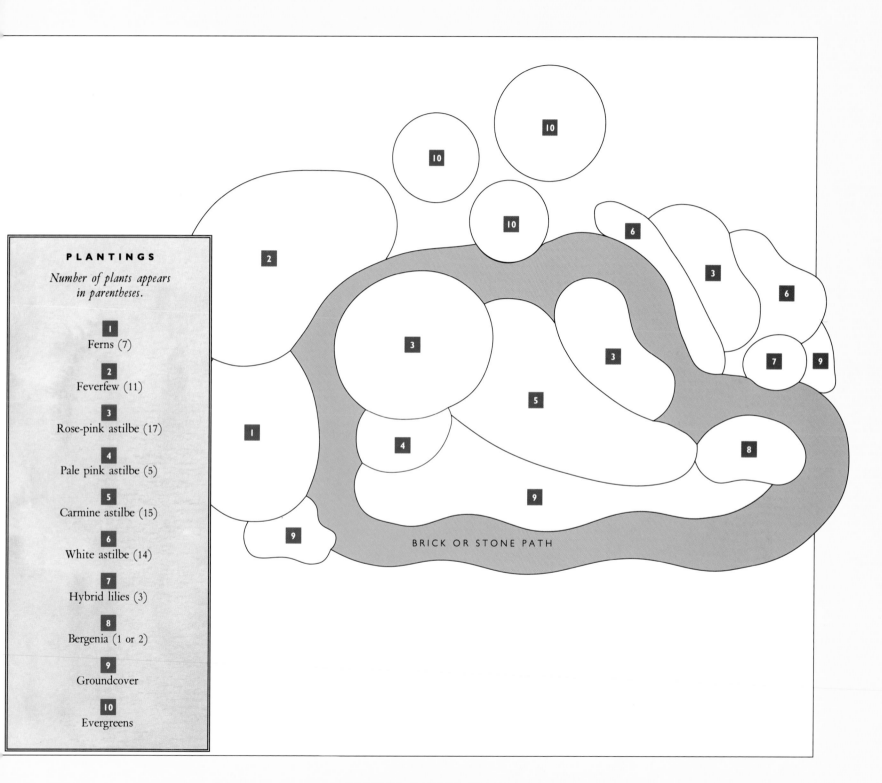

PLANTINGS

Number of plants appears in parentheses.

1 Ferns (7)

2 Feverfew (11)

3 Rose-pink astilbe (17)

4 Pale pink astilbe (5)

5 Carmine astilbe (15)

6 White astilbe (14)

7 Hybrid lilies (3)

8 Bergenia (1 or 2)

9 Groundcover

10 Evergreens

BRICK OR STONE PATH

A SUNNY MIXED GARDEN

This garden combines sun-loving perennials and annuals in a bold scheme of primary colors softened with white. The plan is based on a garden with the outer dimensions of roughly 15 by 20 feet. The flowers are planted in drifts, with violet-blue larkspur running like a ribbon through the center of the garden. If you would rather not wade into the garden to cut flowers, allow a little space between some of the adjoining drifts of plants to permit easier access.

The stone wall behind the garden in the photograph provides a handsome backdrop. A hedge, or a planting of evergreen shrubs or trees, would also beautifully set off the bright, clear colors of the flowers.

If you would rather achieve a softer, more harmonious color scheme, you can plant poppies in shades of salmon and peach instead of red and choose a pink cultivar of beebalm, such as 'Croftway Pink'. If you opt for snapdragons in the annual section of the garden, the best choice is 'Rocket' or another long-stemmed cultivar; plant it in white or yellow, or in mixed pastel shades.

PLANTINGS

Number of plants appears in parentheses.

1 Shasta daisy (36)

2 Rocket larkspur (50 to 60)

3 Red oriental poppy (12)

4 Coreopsis (75)

5 Beebalm (40 to 45)

6 Bachelor's button or snapdragon (40 to 45), or annuals of your choice

This garden of classic perennials fills a sunny spot with drifts of bright color.

STONE WALL

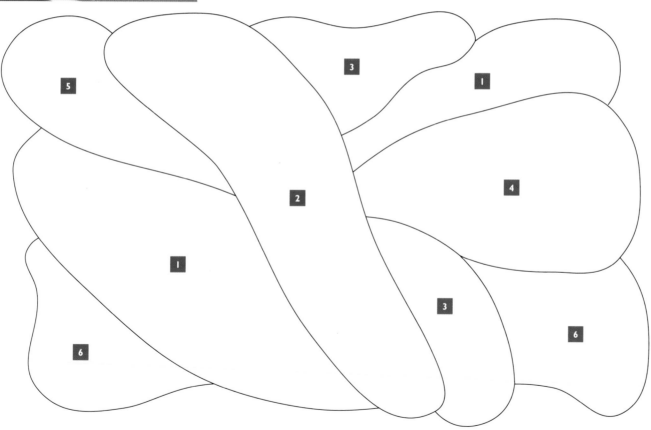

A MONET-INSPIRED GARDEN

This exuberant, multicolored garden contains some of the same flowers planted by the great impressionist painter Claude Monet in his beloved gardens at Giverny, as seen in the photograph. The design calls for two modest-sized beds, each approximately 4 by 12 feet, planted as mirror images of one another. A mulched path runs between the beds, and at each end is a trellis on which climbing roses are trained. You can modify the garden by making the beds longer or, if space is limited, by planting just one bed and eliminating the climbing roses.

The addition of some white nicotiana to the garden slightly softens the intense blend of warm colors. Planting the cosmos and nasturtiums in single, rather than mixed colors would further tone down the color scheme if it is too polychromatic for your taste.

All of these flowers are easy to grow if you give them full sun and well-drained soil.

Monet's gardens at Giverny are lush with flowers in a rich palette of colors. The plan here will let you achieve a similar effect on a small scale.

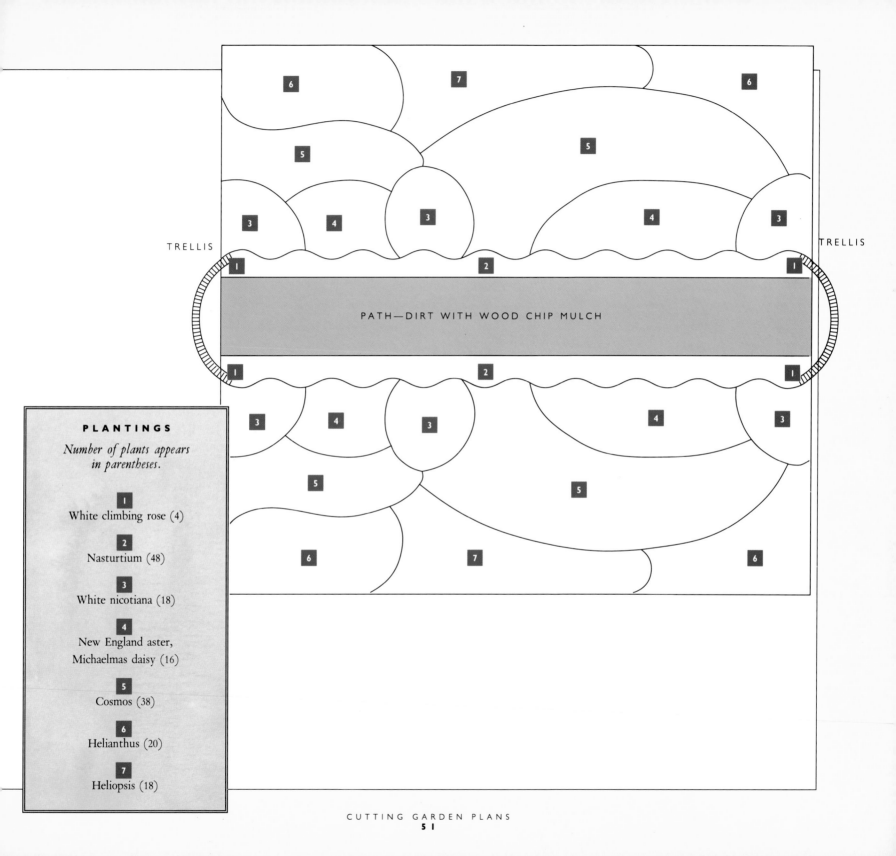

TRELLIS

TRELLIS

PATH—DIRT WITH WOOD CHIP MULCH

PLANTINGS

*Number of plants appears
in parentheses.*

1
White climbing rose (4)

2
Nasturtium (48)

3
White nicotiana (18)

4
New England aster,
Michaelmas daisy (16)

5
Cosmos (38)

6
Helianthus (20)

7
Heliopsis (18)

A BAKER'S DOZEN GARDEN

Roses are favorites with so many gardeners and flower arrangers that we had to include a rose garden. The range of warm colors—reds, pinks, oranges, yellows—available in roses today is astonishing. Fragrant roses are especially wonderful in bouquets.

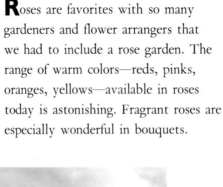

This kidney-shaped rose garden would work just as well as an island bed in a lawn as it does in this paved setting.

This garden consists of a main bed of hybrid tea roses about 5 by 18 feet, and a smaller front bed, roughly 3 by 10 feet, of easy-care shrub roses. The narrow kidney shape and the staggered planting pattern of the main bed make all the hybrid teas easy to see and easy to get to.

The garden shown is built on a simple color scheme of red, yellow, and pink. Some especially good hybrid tea roses to consider planting are 'Chrysler Imperial' (red), 'Mister Lincoln' and 'Perfume Delight' (red, fragrant), 'Double Delight' (red and white bicolor, fragrant), 'Fragrant Cloud' (orange-red, fragrant), 'Eclipse' (yellow), 'Sutter's Gold' (yellow, fragrant), 'Electron' (rose-pink), 'First Prize' (pink-ivory blend), and 'Tiffany' (orchid pink, fragrant). For the shrub roses try 'Bonica' (pink), 'Scarlet Meidiland' (red), or 'White Meidiland' (white).

If you live in zones 8 to 10, plant your roses 3 to 4 feet apart. In zones 5 to 7, plant 2½ to 3 feet apart. Farther north, plant 1½ to 2½ feet apart.

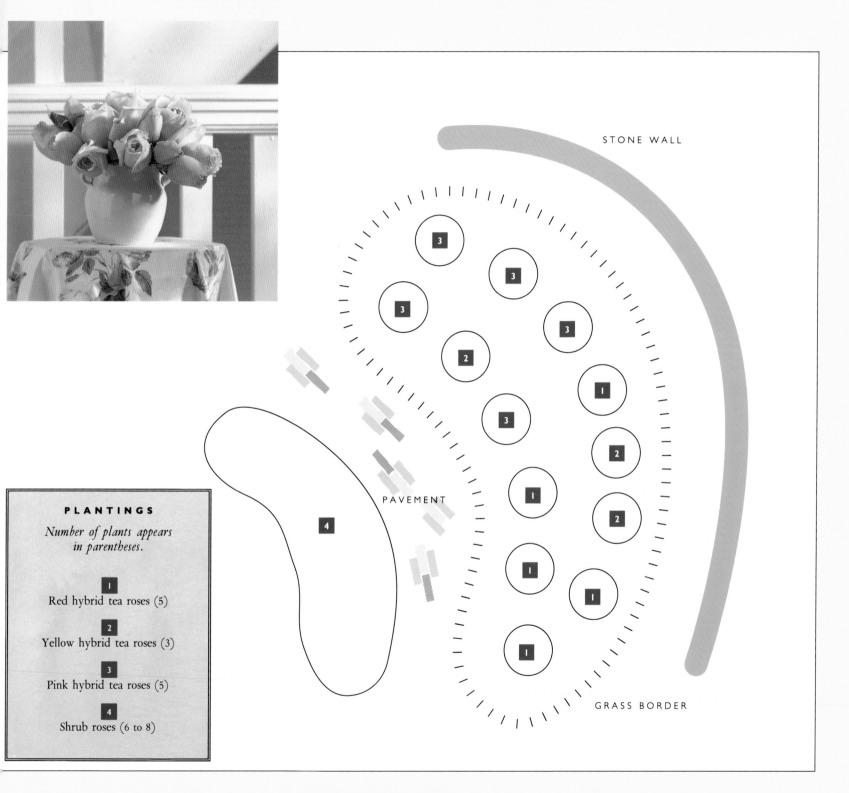

STONE WALL

PLANTINGS

*Number of plants appears
in parentheses.*

1

Red hybrid tea roses (5)

2

Yellow hybrid tea roses (3)

3

Pink hybrid tea roses (5)

4

Shrub roses (6 to 8)

PAVEMENT

GRASS BORDER

MODULAR ISLAND BEDS

In a variation on the garden shown in the photograph, here are six modular beds of classic, mostly perennial cutting flowers, laid out in a formal geometric pattern. The plan is based on individual beds of 6 by 6 feet; each triangular section covering 9 square feet. The color scheme is a harmonious blend of purples, blues, pinks, cool reds, and white. You will find several spiky flowers here for linear elements in arrangements, as well as an assortment of round flowers to use as focal points and accents. All you need to add to complete an arrangement is filler material.

You can expand the size of the individual beds, change their arrangement, plant one bed or two or all six, or modify the plan to suit your space. Or substitute your own favorite flowers for the ones suggested here.

Separate the beds with lawn that is kept neatly mowed, or surround them with low boxwood hedges to create formal French parterres. This garden needs a location in full sun.

This garden of small beds offers lots of flexibility; lay out the beds however you like, and mix and match modules of your favorite flowers.

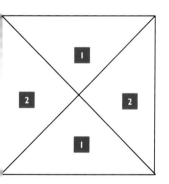
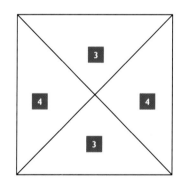

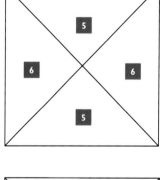

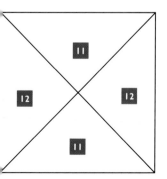
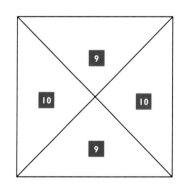
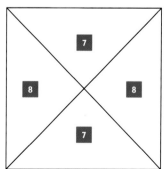

A GARDEN OF LILIES

Lilies are traditional favorite cutting flowers. Lilies bring their own special elegance to arrangements, and many of them contribute a sweet fragrance, too. This plan is for a small circular garden with a radius of about 3 feet, filled with lilies in assorted warm colors.

To allow the central group of flowers to be visible, either plant a tall-growing cultivar or make a mound of soil to raise the central plants above the surrounding ones. The garden shown here is in full sun, but many lilies grow well in partial shade.

Many lily species and cultivars are available to gardeners today. Here are just a few suggestions. Good golden yellow cultivars include 'Golden Temple' and 'Golden Splendor'. A pretty peachy buff can be found in 'Chinook'. For a rich red-orange, try easy-to-grow 'Enchantment'; for a lighter shade of orange, try 'Fair', 'Fiesta Gitana', or 'Yolanda'. An interesting peach-toned lily with reflexed (backward-curving) petals and orange spots is *Lilium amabile*. 'Golden Showers' has clear yellow blossoms. For a deep, rich red, plant 'Firecracker'.

Some fragrant lilies to consider for your garden are the hybrid Regale Strain (white with a reddish purple flush on the outside of the petals), the Madonna lily, *L. candidum* (pure white), *L. speciosum* 'Rubrum' (white and deep pinkish red with reflexed petals), and *L.* 'Stargazer' (deep pink edged in white). If you're looking for pink and melon shades, consider 'Côte D'Azur', 'Alpenglow', and 'Parisienne'.

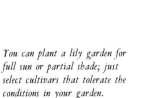

You can plant a lily garden for full sun or partial shade; just select cultivars that tolerate the conditions in your garden.

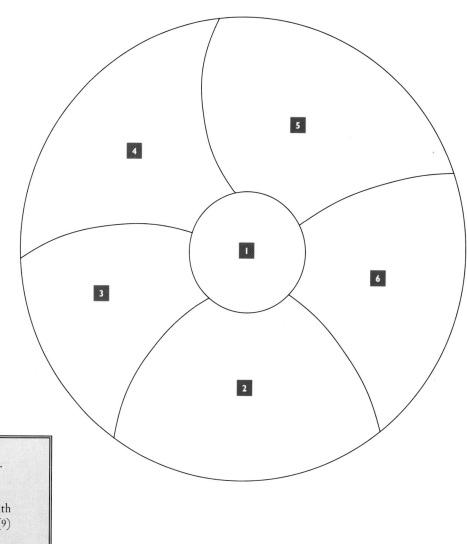

growing flowers for cutting

When the garden plan is complete, and seeds and plants are ordered, we gardeners anxiously await the start of planting. The majority of planting is done in spring, although hardy bulbs and some perennials are usually planted in fall. ❧ This chapter takes you through the growing season, starting with soil preparation in early spring. Instructions on starting seeds indoors follow, along with tips on caring for seedlings indoors. You will also learn how to plant seeds outdoors. For last minute purchases there's always the local garden center, which can be a fine source of common plants if you know how to pick out the healthiest, sturdiest specimens. There's information on how to buy the best plants at the garden center, and on how to transplant them into the garden. ❧ As the plants grow, you will need to care for them. Sections on watering, fertilizing, weeding, and deadheading provide the necessary guidance. Pests and diseases can be a problem too. We prefer to use organic methods and products to combat pests and diseases in our gardens, and that's what you'll find discussed in this chapter. ❧ Annuals come out of the garden at the end of the season, but bulbs and perennials remain in the ground. Occasionally they need to be dug up and divided to keep the plants vigorous and producing the best quality blossoms. A fall cleanup is an important wrap-up for the gardening year, preparing the garden for its winter rest.

Preparing for planting

Good soil is the foundation of a good garden, and the first step in planting a cutting garden is preparing the soil. If you are starting a new garden, try to prepare the soil the autumn before you plan to plant. Loosen the soil to a depth of at least 6 inches; 8 to 10 inches is even better, especially if you will be growing bulbs. Break up large clods and remove any large stones. Spread a layer of compost, manure, leaf mold, and/or other organic matter, and turn it under. At this stage, organic gardeners can sprinkle rock or colloidal phosphate, granite dust, or other sources of phosphorus and potassium over the soil. Organic materials need time to release their nutrients, and rock powders, which decompose particularly slowly, should be applied a season ahead of when their nutrients will be needed by plants. Be sure to till rock powders into the soil.

In spring, turn over the soil as soon as it is dry enough to work. Squeeze a handful of soil in your hand; then open your fingers. If the soil sticks together in a ball, it is still too wet to dig. If the ball crumbles, the soil is ready. After digging, rake the surface to smoothe it out and get rid of small stones.

Spring is a good time to plant many perennials and annuals. Plants that can tolerate cool weather can go into the ground while there is still a chance of some light frost. Tender plants must wait until all danger of frost is past. One to two weeks after the average date of your last spring frost is usually considered safe for planting tender plants. This date is sometimes called the frost-free date.

Calendar dates are notoriously unreliable in predicting weather conditions, which shift from year to year, and just because the calendar says you won't get any more frost does not necessarily make it so. A more reliable guide to safe planting times is natural indicators. Wait to plant tender annuals, tender perennials you will grow as annuals, and tender bulbs until the leaves on nearby oak or elm trees are a few inches long, and you will probably be safe. These are the last trees to leaf out in spring and have long been used by farmers and gardeners to gauge safe planting times for cold-sensitive plants.

Fall is the time to plant hardy bulbs, and it is also a good time to plant many perennials and shrubs. Gardeners in warm climates can plant annuals in fall as well, that the rest of us plant in early spring, to have flowers in winter.

You can sow seeds of fast-growing plants directly in the garden where you want them to grow. For an early start for slow-growing flowers, especially in the North, where the frost-free growing season is short, sow seeds indoors in February or March. You can also buy transplants at the garden center, although your choices will be more limited than when you order from seed and nursery catalogs.

Starting seeds indoors

You can start seeds in just about any container that holds soil and allows excess water to drain off. Many gardeners prefer standard nursery flats or plastic market packs divided into four, six, or more sections. These plastic cell packs are set inside plastic trays that catch runoff water. Clay and plastic pots also work well, as do peat pots and peat pellets.

The best medium for seeds and young seedlings indoors is one that is light and porous so that it retains moisture and also drains well. A sterile, soilless medium reduces the chance that damping-off (fungus disease that kills seedlings by attacking the stem near the soil line) or other diseases will attack the seedlings. One good potting mix is equal parts of peat moss, perlite, and vermiculite; another combines equal parts of peat moss and sharp builder's sand. The only drawback to such soil-less media is that they contain no nutrients, and the seedlings will be totally dependent on you to supply their needs until they go into the garden. As soon as plants develop their first true leaves (the first leaves to have the shape typical of that plant; usually the second set of leaves on the plant), mist or water them with a half-strength liquid fertilizer or fish emulsion.

Covering flats of seeds with plastic helps keep humidity high until germination occurs.

face of the medium feels moist, or mist them gently but be sure you are thorough. Use lukewarm water to avoid shocking seeds and seedlings with water that is too hot or cold.

When the shoots appear, move the containers to a sunny windowsill or a light garden where they will be under fluorescent lamps. The lamps should be 4 to 6 inches above the tops of the plants; you will have to adjust them as

If you would prefer to start your seeds in a mix that contains some soil, try equal parts of peat moss, sand, and pasteurized garden soil or commercial potting soil. If you buy packaged potting soil, try to get a kind that contains no fertilizer. Fertilizers in packaged potting soil can often be too strong for delicate young seedlings.

Moisten the mix before sowing any seeds. A peat-based mix may be difficult to moisten because peat moss actually repels water when it is dry. Pour some warm water onto the mix and knead it in with your hands. Continue adding water until the mix is thoroughly damp, but not soggy.

Fill your containers of choice to ½ inch from the top to allow for watering. Sow seeds to the depth recommended on the seed packet. Place the containers out of direct light.

Keep the medium evenly moist until shoots appear. To water flats and pots of seeds, set them in a pan of water until the sur-

the plants grow taller to keep the distance constant. Bear in mind that while seedlings need lots of bright light, most of them do not grow well in hot conditions. If you live in the North, a south-facing window is probably the best source of natural light, but in southern areas a window that faces east is preferable. A windowsill that is painted white or lined with aluminum foil will reflect extra light back onto the young plants. Give seedlings growing on windowsills a quarter turn each day or two, so the stems will grow straight.

Seedlings of cool-season plants—hardy annuals and spring perennials, for example—grow best in cool temperatures, between 50 and 65 degrees Fahrenheit. Tender plants like impatiens do better where the temperature is warmer: 60 to 75 degrees Fahrenheit.

Indoor seedlings need lots of humidity, but they also need good air circulation, otherwise they're likely to develop mildew, damping-off, or other problems. Don't crowd the plants together; the leaves of neighboring seedlings should not touch one another. A small fan placed in the room but aimed away from the plants will circulate the air without damaging delicate stems.

Water the seedlings from the bottom, if possible, when the growing medium feels dry below the surface. A reliable way to provide steady, even moisture for seedlings is to set the containers on capillary matting, which keeps constantly moist by absorbing water from a reservoir. The mats are available from garden supply companies. Setting the containers on trays of pebbles filled with water, so that the bottoms of the containers are above the water level, will boost humidity without waterlogging the soil.

Fertilize seedlings regularly with an all-purpose liquid fertilizer or one formulated for flowers. If you garden organically, use fish emulsion or a fish-and-seaweed product. Use any of these fertilizers at half the recommended strength while the seedlings are small and still indoors. Feed seedlings in a soilless medium every seven to ten days, and feed plants in a mix containing soil every two to three weeks. Transplant the seedlings to larger containers when they become crowded and the leaves of adjoining plants touch one another.

Starting seeds outdoors

Flowers that grow quickly and can tolerate some cool weather can be sown directly in the garden, or in a cold frame. Prepare the soil as previously described, to create a crumbly, fine-textured seedbed. Sow the seeds in rows or blocks, to the depth recommended on the seed packet. Firm the soil gently in place, and water with a fine spray to settle the seeds in the soil without dislodging them. Keep the seedbed evenly moist—but not sopping wet—until germination occurs. If the seedlings are in a cold frame, remember to open the lid on days when the temperature rises above 40 degrees Fahrenheit.

Buying plants

Almost all gardeners buy at least some of their plants from mail-order nurseries or local garden centers. Most of us don't have the time to start a whole garden full of plants from seed, and some plants, such as lavender, are very difficult to start from seed at home. But plants are a lot more expensive than seeds, so it is important to seek out good-quality stock.

The best way to get good plants by mail is to buy from a reputable source. Ask gardening friends which companies they like. Read catalogs carefully for information on where the different plants offered will thrive and what conditions they need. If this information is not readily available, be wary. Also avoid companies that run hyperbolic ads in general-interest magazines touting miracle plants and exotic flowers for which no botanical name is given, and which are illustrated with brightly colored artwork instead of photographs. Remember, if a plant sounds too good to be true, it probably is.

There are several guidelines you can use to pick out the best plants at a local garden center or nursery. It can be tempting to buy big container plants already in bloom, especially if you are late in planting the garden, but it's not a good idea. Such plants are very expensive—usually $6 to $10 or more *per plant*—and they often have difficulty making the transition from container to garden.

Instead, choose plants in smaller containers that are just beginning to set buds. Pick out sturdy, stocky plants with strong stems, leaves spaced close together on the stems, and a good green color. Avoid plants that are tall and lanky, with weak, floppy stems and pale green leaves; these plants have been stressed by too little light and possibly too little water. Examine the soil

*Buy stocky, compact seedlings with strong stems and healthy color
to get the best results in your garden.*

in the pot or the market pack. Do you see moss or mold growing on the surface? If so, the soil is waterlogged; don't buy these plants. Examine the plants for signs of insects and disease. Check the growing tip, the leaf axils (where the leaves join the stem), and the undersides of leaves for signs of insects or their eggs. If you see fine webbing, sticky patches, or scaly patches, it is a bad sign. Shake the container gently; if tiny white insects appear like a cloud above the plant, it is infested with whiteflies. And lastly, if the leaves are yellow (unless the plant is a gold-leaved or variegated cultivar) or brown and brittle around the edges, the plant is not in peak condition.

A healthy plant will adapt more quickly to life in your garden, and it will grow more quickly and produce more flowers than a stressed or pest-ridden plant, even if the less healthy specimen is bigger when you buy it.

Examine bulbs carefully as well. Look for large, firm bulbs with no soft spots, no blackening, and no signs of rot or mold.

Transplanting into the garden

Seedlings raised indoors must be gradually acclimated to outdoor conditions before they are planted in the garden. That way, they can make the transition easily, without a shock to their system that will set back their growth. The process of adjustment is called hardening off, and it takes about ten days. Harden off seedlings by setting them outdoors in a sheltered location for a couple of hours the first day, and for gradually lengthening periods over the next seven to ten days. On the last night the plants can remain outdoors overnight.

If you will be transplanting seedlings from undivided nursery flats, it is a good idea to "block" them several days before you expect to plant them. Using a sharp knife, cut down through the soil in the flat to divide the soil into blocks—as if you were cutting a pan of brownies. Each seedling should be in the center of its own little block of soil. Blocking separates the root systems of the plants and allows the cut roots to heal somewhat before they are transplanted, decreasing the amount of shock the plants will suffer during the transplanting process.

The least stressful time to transplant (from the plants' point of view) is a mild, overcast day with little or no wind. If you have to transplant on a sunny day, do it early in the morning or late in the day, when the sun is at its least intense and temperatures are lower.

Dig the hole before removing the plant from its container; the goal is to transfer plants from pot to garden quickly, so the roots don't have a chance to dry out. For plants that grow from a rosette of leaves at ground level, dig a hole that will allow you to set the plant at the same depth it was growing at previously. If you set the plant deeper, you run the risk of burying the

Mulching with black plastic warms the soil in spring, helping tender plants get off to a good start. It also conserves soil moisture.

crown, the point from which the top growth emerges, which would hinder growth and could even kill the plant. Plants that have upright, branched stems can be transplanted deeper, up to right below the lowest leaves, and new roots will grow from the buried part of the stem. Planting deeply is especially helpful in light soil and windy locations, for the additional roots help anchor the plant more securely.

When the hole is dug, loosen the plant in its container. For a plant in a pot, place one hand over the top of the pot, supporting the stem between your fingers, and turn the pot upside down onto that hand. Tap the bottom and sides of the pot lightly with the handle of a trowel to loosen the soilball; then slide the plant out of the pot. If the plant is still stuck, set the pot on the ground and slide the blade of an old kitchen knife around the inside wall of the pot. To remove plants from cell packs, push on the bottom of each section to loosen the soilball.

Support the rootball with one hand and gently hold the plant's leaves in your other hand to transfer the plant to the hole. Don't pick up small seedlings by their stems; they may snap. Try to leave as much of the soil around the rootball as you can. Fill in the hole with soil, working it around the rootball with your fingers (you can wear gloves to keep your fingers

clean). Water to settle the plant in the soil and get rid of air pockets, so the roots will be in good contact with the soil.

If you are setting out transplants in peat pots, you can plant pots and all in the garden. Tear the sides of the pot to make sure roots will be able to escape easily. Also make sure to completely bury the rim of the pot; if left exposed, the peat rim will act as a wick when it dries out, drawing moisture out of the soil and away from plant roots and allowing it to evaporate.

If you are transplanting during very hot weather, it is a good idea to cover the new transplants with shade netting or floating row covers for their first few days in the garden, until they adjust to outdoor conditions.

Keep the soil evenly moist for the first several days, until the plants have a chance to start developing new feeder roots.

Caring for a cutting garden

A cutting garden needs the same kind of maintenance as any other flower garden: You will have to weed, fertilize, water during dry weather, and remove spent flowers that you didn't cut to bring indoors. Most perennials need to be lifted and divided every two to five years, and bulb plantings also need periodic renewal. Tender bulbs must be dug and brought indoors for storage every autumn before frost arrives.

But working in the garden isn't drudgery if you approach it in the right frame of mind. Think of the time you spend in the garden as creative time, an opportunity to get to know your flowers better. As you work among the plants, take time to observe how they grow, to appreciate the nuances of their colors, textures, and forms. Notice which flowers look especially good together. Getting better acquainted with the flowers in the garden will suggest new ways to use them in arrangements. You may find new combinations of color and form that you hadn't thought of before. And understanding how flowers look and grow in the garden will help you to place them in arrangements in ways that really suit them. You will be able, for example, to capture the way bleeding heart blossoms dance on their slender stems by positioning the arching stems near the outside of the arrangement, where the heart-shaped flowers can dangle freely. In time, you will develop a knack for arranging your flowers in ways that show them off to their best advantage.

Watering

Most cutting flowers require ample water, so during spells of dry weather you will need to water them. Light sandy soils dry out more quickly than heavy clay soils and will need more frequent watering. The old rule of thumb is to give plants 1 inch of water per week if rainfall does not supply that amount. But water needs vary with the plant, the soil, and the climate.

In most soils, one good, soaking rain a week should be sufficient to meet the needs of most plants. But the best way to judge when the garden needs water is to poke a finger down into the soil. Don't just feel the soil surface; there may still be plenty of water in the root zone although the soil is dry on top. If the soil is dry 2 or 3 inches below the surface, it's time to water. On the other hand, don't wait to water until your plants wilt and look floppy. Many plants look a bit limp on hot, sunny afternoons, but if they appear wilted early or late in the day, they are in water stress, and their growth will slow down or even halt. The best

time of day to water is in the morning or late afternoon. Avoid watering at noon, when more water is lost to evaporation. On the other hand, watering at night can lead to disease problems.

When you do water, water slowly and deeply. Frequent light waterings encourage plants to produce shallow feeder roots that leave them more vulnerable to drought. Water less often, and more deeply, so roots will grow downward in search of moisture.

For the most abundant blooms, water plants that need even moisture during dry weather.

Planting intensively decreases the amount of weeding you will need to do, because there's less space for weeds to grow. But you need good, fertile soil to support intensive plantings.

While too little water is bad for plants, too much water is no better. Overwatering can actually suffocate plants. Waterlogged soil containing little oxygen, which roots need to fuel growth and transpiration, will cause plants to drown.

A 1- to 2-inch layer of loose mulch helps slow the evaporation of moisture from the soil and also helps keep the soil surface loose and the root zone a bit cooler. If you mulch with wood chips, sawdust, or another wood product, the mulch will take nitrogen from the soil as it decomposes, so you will need to fertilize with extra nitrogen to compensate for the loss.

The most efficient watering systems are drip irrigation and soaker hoses, both of which deliver water directly to the soil where plants can use it. Systems that water plants from above lose a lot of water to evaporation. If you water with a standard garden hose, attach a bubbler and lay the hose in the garden, moving it from place to place. If your garden is very small, simply dip water from a bucket and apply it around the base of each plant. Especially if you live in a dry climate, make a shallow depression in the soil around the base of each plant to catch and hold runoff water.

Fertilizing

A well-prepared soil that is rich in organic matter will support the growth and good health of your plants. Additional fertilizing can correct deficiencies in the soil and give plants an extra boost. However, it is important not to overfeed plants or they will produce fast, weak growth that is a favorite target for pests and diseases, and very susceptible to their damage.

To fertilize a cutting garden, use a balanced formula, such as 20-20-20, or one blended for flowers that is higher in phosphorus and potassium than in nitrogen, such as 10-30-20. The numbers on a bag of fertilizer indicate the content of the three major nutrients. The first number indicates nitrogen, the second, phosphorus, and the third, potassium. Organic gardeners can use a preblended product (read the label carefully to see what's in it) or work in bonemeal, rock or colloidal phosphate, and greensand or granite dust. Organic materials need time to release their nutrients in a form that allows plants to use them, so you must apply them in advance of when the plants will need them. Apply organic fertilizers to the soil before planting, and again in the middle of the growing season, or when perennials finish blooming. Bulbs appreciate a handful of good-quality bonemeal worked into the soil at the bottom of the planting hole.

Many flower gardeners like to feed annuals with a mild liquid fertilizer every few weeks during the growing season, to keep them producing lots of blossoms.

Whatever type of fertilizer you use, follow the directions on the package for how much and how often to apply it.

Weeding and deadheading

Weeding and deadheading are two necessary chores in any flower garden, and they can be made less tedious if you regard them as an opportunity to spend time outdoors on a nice day and enjoy the weather.

Weeds are tough plants, and they will compete with your flowers for water, nutrients, light, and space. If weeds are allowed to become too large and vigorous, your flowers will disappear

Mulching helps conserve precious moisture during hot, dry summer weather, and also keeps the soil loose and crumbly.

amid a tangle of rank, leafy growth, to languish and perhaps, in the case of the more delicate plants, even to die. If you want lots of flowers for cutting, and if you want to be able to see those flowers in the garden, keep the weeds pulled.

Weeding thoroughly once a week is usually sufficient for most gardens. Mulch will help keep weeds down, but the most important management technique is simply to keep up with the weeding. Pull weeds while they're small, when they are easier to get out of the ground and before they go to seed and produce new armies of their fellows. There are numerous weeding tools available, and in a large garden, a flat-bladed hoe or a scuffle hoe, which has an open blade, is invaluable. But the best way to get rid of weeds is still to pull them out, individually, by hand. A kneeling pad or bench makes the job immensely more comfortable. Hoeing and cultivating will remove small weeds but will only chop off larger ones at ground level, after which they will inevitably grow back.

If your garden is close to the house, you can pull a few weeds every day as you pass by, to make the main weekly task less time-consuming.

Deadheading—removing spent flowers from the plant—is also important, although in a cutting garden you will to do less deadheading than in a garden where no flowers are cut for indoors. Deadheading prolongs the blooming period of annuals by preventing them from setting seeds, and it encourages many perennials to rebloom as well. It also improves the overall appearance of the garden.

Use flower shears to deadhead soft-stemmed plants, and use pruning shears for thick-stemmed and woody plants. Cut back the stem to right above a pair of leaves or a dormant bud on the stem or in a leaf axil (usually a small, green bump) to promote new growth and more flowers. Proper deadheading encourages plants to grow bushier and, in many cases, to produce more flowers.

When deadheading roses, cut back to right above a stem with five—not three—leaflets, to stimulate reblooming. Deadhead lilacs right after they finish blooming; later in the season you might accidentally snip off next year's flower buds. Remember, when deadheading narcissus, tulips, and other bulbs, the foliage must be left in place until it yellows and dries, in order to nourish the bulb.

Battling pests and diseases

The best treatment for pests and diseases is to prevent them in the first place. A well-tended garden in good-quality soil will have fewer pest and disease problems than a garden of weak, poorly nourished plants in soil that is exhausted and low in organic matter. Strong, healthy plants are less likely to be attacked by pests and disease organisms and are more likely to survive when they are attacked. Keep the garden clean to remove hiding places and points of entry for the bad guys. Pick off spent flowers and dead leaves; pick up any debris that drops to the ground.

Check the plants often for signs of trouble. Examine the plants' growing tips and developing buds. Check the leaf axils and undersides of leaves for pests and their eggs. Look for tiny holes punched in leaves and for ragged, chewed leaf margins. If you do see problems, address them right away, before those first few bugs turn into a major infestation.

Learn to recognize which bugs are harmful and which ones are helpful predators that feed on the bad bugs instead of your flowers. Ladybugs (more correctly called ladybeetles), lacewings, spiders, and praying mantises are four beneficial insects to have in the garden. If you wish to use biological controls to fight pests in your garden, you can purchase a variety of predators through mail-order sources like Necessary Trading Company (see Suppliers on page 140). Lacewing larvae, ladybugs, aphid lions, predatory mites, *Trichogramma* wasps, and fly parasites are some of the beneficial insects available by mail. Bear in mind that in order for the beneficials to stay in your garden, you must provide additional food for them, especially when you first release them. You can purchase this food from the company supplying the insects.

Another very effective biological control is milky spore disease, which is sold under various trade names. It is applied to the lawn to kill the grubs of Japanese beetles, which would emerge as adults the following year.

Small insects like spider mites, aphids, and whiteflies can be controlled with insecticidal soap. Be aware that it usually takes several applications to get rid of all the bugs. For larger pests, you can handpick if the infestation is not a major one, or try botanical insecticides such as pyrethrum and rotenone, which are available in various products sold in garden centers. The advantage of these insecticides is that they break down quickly in the environment after application. However, they are toxic when applied, and they will kill beneficial insects along with pests, so use them with caution and only as a last resort.

Garden flowers are subject to an array of mildews, molds, fungus infections, rots, smuts, blights, and other diseases. Along with good sanitation, correct cultural practices will go a long way toward keeping diseases out of the cutting garden. Don't crowd plants together in the garden; good air circulation is important. Don't work in the garden when the plants are wet, disease can be introduced or spread this way. If you smoke, never do it in the garden, and wash your hands before touching soil or plants. Tobacco mosaic virus is a serious problem for members of the nightshade family such as petunias and nicotiana, and for other plants as well.

Symptoms of plant disease include yellowing, wilting, browning, or dropping leaves; fuzzy white or sooty patches on leaves; and soft, mushy areas on leaves and stems. Buds may drop from the plants before they open. Flowers that do open may be misshapen and discolored.

At the first sign of disease, remove the affected plant parts. Dispose of the diseased material in the garbage. Do not put it on the compost pile or you will spread it throughout the garden; even hot compost is not hot enough to kill all disease organisms. Sterilize your tools after using them to cut away diseased plant material by dipping them in a solution of one part liquid chlorine bleach to nine parts water. If the plant develops more disease symptoms, pull it up and get rid of it to prevent problems from spreading. Unless you want to resort to chemical fungicides, discarding diseased plants is about all you can do.

Dividing perennials and bulbs

Many bulbs and perennials become crowded after several years because they have been spreading and forming clumps by means of underground offsets, rhizomes, suckers, or other structures.

Dividing the clump into several pieces renews the old plant and yields several new ones.

Plants differ in their need for division. Some, such as hardy chrysanthemums, should be divided every year or two to produce the best flowers and stay vigorous. Others, such as bleeding heart and Oriental poppy, don't like to have their roots disturbed and should be divided only when the plants appear weak and the quantity and quality of the flowers noticeably decline. Information on how often to divide perennials and bulbs is widely available. But watch your plants as well. You may notice one year that the plants look crowded and just aren't blooming as well as they used to—the flowers are fewer and smaller. If this happens, the plants are showing you that they need to be divided.

Fall is a good time to divide many perennials and bulbs. Do it early enough so that four to six weeks of mild weather are left before you expect the first hard frost. That way, the new divisions will have a chance to send out new roots and establish themselves in the garden before the weather turns cold. Plants that bloom in fall should be divided in spring.

Cut the stems back to the ground, and dig up the clump of roots. Carefully remove the topsoil from around the base of the plant, and insert a spading fork or shovel into the soil at an angle, all around the base of the plant. Push back and forth on the handle to loosen the roots in the soil. Using the handle as a lever, carefully lift the rootball out of the soil. Brush away loose soil so you can see what you are doing. Try to leave as many of the roots intact as you can.

Look for growth buds on the crown of the plant (the point where the stem meets the roots). When a clump of roots is divided, each division must have several growth buds in order for new plants to grow. To divide a clump of fibrous roots, like those of

When clumps of perennials become crowded, you need to dig them up and divide them to maintain the vigor of the plants.
Some of the plants in this garden will be ready for division at the end of the growing season.

astilbe, cut down through the rootball with a sharp knife, or pull the clump apart with your fingers. If the plant has a large, tough clump of crowns—a large clump of daylilies, perhaps—you and an assistant can separate it by driving two spading forks into the rootball back to back, then pushing and pulling on the handles to lever the mass apart. With plants that form thick clumps of tough, almost woody roots, such as phlox and long-neglected bearded iris, you may have to chop apart the rootball with a hatchet. This can be hard work; get assistance if you need it.

Fleshy-rooted and rhizomatous plants like peonies, daylilies, and many irises will have eyes on the fleshy roots and rhizomes that contain growth buds. Pull the clumps of roots apart so that each clump contains one or more of these eyes.

Your goal in dividing rootballs is to remove and discard the old, tough roots in the middle of the clump, and to replant the younger roots around the outside. Replant the new divisions immediately, before they begin to dry out. In most cases the divisions should be planted at the same depth they were growing at before.

Keep the soil evenly moist while the divisions form new roots. If you live in the North, give newly divided perennials a winter mulch to protect them from the soil heave caused by alternating freezes and thaws. When the soil freezes in fall, put down a 6- to 12-inch layer of shredded leaves, salt hay, or other loose material to keep the ground frozen until spring.

Many bulbs also benefit from periodic division. Narcissus, tulips, and many other true bulbs produce small offsets that will develop into new plants. The offsets form around the outside of the main bulb, and they compete with it for water and nutrients. If you notice that a bulb planting that is several years old seems to be producing leaves but few flowers, division is in order.

In summer after the foliage has turned yellow, then dried and died back, dig up the bulbs and carefully remove the offsets without cutting them. Discard diseased or damaged ones. You can replant the bulbs and the offsets right away or let them dry out for a day in an airy location out of direct sun. Store them in a cool, dry place out of direct sun. Then replant them in fall when you plant your new bulbs. Given room, offsets will eventually grow to full-size, blooming bulbs.

Scaly bulbs, such as the bulbs of many lilies, produce structures called scales, which resemble the cloves of a garlic bulb. To divide scaly bulbs, dig them in fall, after the plants have finished blooming, and pull off the loose scales on the outside of the bulb. Plant the scales upright in a container of moist vermiculite or a peat-based potting medium. The scales will produce bulblets, which can in turn be planted to grow new plants. Some lilies form tiny bulbils in the leaf axils, or along the underground portion of the stem. Remove and plant these bulbils to produce new plants. Don't expect your new plants to flower the next year, however. It takes a few years for the bulbs to reach blooming size.

Plants that grow from bulblike structures called *corms* (gladiolus and crocus are two examples) are divided differently from true bulbs. A corm dies after one year and is replaced by a new one.

The corm also develops little structures called *cormels* around its base. Dig corms of hardy plants like crocuses after the leaves have died back; dig tender corms like gladiolus in fall when flowering is finished. Separate the new corm from the old, withered one, and detach the cormels. Immediately replant new corms and cormels of hardy plants; store those of tender plants indoors until spring, and plant them when the danger of frost is past.

Fall cleanup

When frost arrives and flowering is over for another year, it is time to clean up the garden. The fall cleanup is important not just from an aesthetic point of view, but also because it eliminates hiding places for pests to live in over winter.

First, pull up and discard all your annuals. Then cut back perennials to a few inches above the ground. Put the plant remains, if healthy, on the compost pile. Dig tender bulbs and store them indoors. Spread a 1- to 2-inch layer of compost and shredded leaves on top of the soil. Turn it under in areas where annuals were planted, and work it carefully around and between perennials and bulbs. If you live in the North and grow hybrid tea, grandiflora or floribunda roses, mound up soil around the base of less hardy cultivars to protect the roots over winter. Fall is also the time to apply rock powders and other slow-to-decompose organic materials in anticipation of early spring planting. If you will be laying a winter mulch, wait until the ground freezes to apply it. It's a good idea to check your cutting garden periodically over the winter to see whether plants have heaved out of the ground. Gently push any exposed roots back into the soil, and cover them with mulch.

CHAPTER FOUR

cutting and arranging flowers

The great joy of having a cutting garden is bringing the flowers into your home. You can go out into the garden and cut armloads of blossoms to fill containers throughout the house, or to use in creating more traditional arrangements for special occasions. You can fashion a horizontal floral grouping to use as a centerpiece for a dinner party, or you can cut a big bunch of blossoms to tie up with ribbon and give to a friend. This chapter discusses how to cut and condition the flowers you grew and how to create your own unique arrangements. ❧ Although the flowers featured in this book are all good for cutting, they respond differently and need different handling. For specific information on the treatment of individual flowers, see the Encyclopedia beginning on page 87. This chapter opens with an introduction to the techniques used for cutting and conditioning flowers. ❧ It helps to realize that cut flowers are still alive and growing, although they have been separated from the plant that nourished them. In caring for cut flowers your aim is to decrease stress and make it possible for the flowers to continue to take up water and nutrients. To do this you need to supply them with a source of nutrients, and to keep out of the vase any dirt and bacteria that would interfere with the flowers' life processes and cause disease. Following the directions here will keep your cut flowers in good condition for the longest possible time.

Informal bouquets like these express the low-key spirit of a country cutting garden.

How to cut flowers

Cut most flowers when they are young, before they are fully open. Many flowers can even be cut when they are still in bud and will open indoors. However, most tightly closed buds will not open after cutting. Instead, cut when the buds are about halfway open and showing color. If the flower is actually a cluster of many small flowers, as are lilacs and spider flowers, cut them before all the florets are fully open. Some flowers, such as asters, marigolds, zinnias, and chrysanthemums, must be fully open when you cut them or they will not last very long. Check the Encyclopedia to find the best stage at which to cut the flowers in your garden.

Cut only the most perfect blossoms. Flowers that have been damaged by severe weather, pests, or disease, in addition to being of questionable aesthetic value, will not hold up well when cut. With most flowers, when the petals begin to droop the flower is past its peak; leave these flowers in the garden, for their vase life would be brief. Of course, there are exceptions to this rule. Flowers such as bearded irises have some petals that are meant to face downward (called *falls*).

When cutting, sever the flowers with the longest possible stems, to give yourself the most options for using the flowers in an arrangement. Later you can recut the stems to just the length you need.

To reduce the stress of cutting, take a bucket of lukewarm water out to the garden with you, and stand the flower stems in it as soon as you cut them. Warm water is easier for the stems to absorb than either cold or hot water.

The best time to cut flowers is in the early morning before the dew has dried. At this time of day the flowers contain the most water, and their tissues are firm. The next best time to cut is early in the evening. Although the flowers contain less water then, the plants have been manufacturing food all day, and the flowers have a good supply of nutrients, which will also extend their life in the vase.

Be sure your flower shears, knife, or pruning shears are sharp; dull tools can crush the water-carrying capillaries in flower stems and hamper the stems' ability to absorb water.

Whenever possible, cut the stem right above a node (a dormant bud), to encourage new growth and more flowers. Handle the flowers with care, both during and after cutting. Double-petaled blossoms, such as *Dahlia* 'Park Princess' or *Helianthus* x *multiflorus* 'Flore Pleno', are especially fragile and tend to shatter easily. Shattered flowers have to be discarded, that is, if you don't want to reattach their petals one at a time with melted wax—an extremely painstaking process.

Conditioning flowers

To help extend the life of cut flowers in arrangements, condition them before you arrange them.

The conditioning process begins as soon as you bring the flowers indoors. First, many flowers benefit from having their stems recut underwater, to ensure that the flowers will be able to take up the moisture they need. You can recut them in a sink or basin, or under a running faucet. When the cut stems of certain flowers are out of water, even briefly, a bubble of air gets inside the stem and seals it, so the flower cannot take up any more water. Even though these stems may be standing firm and straight, the flower heads will quickly droop and wilt. When you recut stems, cut them on a slant so they will be able to absorb water even when resting on the bottom of a container. Some of the flowers that benefit from having their stems recut underwater are carnations, sweet williams, and other *Dianthus*, China asters, marigolds, marguerites, snapdragons, and sweet peas.

If the flower has a hollow stem, like those of delphinium, dahlia, or hollyhock, it will help if you turn the flower upside down, fill the stem with cool water, and plug the end with a tiny piece of cotton. Or you can dip the end of a hollow stem in boiling water for about twenty seconds to seal it; then condition the flowers in warm water that cools gradually to room temperature.

Some flowers contain a milky sap that oozes from the stem when it is cut. The stem loses nutrients along with the sap, and when they're in water these nutrients support the growth of bacteria. To prolong the vase life of flowers that "bleed," you can seal the ends of the stems to prevent the sap from leaking out. Dip the end of the stem in boiling water for about twenty seconds, or hold it over the flame of a candle. You will prevent the sap from bleeding out, but the water-conducting cells in the stem will still be able to draw in moisture. A few of the flowers that benefit from sealing are campanula, hardy mums, daffodils and narcissus, dahlia, forget-me-nots, heliotrope, hollyhocks, hydrangea, lantana, lobelia, poppies, and stephanotis.

Flowers with woody stems also need special treatment so they can continue to absorb sufficient moisture. Split—do not crush—the ends of the stems of lilacs, butterfly bush, mock

To get the longest vase life from poppies, sear the ends of the stems before arranging the flowers.

orange, rhododendron, and other shrubs with a sharp knife, or tap them gently with a hammer.

For flowers with tough but non-woody stems, such as asters and chrysanthemums, split the end of the stem; then dip it in boiling water for about twenty seconds.

Before conditioning any flower, remove all the leaves that would be underwater in the conditioning vessel. If left on the stem they would just rot in the water, fouling it with bacteria.

To condition cut flowers, stand them *loosely* in a tall container of water, allowing air to circulate freely around the stems. Galvanized metal flower buckets are available from several mail-order garden suppliers, but you can also use a household pail or an old pitcher or any other container you have around the house that's the right size. Lukewarm water is best for conditioning most flowers, although some, such as dahlias, daffodils and narcissus, forget-me-nots, hydrangea, and poppies, prefer cold water. See the Encyclopedia for details on each flower's needs.

Leave the flowers in a dark place, at room temperature or a bit cooler, for several hours or overnight. The darkness causes the stomata (tiny pores in the leaves and stems) to close, reducing the amount of water that will be lost by transpiration.

Flowers with weak stems, such as tulips, should be wrapped in paper before conditioning to support the stems. Green florist's tissue (available in some craft shops) works best because it will not disintegrate easily in water, but you can also wrap the stems in plain tissue paper or newspaper. Wrap the flowers the way a florist would wrap a bouquet: lay the flowers diagonally across the sheet of paper and roll up the paper around the stems. Leave the ends of the stems exposed.

If you wish, add a flower preservative to the conditioning water to extend the life of the cut flowers. You can also add a tablespoon or two of sugar to the water instead of a preservative, to nourish the flowers, although sugar encourages the growth of bacteria. An additional tablespoon of bleach will help prevent bacterial growth. Floral preservatives (available in garden centers and craft shops selling florist supplies) nourish the flowers but also contain chemicals that encourage water-conducting cells to continue functioning, and they hinder the growth of bacteria.

To condition foliage, lay it flat in a pan of water, with or without preservatives, and soak it. Yellow leaves, however, are best treated like flowers and conditioned in an upright position; yellow foliage may spot or turn brown if laid in water, especially cold water. To condition silver leaves, wrap them in cloth or florist's tissue, and dip the stems ends in boiling water for about twenty seconds, then in cold water.

Containers for flowers

There are all sorts of containers in which you can show off your flowers: glass vases, clear or opaque, in a range of sizes, shapes, and colors; ceramic jugs, bowls, and pots, glazed in any color of the rainbow; fancy pedestal vases atop figurines; oriental porcelain vases and ginger jars; charming delftware, silver, pewter, or brass containers; wicker or woven baskets lined with plastic; glass or pottery pitchers; reproductions of antique pieces—the choices are limited only by your imagination. Yard sales, antique stores, and thrift shops are great places to look for interesting containers.

A container helps set the style of an arrangement. Figurine and pedestal containers are lovely for formal arrangements in formal rooms. Sleek glass vessels are ideal for a contemporary look. Antique pieces are especially suited to settings and arrangements from the same historical period. Pottery, earthenware, and wicker and woven baskets are charming in country-style settings.

The color and style of a container should complement both the flowers and the furnishings in the room. Opaque containers in leafy green are easy for beginners to work with; the container's opacity hides pinholders, foam, and other underpinnings from view, and the green color becomes a visual substitute for the stems and focuses attention on the flowers. Neutral browns, beiges, and grays are also easy to work with because they go well with flowers of practically any color, from pastels to brights.

Your job will also be easier if the container has a rather narrow neck that can help support the stems, and if it is tall enough for the water inside to cover the stems to half their length.

Glossy containers look especially nice with shiny leaves and flowers. If you have a favorite silver or marble container that you would like to use, treat it carefully, for these materials scratch easily. Consider using the container as a cachepot, and create the arrangement in a smaller container that will fit inside it. This is also a good way to work with a big, wide container that you especially love but that would be difficult to fill with flowers.

You might also purchase a set of candle cups that fit onto candleholders and allow you to create small arrangements of flowers and candles to dress up a dining table or mantelpiece.

If you wish, you can place the container on a base for additional emphasis. A base might be a straw mat, trivet, cutting board, place mat, or piece of colored fabric.

Whatever container you choose, be sure it works *with* the flowers and the room, and not against them. In a room filled with antiques and bric-a-brac, a simple container with a simple arrangement would be most appropriate. An elaborately patterned container will be shown off to its best advantage by an uncomplicated arrangement in a simple color scheme. If, on the other hand, you want the flowers to be the stars of the show, create a big, colorful composition in a simple container.

Tools and equipment

In addition to containers you will need some tools and supplies for cutting and arranging your flowers. Several types of shears are available for cutting tender-stemmed blossoms. The smallest have smooth, pointed blades just a few inches long and are meant for snipping tender stems. There are also scissorlike shears that cut stems in a variety of sizes. Flower-gathering shears allow you to

JAPANESE FLOWER SHEARS

ANVIL PRUNER

FLOWER GATHERER

cut flowers and strip thorns and leaves from the stems. Or if you prefer, buy a florist's knife. If your cutting gardens will contain some woody plants, invest in a good pair of pruning shears.

Metal flower buckets, imported from England or France and available from mail-order garden suppliers, are tall and narrow, and ideal for conditioning flowers before arranging them.

Florist's foam (Oasis) is indispensable. You can buy it in blocks of various sizes and densities, and with a sharp knife carve it into a globe or a cone or whatever shape you need so the block fits your container. Cut the foam slightly smaller than the container so there is space for a water reservoir. Foam is extremely useful in large and wide-mouth containers, because you can insert flower stems at whatever angle works best. In a pedestal container the foam can be higher than the rim of the container so that you can place flowers to cascade down the sides of the container. Flowers also tend to last longer in foam than when they sit in a vase full of water. They draw as much moisture as they need from the foam, but they will not drown. Rinse the foam thoroughly to help remove salts which may harm flowers, then soak the foam before you use it, for about fifteen minutes or until it cannot absorb any more water. If you use a floral preservative, add it to the water as you soak the foam. It is a good idea to also use a preservative in the water when arranging the flowers, to counteract any salt residues that may remain in the foam.

To hold the foam in place you will need some waterproof florist's tape, which is usually green. Adhesive clay is also useful, especially for anchoring a pinholder in the bottom of a container.

Pinholders come in handy for simple arrangements in shallow containers, and a complex arrangement can be held in place with a combination of a pinholder and a piece of chicken wire. Place the pinholder in the bottom of the container and secure it. Lay the chicken wire over the top and press it down among the pins; then fold the ends in and over so that all the chicken wire is inside the container.

A layer of marbles or pebbles in the bottom of a container can provide minimal control for very loose, informal arrangements. Use clear marbles if you have a clear glass container.

Basics of floral design

There are so many ways to show off the flowers from your garden. You can make loose bunches, or bouquets lavish or simple, to place in your favorite containers. Or you might want to feature a single perfect blossom in a bud vase, or a few flowering stems in a long-necked container. Or perhaps you want to try your hand at traditional flower arranging.

If all you want to do is fill pitchers and bowls with loose bunches of flowers, you need not be bound by any rules. Just create a bouquet that looks pretty to you. On the other hand, if you want to learn about the traditional techniques of flower arranging, there are a number of guidelines with which you can work. This section will explain some of the basic rules. But remember, you are creating these arrangements to please yourself; if you don't like a rule, break it and see what happens.

The art of flower arranging is built on a set of formal rules, similar to the rules that govern painting, sculpture, and other visual arts. The flowers and plant materials in an arrangement, their placement, and the way they relate to one another may be expressed as a set of artistic principles. These principles (known as elements of design) indicate, in formal terms, the elements that go into an arrangement.

An all-white arrangement of delphiniums in an elegant silver urn is lovely in a formal room.

Line is an important structural element. It can be vertical, horizontal, diagonal, or circular, and it gives the composition its movement, direction, and two-dimensional shape. The arrangement might be in the shape of a circle, an oval, a crescent, a triangle, a rectangle, or a fan and the lines that make up this shape can be straight or curved, continuous, or broken.

Form is the three-dimensional shape of the arrangement. The composition might take the form of a sphere, a pyramid, or a cube, or it might be freeform.

Space is an external element: the area around the arrangement, its setting, and frame of reference. It is important that the overall size of the arrangement be kept in scale with the space around it. If the arrangement is too big for the space, it will be overwhelming; if it is too small, its impact will be lost.

Color is always an essential part of a floral composition. Colors can be subtle or dramatic, harmonious or contrasting, and can evoke moods. Colors are discussed briefly later in this chapter, and in more depth in Chapter One.

Be aware of both the visual and the tactile textures of the plant materials you use, that is, both how they look and how they would feel if you were to touch them. Visual textures include glossy, dull, feathery, delicate, lacy, chunky, and bold. Tactile textures include fuzzy, smooth, rough, velvety, prickly, and soft. Develop a sensitivity for textures, and you will add an extra dimension to your arrangements.

Principles of design

The rules that govern the ways in which you actually use the elements of design to create an arrangement are called the *principles* of floral design. These principles are sometimes applied in actual terms, such as balancing three flowers on one side of an arrangement with three flowers on the other side. In other cases the principles are applied in visual, or apparent, terms, based on the way things appear to be. Thus the three flowers could be balanced with one larger flower of equal visual weight.

Balance is the sense of stability created by building the arrangement around an imaginary axis running vertically through the center of the design. Balance can be symmetrical, with equal weight on both sides of the axis, or asymmetrical. In either case the design should not appear to tilt to one side or the other, or to lean forward or backward when viewed from the side. To achieve balance, place the largest, heaviest flowers and the darkest colors low and in the center of the composition, gradually working outward to position the lighter, more delicate flowers toward the top and along the outside.

When a composition has a dominant element or focal point, it means that some parts of the composition are more important than others. Perhaps a large flower is featured, or a particular color is emphasized. The focal point is the center, the heart of the arrangement, to which the viewer's eye is drawn. All the lines in the composition converge at the focal point. The greatest weight of material is placed at this point: round shapes; large, weighty flowers; and bright colors. A focal point or dominant element adds interest and excitement to a design.

Scale and size are important considerations in the relationships between the materials and the arrangement, the arrangement and the container, and the arrangement and the room. Choose flowers that are of an appropriate size for the container. Johnny jump-ups and miniature roses would be lost in a big

ARRANGEMENTS

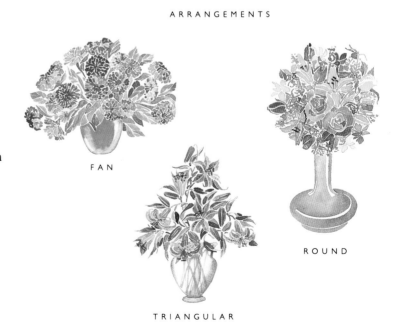

FAN

ROUND

TRIANGULAR

pewter bowl, and a peony or sunflower would dwarf a bud vase. A large arrangement made entirely of tiny flowers would look silly, as would a small arrangement composed of large flowers. Generally speaking, the individual flowers should be no larger than one-quarter to one-third the size of the container in which you arrange them. Also consider the size of the finished arrangement in relation to the furnishings in the room. A big arrangement in a tall pedestal vase would look quite out of place on a small end table.

The term proportion refers to the way the size and shape of the arrangement relate to the container, and to the relative quantities of things in the composition. For the most interesting design, use different proportions of flowers and foliage, or different proportions of the colors in your color scheme. For example, a blue and white arrangement with equal numbers of blue and white flowers is less successful than a composition in which one color or the other dominates.

The proportion of the arrangement to the container is important as well. A horizontal arrangement looks best when it is two to three times the width or length of the container. A good height for an upright arrangement is one and one-half to two times the largest dimension of the container. In an S-curve, two-thirds of the design is usually positioned above the edge of the container and one-third below.

Rhythm is the movement or activity in an arrangement; it leads the viewer's eye to different parts of the composition. Rhythm can come from linear elements, such as a spiky stem or a trailing vine, and it can also be created with a sequence of sizes. Including different sizes of a particular flower encourages the viewer to look at one, then another, and thus travel visually through different parts of the arrangement. To enhance rhythm,

use straight-sided containers for angular, straight materials and designs and curved or round containers for curved designs and materials. Remove any stems that create crossed lines, which interfere with the rhythm.

Harmony and contrast are also important in bringing cohesiveness and interest to a floral composition. To create harmony, repeat flowers in an arrangement as you would in a garden border to create unity. Or use colors that are related, and thus harmonious. Choosing flowers that would grow in the same outdoor environment—a shady woodland, a bog, a seashore garden, a sunny meadow—is yet another way to create harmony. A container that echoes the feeling of the flowers and the arrangement adds harmony too. A bold, contemporary composition of calla lilies might look strange in a wicker basket but is elegant in a shiny black, sleekly shaped ceramic vase. To create contrast in an arrangement, juxtapose materials with opposite qualities: large and small flowers, smooth and frilly textures, heavy and delicate lines, complementary colors.

The role of plant materials in arrangements

Arrangements are built from flowers, leaves, and other plant materials that fall into three broad categories: spiky shapes, round shapes, and filler.

Spiky, linear materials form the framework of a floral composition and establish its line, direction, and movement. Linear materials include spiky flower forms like salvia, gladiolus, liatris, snapdragon, and larkspur; tall, pointed leaves like those of iris and yucca; vines and trailing stems such as ivy; and branches from flowering cherry, pussy willow, and other shrubs and trees.

FLOWERS, BERRIES, BRANCHES, VINES, AND STEMS FOR LINE

Acanthus, bear's breeches

Alcea, hollyhock

Amaranthus, love lies bleeding

Antirrhinum, snapdragon

Artemisia

Buddleia, butterfly bush

Campanula, bellflower,
   Canterbury bells

Celosia, cockscomb, plume type

Chaenomeles, flowering quince

Consolida, larkspur

Cotoneaster

Cytisus, broom

Delphinium

Dicentra, bleeding heart

Digitalis, foxglove

Eremurus, foxtail lily

Forsythia

Genista, broom

Gladiolus, sword lily

Hamamelis, witch hazel

Hedera, ivy

Hesperis, dame's rocket

Heuchera, coral bells

Iris

Kniphofia, red-hot poker

Lavandula, lavender

Lavatera, mallow

Liatris

Limonium

Lunaria, honesty

Lupinus, lupine

Lysimachia, loosestrife

Lythrum, purple loosestrife

Malus, crabapple, apple

Matthiola, stock

Miscanthus, eulalia grass

Molucella, bells-of-Ireland

Penstemon

Philadelphus, mock orange

Physostegia, false dragonhead,
   obedient plant

Polemonium, Jacob's ladder

Polianthes, tuberose

Polygonatum, Solomon's Seal

Prunus, almond, cherry, peach, plum

Salvia, sage

Solidago, goldenrod, some types

Talinum, jewels of Opar

Veronica

FLOWERS FOR FOCAL POINTS AND ACCENTS

Agapanthus, lily of the nile

Allium

Alstroemeria, lily of Peru

Anemone

Aquilegia, columbine

Calendula

Callistephus, China aster

Camellia

Centaurea, cornflower,
   bachelor's button

Centranthus, red valerian

Chrysanthemum

Clarkia, godetia

Clematis

Cleome, spider flower

Coreopsis

Cosmos

Dahlia

Dianthus, carnation, pink

Doronicum

Echinacea, purple coneflower

Echinops, globe thistle

Eschscholzia, California poppy

Eustoma, lisianthus, prairie gentian

Freesia

Fritillaria

Gaillardia, blanket flower

Gazania

Gerbera, Transvaal daisy

Geum, avens

Helianthus, sunflower

Helichrysum, strawflower

Helleborus, Christmas rose, Lenten rose

Hyacinthus, hyacinth

Hydrangea

Iris

Lavatera, mallow

Lilium, lily

Lycoris, magic lily

Monarda, beebalm, bergamot

Narcissus

Nigella, love-in-a-mist

Ornithogalum

Paeonia, peony

Papaver, poppy

Pelargonium, geranium

Petunia

Primula, primrose

Ranunculus, Persian buttercup

Rhododendron, rhododendron, azalea

Rosa, rose

Rudbeckia, gloriosa daisy,
   black-eyed Susan

Scabiosa

Schizanthus, butterfly flower

Stokesia, Stoke's aster

Syringa, lilac

Tagetes, marigold

Tithonia, Mexican sunflower

Trachymene, blue lace flower, didiscus

Tropaeolum, nasturtium

Tulipa, tulip

Viola, pansy

Zantedeschia, calla lily

Zinnia

Linear materials can be petite or grand, depending on the scale of the arrangement you are making. See the above list of Flowers, Berries, Branches, and Vines for Line.

Large round forms provide focal points in an arrangement, the heaviest weight of the design, the heart of the composition. Smaller round forms are used as accents, to call attention to a line or direction of movement, or to add mass to the design. The lines in the arrangement meet at the focal point, and the movement created by the linear elements stops. Your eye comes to rest in

SMALL FLOWERS AND FOLIAGE FOR FILLER

Ageratum

Alchemilla, lady's mantle

Anaphalis, pearly everlasting

Anthemis, golden marguerite

Armeria, thrift

Asclepias, butterfly weed

Asparagus

Aster, Michaelmas daisy

Avena, oat grass

Brunnera

Cheiranthus, wallflower

Chrysanthemum parthenium, feverfew

Convallaria, lily of the valley

Cotoneaster

Dianthus, sweet william, garden pink

Dicentra, bleeding heart

Elaeagnus, Russian olive

Erica, heath

Euphorbia, spurge

Ferns, many genera and species

Filipendula, meadowsweet

Geranium, cranesbill

Gomphrena, globe amaranth

Gypsophila, baby's breath

Hedera, ivy

Hyacinthoides, wood hyacinth

Iberis, candytuft

Lantana

Lathyrus, sweet pea

Linaria, toadflax

Limonium, statice, sea lavender

Muscari, grape hyacinth

Myosotis, forget-me-not

Pieris, andromeda

Spiraea, Spirea

Talinum, jewels of Opar

Thalictrum, meadow rue

Torenia, wishbone flower

Verbena

Zinnia, miniature sizes

this part of the composition. Roses, daisies, zinnias, peonies, and mums are obvious examples of flowers to use as round focal points. Trumpet-shaped flowers like lilies also fall into this category, as do large, dense clusters of smaller blossoms, such as lilacs. Smaller round flowers such as coreopsis and cosmos make good accents, although in a small arrangement such flowers could serve as focal points.

Which flowers will work as focal points depends on the overall size and scale of the arrangement. A medium-sized flower such as columbine would function as a focal point in a small bouquet of baby's breath and forget-me-nots but would be a minor accent in a large composition with peonies and bearded iris. See the list of Flowers for Focal Points and Accents on page 81 for additional flowers in this category.

Filler materials are small, airy flowers and leaves used to fill gaps in an arrangement and give it a finished, unified look. Fillers are not stuffed into every empty space; rather, they are used to provide continuity among the accented lines and focal points in the composition. Baby's breath, heather, statice, asparagus fern, and boxwood are some classic fillers. Tiny filler flowers like baby's breath can be used by themselves in soft, cloudlike bouquets. One of our favorite fillers, *Talinum*, or jewels of Opar, has 2-foot plumes of glossy scarlet berries a quarter of an inch across, and it's striking on its own, fresh or dried.

Fillers, like focal points, are relative to the overall size of the arrangement. In large arrangements, slightly bigger flowers, such as freesia and dianthus, can serve as fillers. See the above list of Small Flowers and Foliage for Fillers for suggestions.

Another way to use flowers is to mass them in bunches of a single type of flower. Massing small flowers can create a soft, cloudlike effect that is delightful in a country-style setting.

Traditional types of arrangements

Traditionally, flower arrangements have been classified into three types: line, mass, and mass-line. Line arrangements are the simplest kind, an uncomplicated shape built from just a few flowers. They are similar to Japanese-style arrangements in their spare simplicity (although Japanese arrangements follow a strict set of rules). Line arrangements are often built from a few well-placed branches, with some flowers added where the lines converge.

Mass arrangements are full of flowers, like the opulent bouquets in Flemish still lifes and other paintings by the Old Masters. They can be formal or informal, depending on the flowers used, the container, shape of the arrangement, and the colors.

Mass-line arrangements, as you would suppose, combine qualities of both line and mass arrangements. They have a linear shape but are fuller and contain more flowers than a line arrangement. They tend to be formal because of their careful structure. A mass-line arrangement might be horizontal in form, or diagonal, or in the form of an S-curve (known in floristry as a Hogarth curve).

Where to begin?

If you are new to flower arranging, the process may seem a bit overwhelming—so many decisions to make, so many factors to consider. A good first step is to stroll through your cutting garden to see what's in bloom. Then go indoors and think about where you would like to place an arrangement, in which rooms the colors of the flowers currently in bloom will work. Remember, flowers need not be confined to living and dining rooms. You can put fresh flowers in any room. Consider a small, intimate design for a bedroom or bathroom or a sunny, informal bouquet in the kitchen. Herbs are delightful additions to kitchen arrangements; consider including lemon balm, mints, pineapple sage, dill, lavender, purple basil, catmint, or tansy. In an entry hall or foyer, flowers offer a gracious welcome to your home.

If the room contains a lot of active patterns, on walls, drapes, rugs, or other furnishings, you might want to try a monochromatic arrangement, perhaps of a single type of flower as well. A more colorful arrangement, if handled well, can be quite pretty, but a very complicated design could compete with the furnishings for attention.

If you want to create a centerpiece for a dinner party, remember that your guests will want to converse, and that a large, tall arrangement would get in the way. A low, perhaps horizontal arrangement, in a shallow bowl, with or without candles

in the center, might work quite well. Or create small arrangements in candle cups to use with your favorite candleholders. A simple design of white flowers against deep green foliage, accented with white candles, is very elegant.

Avoid using fragrant flowers in an arrangement for a dining table. Heavily scented blossoms such as jasmine and orange blossoms will detract from the enjoyment of the meal and can become quite overpowering in a small room.

When planning the color scheme for an arrangement, consider the lighting in the room. Incandescent light casts a golden glow

This bouquet of sunflowers and salvia juxtaposes yellow and purple, which are complementary colors.

that brightens yellows, oranges, and orangey reds but dulls blues, purples, and cool reds. Fluorescent light is cool and enhances pink, blue, violet, and white.

If you want a relaxed, country-style arrangement, choose a container in a rustic or natural material: wicker, a woven basket, crockery, or earthenware. Opt for cottage garden and old-fashioned flowers, or wildflowers. For a romantic touch, use soft, pastel colors and a profusion of flowers with many delicate textures and flowing lines. Gracefully curving vines enhance the mood as well.

If you prefer a more sophisticated, urban style, use formal flowers in a simple combination of restrained colors, such as blue and white, or all white. Flowers that are associated with florists—roses, irises, tulips, lilies, and tuberoses, for example—are usually considered more formal, even though you can grow them at home.

If your taste runs to the contemporary, choose simple containers with sleek lines and a shiny finish, or perhaps a clear glass vase, or a one-of-a-kind art piece. Spare, elegant arrangements of big, bold flowers and leaves work well in such containers.

Creating an arrangement

When building an arrangement, start off simply. Until you gain experience, work with simple shapes such as circles or triangles, use your favorite flowers, and choose colors to match your decor. Leave artistic statements for later, when you have gained more facility in the language of floral design. Instead of setting out to create a work of art, just work toward creating a simple arrangement of flowers and colors you love.

Choose your container and color scheme before you cut the flowers. The colors in the arrangement will connect the flowers to other furnishings in the room. Colors can help to express a theme (Christmas or the Fourth of July, for instance). They can help create a mood: Cool colors evoke serenity and restfulness, while warm colors are active and upbeat. And color can express the personality of the arranger; you may find over time that you develop certain signature colors. Concoct color schemes for flower arrangements just as you do when designing the garden. See the discussion on color in Chapter One beginning on page 27.

When considering colors, don't forget to think about the colors in your foliage as well as in your flowers. Leaves can be deep green, bright green, yellow-green, golden, variegated, purple-bronze, silver-white, and fiery red or orange in autumn.

Once your flowers have been cut and conditioned, it is time to arrange them. It is essential to start with a clean container. Wash it in soapy water, rinse, then rinse again with a mild solution of ammonia or white vinegar in water to get rid of any bacteria that may have lingered from the last time you used it.

Remove from the stems all leaves and thorns that would be underwater in the arrangement after the stems are cut, to help minimize the growth of new bacteria. For some flowers it's best to remove even the foliage that would be above the water level; zinnias, lilacs, and mock orange, for example, last longer with all their leaves removed. You can add foliage to the arrangement to avoid a stark, bare-stemmed look.

Most flowers like the pH of their water to be about the same as their soil pH, usually neutral or slightly alkaline. But some flowers do have decided pH preferences. Azaleas and rhododendrons, delphiniums, larkspur, stocks, and carnations like acid water. If your tapwater is naturally alkaline, or if you use a water softener, add a teaspoon or two of white vinegar to the water

A horizontal arrangement is ideal for a dining table.

For a square or fan-shaped arrangement, cut all the stems to the same length and place them in the container vertically or fanned out.

Use filler materials to fill gaps between larger materials. But don't plug every hole. Leave some air and space in the design or the arrangement will look crowded. With practice you will develop a feel for how much filler is needed. Positioning the filler material slightly behind the focal points and accents will add depth to the design.

when you arrange these flowers. Test the pH of your water with litmus paper from a scientific supply company, or use a soil pH test kit from the garden center.

To begin, fasten a wet block of foam in the bottom of the container, or put in place whatever other anchoring material you wish to use to position and support the flowers.

To build an arrangement, start by placing the linear elements to form the basic shape of the arrangement—triangle, rectangle, fan, or whatever. For oval or round designs, or for a line arrangement, position an upright stem to establish the vertical axis of the design. In a simple oval composition, that axis goes right up the middle. When you've established the axis, place one or two horizontal materials to define the width of the arrangement.

With the framework in place, position the round forms to provide the mass and focal points of the composition. Try to group the round flowers in pairs or trios, as you would in the garden, for greater impact. Place the largest, heaviest-looking blossoms and thickest stems first, and put them in the center and bottom of the arrangement. Work up and out toward the edges of the form with gradually smaller, lighter flowers.

Caring for flower arrangements

To get the longest possible life from a flower arrangement, change the water often, and replace it with fresh water containing a flower preservative. If the arrangement is in foam, make sure the foam stays constantly wet. A bouquet simply standing in a vase of water will last longer if you change the water every day and cut about ½ inch from the bottoms of the stems every couple of days.

Adding some charcoal (filter charcoal, not barbecue briquettes) to opaque containers will help keep the water fresh.

The key to extending the vase life of cut flowers is to prevent the growth of bacteria. Clean containers and tools, plenty of fresh water, and properly conditioned flowers are most important. Keeping the arrangement out of direct sun and in a cool place with relatively high humidity will also help. When the first flowers fade, you can remove them and get a few more days' life from the rest.

Best of all, when an arrangement must finally be discarded, you can go out to your cutting garden, harvest a new bunch of flowers, and create a fresh new arrangement.

encyclopedia of plants

These illustrated entries are your guide to growing 200 of the best garden and landscape plants for use in spectacular fresh floral arrangements. Each entry describes the appearance of the plant and how to grow it, where it grows best, and how to use it. These recommended selections can be grown without a greenhouse or special equipment. ❧ We have included plants for a wide range of climates and soil types: plants which grow in many diverse regions as well as special selections limited to warm- or cold-winter areas. We have included some plants for good garden conditions and others that are naturally suited to shade and hard-to-use garden spots, so that any garden, in any exposure, can be used to grow something for bouquets. The 200 selections offer a wide range of colors, shapes, and textures in their flowers, leaves, berries, and seedpods. They include many traditional garden favorites as well as some unusual possibilities. There is plant material for all seasons, including winter holidays. ❧ Where possible, we have selected plants that produce more flowers or foliage for arrangements in less space or with less effort. The encyclopedia listings include cut-and-cut-again annuals, spring bulbs which share space with later blooming flowers, reliable perennials which rebloom each year, and fast-growing landscape shrubs and trees suitable for cutting. With these choices, you can harvest freely for bouquets without stripping your landscape.

Encyclopedia entries

Alphabetized by botanical genus, the encyclopedia entries also include common and species names. If species within a complex genus require different treatment, an entry may be split into several parts. Some genera, such as *Rosa* (rose) and *Clematis*, which include many species and cultivars that thrive under similar growing conditions but vary in appearance and preferred pruning technique, are discussed briefly in one entry.

"Description" provides information on flower and leaf color, shape, and size; plant shape and size; growth habits such as invasiveness; time and duration of productivity; and how well the material lasts when cut.

"Hardiness" indicates the geographical areas where the plant is hardy, with reference to the standard zones established in the U.S. Department of Agriculture Plant Hardiness Zone Map, published in 1990 (USDA publication #1475). The zone range can sometimes be extended by giving extra protection or ideal conditions. For instance, a zone 3 gardener can mulch deeply in winter to protect a zone 4 plant, or a zone 8 gardener can grow a zone 10 plant in a pot and take it indoors in winter. Since USDA zones are based on average minimum winter temperature, but summer temperatures within a zone vary widely, notes such as "prefers cool summers" are included.

"Growing conditions" covers plants' preferences for wet or dry conditions; for soil that is acidic or alkaline, rich or average in fertility (nutrient content), or loamy or sandy; and for sun or shade. Loamy soil is dark and crumbly, a balanced mixture of sand, clay, and silt particles. It contains a high proportion of organic matter, such as peat moss, compost, manure, and leaf mold. Other soil types are predominantly clay or sand. Fertile soil is high in trace elements and major nutrients such as nitrogen (N), phosphorus (P), and potassium (K); the NPK percentages in fertilizer products are given, in order, on the label, such as 5-10-5. Where possible, use soil-conditioning natural fertilizers such as manure, earthworm castings, cottonseed meal, rock powders, or compost. Chemical fertilizers add nutrients but do not improve soil texture. All purpose, flower, and tomato fertilizers have lower N and higher P and K values than lawn fertilizers, which are higher in nitrogen. Soil pH —that is, acidity, neutrality, or alkalinity (sweetness)—is mentioned only for plants with a strong pH preference; others prefer a pH near neutral or adapt to a wide range.

A site in full sun receives six or more hours of unimpeded sunlight per day. Partial shade refers to a spot that either gets strong sunshine for only three to five hours per day or gets filtered sunlight all or most of the day. Shade refers to a spot that gets little or no direct sunlight.

Most plants will survive in less than ideal situations, but they usually produce fewer, poorer flowers. An ability to tolerate a range of conditions is mentioned in an entry only if the plant remains attractive under varying or adverse conditions.

Recommendations for the spacing and depth of planting are given at the end of the "Growing conditions" section.

"Planting" covers the recommended times for setting out divisions, transplants, or potted plants; for planting seed indoors or outdoors; and for taking softwood (still green and flexible) or hardwood (mature, woody) cuttings. The application of rooting-hormone products such as Rootone™ usually increases the percentage of success with cuttings, and we recommend their use, though this recommendation is not restated in each entry.

Plant propagation is complex, but the guidelines here will get you started. Also, partly as a warning, the amount of time to allow for germination and growth is indicated, especially of slow, erratic, or difficult species.

"Care" gives an indication of how much attention a plant needs and what procedures, such as protection from pests, pruning (time and method), fertilization, mulching, deadheading, and staking, are involved. Deadheading means the removal of spent flowerheads; harvesting the flowers while still fresh gives the same benefit. Mulch materials and recommended depth of mulch vary greatly with local conditions. More detailed descriptions of these operations are given in the text.

"Harvesting and conditioning" covers the times and methods of cutting, sealing, and conditioning materials for the longest possible vase life. Commercial floral preservatives can be used for all flowers in both conditioning and arranging water, and we recommend their use. Because formulations vary, specific brands are not mentioned. However, most include several substances which feed flowers and prevent the growth of bacteria in the water.

At times, we mention using sugar, salt, or bleach in the water. Sugar, used at 1 teaspoon per quart of water, feeds the flowers. Salt, used at 1 teaspoon per quart, increases the plant's uptake of water and helps certain flowers, such as begonias, reach a firm state of conditioning but is not good for all types. Bleach, used at 1 teaspoon per quart, prevents the growth of bacteria in the water. While it can be used with all flowers, it is most needed in the water of long-lasting ones or those unusually prone to bacterial infection. These additives should be used in the conditioning water but may also be included in the arranging water. If you use sugar and expect the bouquet to be a lasting one, be sure to use bleach, too, or to change the water often, as the sugar favors the growth of bacteria.

"Stand in deep water for several hours" means stand in water up to the flower heads or, for foliage, the uppermost leaves. Floral materials can also be cut and used instantly if their longevity is not important, or if they do not wilt at first when massed in a deep container which holds enough water to condition them even as they decorate the room. A few flowers serve well without conditioning, but the majority are greatly improved by it.

"Uses" indicates the plant's most popular uses in a bouquet, as a filler, focal, linear, accent, or massed element. Function is related to color, scale, and context. For instance, a mid-sized round blossom such as a columbine can be used as a focal point in a small bouquet, but as a filler or accent when used with bigger blossoms in a larger-scale arrangement. Flowers for drying have not been emphasized, but we do cite those easily air-dried. The same is true of those for edible garnishes and for winter forcing.

Using this encyclopedia

How you use this part of the book depends on your priorities. You may browse through the photographs for plants that appeal to you, then read the entries to see whether they will grow in your garden's unique conditions. Or you may decide to locate all the perennials (under "Description"), then find those in the colors and shapes you like, which suit your climate, soil type, and exposure. You may prefer to start from lists of plants for shade, dry areas, and so on in the text. If you live in a difficult climate, you can look for plants in your zone (under "Hardiness"). You can even use those glossy nursery catalogs to make your wish list and then, using the entries, choose favorite plants that are most likely to succeed in your garden.

ACANTHUS
BEAR'S BREECHES
A. mollis

DESCRIPTION: Perennial. Tall violet flower spikes above spiny, deeply cut, dark glossy leaves. Semievergreen, somewhat shrublike. Blooms late summer. Species and cultivars range from 2 to 5 ft. tall and wide. Plants bloom for a month, last 2 weeks when cut.

HARDINESS: Zones 6 to 10. Likes heat; killed by deeply frozen ground.

GROWING CONDITIONS: Prefers well-drained, sandy loam enriched with compost, partial shade, average moisture, and winter protection. Space plants 3 to 4 ft. apart. Grow in a confined spot or add underground barriers to control invasiveness if space is limited.

PLANTING: Plant divisions in early spring as new growth begins, acclimatized potted plants at any time during growing season. Start seeds indoors in March; then grow outdoors for two years in large pots that will accommodate deep taproots before moving to permanent spots.

CARE: Apply 2 handfuls of manure or compost to each established plant in fall or early spring. Divide in late winter or early spring if crowded, digging about 2 ft. deep. Mulch around crowns winter and summer; remove mulch if soil becomes soggy. Protect young plants from slugs. Cut off flowering stems at base when blooms have faded.

HARVESTING AND CONDITIONING: Cut when lower flowers have opened, in morning or evening. Recut stems and slit, dip stem ends briefly in boiling water, then condition in deep water for several hours.

USES: Flowers as imposing linear element, leaves as filler.

ACHILLEA
YARROW
A. filipendulina, A. millefolium,
A. ptarmica

DESCRIPTION: Perennial. *A. ptarmica* has small, buttonlike white flowers in loose sprays; *A. filipendulina* has wide, tight, flat-topped gold clusters several inches wide; *A. millefolium* has smaller flat-topped clusters in white, yellow, or pink. Ferny leaves, pungent aroma. Most cultivars 2 to 4 ft. tall. Blooms in summer for about 4 weeks. Cut flowers last 1 week.

HARDINESS: Zones 3 to 8. Tolerates cold and heat.

GROWING CONDITIONS: Prefers average to fertile, well-drained, loamy soil; average moisture; and full sun or partial shade. Space plants 1 to 3 ft. apart.

PLANTING: Plant divisions in spring, acclimatized potted plants at any time during growing season. Grows easily from seed; takes 2 years to bloom. Sow seeds thinly in prepared beds in summer or start indoors in spring and transplant.

CARE: Apply 1 handful manure or compost to each established clump in fall or early spring. If crowded, divide or transplant plants in spring or fall. Mulch around crowns unless soil is soggy. Deadhead.

HARVESTING AND CONDITIONING: Cut flowers when half the florets have opened, before pollen shows, in morning or evening. Recut and slit stem bases, remove lower leaves, and condition in deep, cool water for several hours. Cut leaves any time; submerge in cool water for several hours.

USES: Flowers as focal points or filler, leaves as filler.

AGAPANTHUS
LILY OF THE NILE
A. africanus, A. praecox subsp.
orientalis

DESCRIPTION: Perennial. Flowers in shades of white to blue-violet are dense globelike umbels 4 to 8 in. wide on straight, leafless stems. Handsome straplike leaves usually vanish in winter. Plants 1½ to 3 ft. tall. Blooms in summer for 1 month. Cut flowers last 2 weeks.

HARDINESS: Zones 8 to 11 without protection. All zones if kept from freezing in winter. Tolerates heat.

GROWING CONDITIONS: Prefers rich, sandy loam soil with excellent drainage. Good for large tubs. Grows best in full sun, 2 ft. apart, with ample moisture.

PLANTING: Plant divisions or potted specimens in spring, giving each a dose of manure tea. Can be grown from seeds sown indoors in spring; will take at least 2 years to flower.

CARE: Apply 1 handful of manure or compost to each clump in fall, adding more compost in spring. Avoid disturbing roots, which are thick and matted. When necessary (every few years), divide with two garden forks. Mulch in zones 8 to 11, but elsewhere bring plants indoors in winter. (An entire tubful, with soil kept fairly dry, may be stored in a cool basement and put out again in spring.) Deadhead after blooms fade.

HARVESTING AND CONDITIONING: Cut when one-fourth of flowers have opened. Stand in deep water for several hours.

USES: Focal element or single specimen.

AGERATUM
FLOSS FLOWER
A. houstonianum

DESCRIPTION: Annual. Clusters of fuzzy little blue, pink, or white flowers whose stems are sometimes too short for cutting; seek out taller types such as 'Cut Wonder' and 'Southern Cross' for bouquets. Blooms late spring through summer. Leaves wide and downy. Plants 6 to 18 in. tall. Cut flowers last 1 week.

HARDINESS: All zones. Takes all weather from cool to hot; does not withstand frost.

GROWING CONDITIONS: Prefers rich, loamy soil and plentiful moisture. Grows in full sun or partial shade. Plant 1 ft. apart in well-tilled soil, incorporating flower fertilizer and compost into the bed.

PLANTING: Set out bedding plants in spring after the danger of frost passes. Easily grown from seed sown indoors or in a frost-free cold frame 8 weeks before the frost-free date. Sow thinly, ⅛ in. deep; keep seedlings moist. Transplant outdoors when weather is stable and plants are large enough to handle.

CARE: Side-dress with compost or flower fertilizer in midsummer. Harvest or deadhead frequently. Remove and replace spent plants; thin others if overcrowded. Mulch in dry or hot climates.

HARVESTING AND CONDITIONING: Cut when half of flowers on stem have opened, in morning or evening. Stand in deep, warm water for several hours.

USES: Filler or accent element.

ALCEA
HOLLYHOCK
A. rosea, A. rugosa

DESCRIPTION: Perennial or biennial. Large, round flowers, single or double, in every color but blue. Bloom several at a time on tall spires. Leaves are roundish and hairy, forming a tidy basal rosette in winter and spring. Species and cultivars range in height from 3 to more than 8 ft. Blooms 1 to 2 months in summer. Cut flowers last 1 to 2 weeks.

HARDINESS: Zones 4 to 8 as perennials or biennials; only as biennials in 9 to 11. Killed by long, hot summers.

GROWING CONDITIONS: Prefers rich, loamy, neutral or slightly alkaline soil; full sun; and average moisture. Space plants 2 to 4 ft. apart.

PLANTING: Plant divisions in early spring, acclimatized potted plants at any time during growing season. Sometimes blooms the first year from seed if planted in winter. Sow ¼ in. deep indoors and transplant, or outdoors at about 65°F.

CARE: Apply 3 handfuls of manure or compost to each established clump in fall. If necessary, divide in spring, while growth is small. Mulch around crowns winter and summer. Stake when planting, especially doubles or in partly shady or windy areas. If plants get rust, destroy them and plant new ones in fresh soil.

HARVESTING AND CONDITIONING: Cut in morning or evening. Dip stem ends in boiling water, fill hollow stems with water, and plug with cotton. Stand in deep, warm water for several hours.

USES: Large-scale linear element.

ALCHEMILLA
LADY'S MANTLE
A. mollis

DESCRIPTION: Perennial. Small greenish yellow starlike flowers in airy clusters above attractively pleated round, silvery green leaves. Plants 12 to 18 in. tall when in bloom, and almost as wide. Blooms from late spring through early summer, up to 2 months if weather is cool. Cut flowers last up to 2 weeks.

HARDINESS: Zones 3 to 7. Cannot tolerate dry heat.

GROWING CONDITIONS: Prefers loamy soil enriched with compost, bright partial shade, and moist but well-drained conditions. Space 2 ft. apart.

PLANTING: Plant divisions in early spring just as new growth begins, potted plants at any time during growing season; overcast day preferred. Self-sows freely; seedlings are sizable in two years. Sow seed ⅛ in. deep in shaded bed in summer, or indoors. Transplant when large enough to handle.

CARE: Apply 1 handful manure or compost to each established plant in fall or early spring. In autumn or early spring, thin or transplant volunteers crowding established plants. Deadheading is optional; leave flowers on for self-sown plants. Mulch around crowns winter and summer; remove mulch if soil becomes soggy.

HARVESTING AND CONDITIONING: Cut stems of freshly opened flowers near the plant's base in early morning or evening. Stand in deep water for several hours.

USES: Flowers as filler, leaves as either filler or focal material.

ALLIUM
ORNAMENTAL ONION
A. aflatunense, A. christophii, A. giganteum, A. neapolitanum, and others

DESCRIPTION: Bulb (most), or perennial. Flowers are round or oval umbels on straight, leafless stems, in white, yellow, rose, or violet. Species vary greatly in umbel width (1 to 12 in.) and stem height (6 in. to more than 4 ft.). *A. neapolitanum* sweetly scented; some species oniony. Blooms once a year for 2 weeks, most species in late spring. Attractive seedheads on some species. Straplike leaves yellow, then vanish in summer. Cut flowers last 1 to 2 weeks.

HARDINESS: Zones 4 to 9 (most species).

GROWING CONDITIONS: Prefers average to rich, sandy loam soil with average moisture, full sun, and excellent drainage. Plant 4 to 5 in. deep, 6 to 12 in. apart.

PLANTING: Plant bulbs in fall, acclimatized plants at any time during growing season, preferably spring. Mark locations to prevent stabbing bulbs. Can be grown from seed sown ⅛ in. deep indoors in spring or outdoors in summer; takes at least 2 years to flower.

CARE: Apply 1 handful of manure or compost to each bulb or plant in fall, adding compost in spring. If crowded, dig and divide after blooms fade and foliage yellows. Mulch in winter. Deadhead after blooms fade. Protect from slugs.

HARVESTING AND CONDITIONING: Cut when flowers have begun to open. Stand in deep water for several hours. Change water often.

USES: Focal or massed element, or as a single specimen.

ALSTROEMERIA
LILY OF PERU
A. aurea, A. ligtu, A. pelegrina

DESCRIPTION: Perennial. Trumpet-shaped, large, loose clusters of 3-in. flowers, sometimes speckled, in all shades but blue. Some types sweetly scented. Leaves narrow and glossy, sometimes twisted; roots tuberous. Stems 3 to 4 ft. tall. Blooms in summer for several weeks. Cut flowers last 1 to 2 weeks.

HARDINESS: Zones 8 to 9, and cooler zones with winter protection. Cannot tolerate deeply frozen soil.

GROWING CONDITIONS: Prefers sandy loam enriched with compost, bone meal, and manure, with average moisture, full sun, and excellent drainage. Protect from wind. Plant 8 to 10 in. deep, 1 to 2 ft. apart. Will fail if planted too shallowly. Can be grown in large tubs.

PLANTING: Plant in spring. Can be grown from seed indoors; germination may take as long as 12 months.

CARE: Apply 1 handful of manure to each clump in early spring. Stake. Difficult to divide because plants are deeply rooted. If in pots, bring indoors for winter. Do not let plants dry out in spring or summer; drier conditions are preferred in fall and winter. Mulch, especially in winter. Deadhead regularly. Protect from mice.

HARVESTING AND CONDITIONING: Cut when flowers have begun to open. Stand in deep water for several hours. Remove foliage below water line. Use floral preservative in water; change water often.

USES: Focal point, filler, accent, or as a single specimen.

AMARANTHUS
LOVE-LIES-BLEEDING, JOSEPH'S COAT
A. caudatus, A. tricolor

DESCRIPTION: Annual. *A. caudatus* (love-lies-bleeding) has unusual long, trailing, fuzzy ropes of small red, pink, or yellowish flowers. *A. tricolor* (Joseph's coat) is grown for its multicolored red, yellow, and green lanceolate leaves in starlike clusters. Both species 2 to 3 ft. tall. Ready for cutting at summer's end. Cut leaves or flowers stay fresh about 1 week.

HARDINESS: Zones 3 to 11. Prefers temperatures above 80°F, killed by frost. Tolerates heat in upper 90s F.

GROWING CONDITIONS: Prefers average fertility and moisture, full sun. Grows in poor soil, if well drained. Drought-tolerant. Space 2 ft. apart.

PLANTING: Set out bedding plants grown in individual pots when the danger of frost ends. Do not disturb roots. Sow seed directly outdoors in warm weather, after danger of frost, 1/8 in. deep, 3 in. apart. Light aids germination.

CARE: Thin seedlings to 2 ft. apart when they have four true leaves or are crowded. Side-dress growing plants with all-purpose fertilizer and compost in midsummer. Mulch in dry regions. Protect from Japanese beetles and slugs. Stake top-heavy plants of *A. caudatus*, if needed. Pinch back *A. tricolor* once for bushiness. Deadhead only if unsightly.

HARVESTING AND CONDITIONING: Harvest in morning or evening. Strip off most leaves. Condition in deep water for several hours.

USES: Large-scale accent or focal point.

AMMI
BISHOP'S WEED
A. majus

DESCRIPTION: Annual. Large, round, lacy white flowers in 6-inch umbels. Florets resemble snowflakes. Freely flowering, branched plants bloom in late spring and early summer. In frost-free climates, blooms late winter. Leaves are feathery, serrated, compound. Plants resemble Queen Anne's lace but are fuller. Height from 1 1/2 to over 3 ft. Cut flowers last 4 or 5 days.

HARDINESS: Zones 3 to 10. Tolerates light frost; dislikes heat.

GROWING CONDITIONS: Prefers rich to average soil, average moisture, good drainage, and full sun. Space 1 ft. apart.

PLANTING: Set out bedding plants in spring near frost-free date. Sow seed 8 weeks earlier indoors at 55 to 65°F, or directly outdoors as early as soil can be worked in spring or in late summer or fall. Sow seeds 1/8 in. deep; prefers individual pots or wide spacing. Germinates in 1 to 3 weeks. Dislikes disturbance of roots. In zones 8 to 10, sow in fall; grow as biennial.

CARE: Thin or transplant seedlings to correct spacing and desired sites when they are 4 in. tall or are crowded. Side-dress with flower fertilizer and compost during growth. Mulch in hot or dry areas. Deadhead.

HARVESTING AND CONDITIONING: Cut when half of flowers on umbel have opened, in morning or evening. Strip off lower leaves. Stand in deep water for several hours.

USES: Filler or massed element.

ANAPHALIS
PEARLY EVERLASTING
A. margaritacea, A. triplinervis

DESCRIPTION: Perennial. Clusters of small, pearly white, starlike flowers for 1 month in summer; grayish, fuzzy leaves. Ranges in height from 8 in. to 3 ft. *A. margaritacea* is taller and withstands drought. Cut flowers last over 1 week.

HARDINESS: Zones 3 to 8. Tolerates cold winters; killed by hot, humid summers.

GROWING CONDITIONS: Prefers well-drained soil of poor to average fertility, with average moisture. Do not overfertilize or plants will be leggy. Benefits from bonemeal. Grows in full sun or partial shade. Space 1 to 2 ft. apart.

PLANTING: Set out divisions in spring before new growth begins, potted plants at any time during growing season. Blooms from seed in 2 years; sow 1/8 in. deep outdoors in spring or fall, or indoors any time at about 65°F. Set out after danger of frost passes.

CARE: Apply all-purpose fertilizer, compost, and bonemeal each spring. If necessary, divide in spring, while growth is small. Replant at same depth. Mulch around crowns winter and summer. Remove mulch if soil becomes soggy. Stake if necessary.

HARVESTING AND CONDITIONING: Select spikes just beginning to bloom but whose centers can be seen. Cut in early morning or evening. Strip off leaves below water line. Stand in deep water for several hours.

USES: Filler element.

ANEMONE
WINDFLOWER
A. coronaria, A. × fulgens, A. hupehensis, A. vitifolia

DESCRIPTION: Perennial. Poppylike, round red, pink, white, blue, or violet flowers 2 to 6 in. wide on strong stems. *A. coronaria* and *A. × fulgens* are 18 in. tall, from tubers. Bloom in spring. *A. hupehensis* and *A. vitifolia* are 3 ft. tall. Bloom in summer. Cut flowers last 4 to 7 days.

HARDINESS: *A. hupehensis*, zones 5 to 8; *A. vitifolia*, zones 4 to 8; *A. × fulgens*, zones 7 to 10; *A. coronaria*, zones 8 to 10, and all zones with winter protection.

GROWING CONDITIONS: Prefers average to rich sandy loam soil with average moisture, full sun to partial shade, and excellent drainage. Space *A. hupehensis* and *A. vitifolia*, for partial shade, 2 1/2 ft. apart. For tuberous types, soak overnight and plant 4 in. deep, 8 in. apart.

PLANTING: Set out plants or tubers in spring or when temperatures remain at about 50°F.

CARE: Apply 1 handful of manure or compost to each plant in spring. If crowded, divide in early spring. Mulch around crowns winter and summer. Mulch tuberous anemones deeply in winter. Harvest or deadhead frequently. Dust with rotenone to prevent leaf rollers.

HARVESTING AND CONDITIONING: Cut when flowers have begun to open. Recut stems under water. Stand in deep, cold water for several hours. Dislikes floral foam. Use bleach in container water.

USES: Mainly focal point, varies with species.

ANETHUM
DILL
A. graveolens

DESCRIPTION: Annual herb. Wide, flat umbels of tiny yellow flowers or fat green seeds ripening to brown. Blooms in summer on strong stems. Green, threadlike, aromatic foliage. Plants 2 to 4 ft. tall, varying with conditions. Cut flowers last 4 to 5 days, seedheads 1 week or more.

HARDINESS: Zones 3 to 11. Tolerates light frost and high heat.

GROWING CONDITIONS: Prefers well-drained soil enriched with compost and leaf mold, full sun, and average moisture. Space 10 in. apart for well-developed heads, closer if grown only for foliage.

PLANTING: Set out plants after danger of frost ends, or 2 weeks earlier. Sow seed ¼ in. deep indoors in individual pots 10 weeks before last frost or outdoors in early spring, several weeks before last expected frost. Needs light to germinate. Sprinkle ripe seeds in summer; plants tend to self-sow. Dislikes root disturbance; transplant with care.

CARE: Transplant or thin seedlings in spring. Cut off flowers to promote foliage growth or to prevent self-sown seedlings, if unwanted. Mulch in hot, dry weather. Protect from aphids and caterpillars.

HARVESTING AND CONDITIONING: Cut newly opened flowers, developed seedheads, or ferny foliage in morning. Stand in deep water for several hours.

USES: Flowers, leaves, and seedheads used as filler or edible, aromatic garnish.

ANTHEMIS
GOLDEN MARGUERITE
A. tinctoria

DESCRIPTION: Perennial. Masses of yellow daisies up to 3 in. wide on strong stems. Plants are up to 3 ft. tall with feathery leaves. Blooms throughout summer and fall. Cut flowers last up to 1 week.

HARDINESS: Zones 3 to 7. Tolerates cold winters; killed by excessively hot, dry summers.

GROWING CONDITIONS: Prefers average, well-drained soil, not too fertile; full sun; and average moisture. Also grows in bright partial shade. Space 2 to 3 ft. apart.

PLANTING: Plant divisions in early spring before new growth begins, acclimatized potted plants at any time during growing period. Grows quickly from seed; sow ⅛ in. deep indoors or outdoors at 65 to 70°F. Shift to larger pots or permanent places when crowded.

CARE: Apply 1 handful of manure or compost to each established clump in fall or early spring. Divide old plants in spring or fall if centers have started to die out, discarding unhealthy portions. Replant at same depth. Deadhead frequently. Cut back stems in midsummer to encourage new growth. Mulch around crowns in winter and summer. Remove mulch if soil becomes soggy.

HARVESTING AND CONDITIONING: Select flowers with tight centers. Cut in early morning or evening. Strip off lower leaves and stand in deep water for several hours.

USES: Focal points or filler.

ANTIRRHINUM
SNAPDRAGON
A. majus

DESCRIPTION: Tender perennial, usually grown as an annual. Freely flowering plants with brilliant spires of blossoms from late spring to fall—a productive choice for small gardens. Available in mixed or individual colors, except blue. Tubular flowers are either in the dragon's head shape, ruffled, or doubled. Height 8 in. to 4 ft., depending on cultivar; 3-ft. types best for cutting gardens. Flowers last up to 1 week when cut.

HARDINESS: All zones, as annual. Tolerates light frost, killed by severe freezing weather.

GROWING CONDITIONS: Prefers fertile, loamy soil, average moisture, and full sun (partial shade in hot areas). Space 2 to 3 ft. apart.

PLANTING: Set out nursery-grown plants 1 to 2 weeks before frost-free date, or grow transplants indoors from barely covered seed sown 3 months ahead of planting time.

CARE: Mulch around crowns in summer. Side-dress with flower fertilizer in midsummer. Remove spent flowerheads. Water more often if plants tend to wilt at midday. Discard plants in fall except in mild-winter areas. Discard plants if prone to disease.

HARVESTING AND CONDITIONING: When lower flowers have opened, cut spikes in early morning or evening. Immediately plunge into a bucket of cool water up to lowest flowers on stems. Strip off leaves; cut stems under water; condition for several hours or overnight.

USES: Linear element.

AQUILEGIA
COLUMBINE
A. chrysantha, A. flabellata,
A. hybrids

DESCRIPTION: Perennial. Nodding, usually spurred flowers of unusual shape. Airy clusters on wiry stems. Come in all colors, often bicolored. Ferny, whitened leaves. Species and cultivars range in height from 6 in. to 3 ft. Choose tall types for cutting. Blooms for 1 month in spring. Cut flowers last 3 days.

HARDINESS: Zones 3 to 8. Short-lived. Tolerates cold winters, killed by heat and drought.

GROWING CONDITIONS: Prefers loamy soil enriched with compost and leaf mold, partial shade, and average to moist conditions. Space 2 to 3 ft. apart.

PLANTING: Set out divisions or potted plants in early spring. Self-sows freely; offspring vary in color and size but are good replacement plants. Sow seeds ⅛ in. deep indoors or out near 70°F; transplant.

CARE: Apply 2 handfuls compost to each established clump in fall or early spring. Easily harmed by strong fertilizer. If necessary, divide clumps in spring, every 3 years, without cutting taproots. Transplant volunteers in spring. Remove and discard leaves spoiled by leaf miners. Mulch around crowns winter and summer. Remove mulch if soil becomes soggy.

HARVESTING AND CONDITIONING: Cut before flowers open fully, in morning or evening. Add bleach to water; stand in deep, cool water for several hours.

USES: Flowers as focal points or filler, leaves as filler; take only one leaf per plant to avoid weakening it.

ARMERIA

THRIFT, SEA PINK
A. maritima, A. pseudarmeria

DESCRIPTION: Perennial. Dense, low mounds of foliage studded with sprightly, round red, pink, or white flowers on firm, straight stems. Narrow, dark green leaves hug the ground. Blooms in spring for several weeks. 6 in. to 2 ft. tall—tall types best for cutting. Cut flowers last up to 1 week.

HARDINESS: Zones 3 to 8 for *A. maritima*, zones 6 to 8 for *A. pseudarmeria*.

GROWING CONDITIONS: Prefers average to rich sandy loam soil with average moisture, full sun, and excellent drainage. Avoid soggy soil in winter. Does well in seaside gardens. Plant 6 to 12 in. apart.

PLANTING: Set out plants in early spring to get bloom the same year. Can be grown from seed sown 1/8 in. deep indoors or out at 60 to 70°F.; presoak seeds overnight for best germination.

CARE: Divide in early spring if crowded or if more plants are needed. Side-dress with manure and compost in fall. Mulch lightly in winter. Deadhead after blooms fade. Transplant divisions to cover bare spots from winterkill. May harbor slugs, though not much affected by them.

HARVESTING AND CONDITIONING: Cut when flowers have begun to open. Stand in deep water for several hours.

USES: Mainly filler or accent element.

ARTEMISIA

WORMWOOD
A. absinthium, A. lactiflora,
A. ludoviciana

DESCRIPTION: Perennial. Grown more for silver foliage than for flowers. Plants range from under 1 to over 3 ft. tall. *A. lactiflora* has small ivory flowers, felty leaves. *A. absinthium* has fine, threadlike leaves. *A. ludoviciana* 'Silver King' has tiny yellow flowers, bold silver leaves. Blooms for 1 month, foliage attractive through summer and well into fall. Lasts more than 1 week in bouquets.

HARDINESS: Zones 3 to 9, most types. Tolerates adverse conditions.

GROWING CONDITIONS: Prefers well-drained, average soil, not too rich (fertilize with bonemeal), and full sun. Gets leggy in shade. Space 1 to 2 ft. apart.

PLANTING: Plant divisions in spring, acclimatized potted plants at any time during growing season. Sow seed indoors 1/8 in. deep, 2 in. apart at 65 to 70°F.

CARE: Side-dress established clumps with compost in fall or early spring. If necessary, divide in spring while growth is small. Restrain stolons of spreading types. Mulch around crowns in winter unless soil is soggy. Pinch back tips for bushiness. Stake tall types if necessary.

HARVESTING AND CONDITIONING: Cut in early morning or evening. Select fresh-looking stems, slit stem bases and recut, then dip stem ends in boiling water. Strip off leaves below water in vase. Stand in deep water for several hours.

USES: Leaves and flowers used as filler.

ASCLEPIAS

BUTTERFLY WEED
A. tuberosa

DESCRIPTION: Perennial. Bright 3-in. clusters of small starlike flowers in hot orange, yellow, pink, or red. Blooms all summer long. Plants 2 1/2 to 3 ft. tall. Tuberous-rooted plants live many years. Narrow leaves, strong stems. Cut flowers last more than 1 week.

HARDINESS: Zones 3 to 10. Tolerates extreme heat and cold.

GROWING CONDITIONS: Prefers average, sandy loam soil with average moisture, full sun, and good drainage. Tolerates drought. Do not plant too close to shallow-rooted trees. Avoid soggy soil in winter. Plant 2 to 4 ft. apart.

PLANTING: Set out divisions in late spring, potted plants at any time during growing season. Grows easily from seed. Sow in sandy soil 1/4 in. deep, 3 in. apart, indoors or out at 60 to 85°F. Plants bloom the following year, sometimes sooner.

CARE: Feed each mature plant in fall and again in spring with 1 handful of manure and 1 of compost. Boost with flower fertilizer in summer to support prolonged bloom. Plants are slow to emerge from dormancy. Divide in late spring very rarely, only if necessary. Transplant outdoor-grown seedlings at the same time. Deadhead after blooms fade.

HARVESTING AND CONDITIONING: Cut when flowers have begun to open. Sear stem ends. Stand in deep water for several hours.

USES: Versatile; filler or focal material.

ASPARAGUS

A. densiflorus, A. officinalis

DESCRIPTION: Perennial. Tuberous roots. Narrow sprouts feather out into ferny plumes in late spring. Inconspicuous white flowers develop into handsome red berries dotting the green leaves. *A. densiflorus* (formerly *A. sprengeri*) is widely grown as an ornamental. The foliage of *A. officinalis*, the edible type, can also be cut for bouquets. Plumes range from 1 to 4 ft. tall and stay green except during freezing weather. Cut foliage lasts 5 to 7 days.

HARDINESS: *A. densiflorus*, zones 9 to 11; all zones if kept from freezing. *A. officinalis*, zones 3 to 8; prefers cold winters.

GROWING CONDITIONS: Prefers moderately rich, sandy loam soil with average moisture, full sun to partial shade, and good drainage. *A. densiflorus* grows well in containers. Outdoors, plant 2 ft. apart.

PLANTING: Set out plants in spring or mild weather. Sow seed 1/2 in. deep, 1 in. apart, indoors in winter or outdoors in spring. Thin first-year plants to 5 in. apart.

CARE: Fertilize at planting time, mulch with compost. Keep moist in first year. Transplant 1-year-old seedlings to permanent places. Bring potted plants of *A. densiflorus* indoors where winters are cold.

HARVESTING AND CONDITIONING: Cut when all leaves have opened on spike. Stand in deep water for several hours.

USES: Leaves used as filler or linear element, berried fronds as accent.

ASTER
MICHAELMAS DAISY
A. × frikartii, A. novae-angliae,
A. novi-belgii, A. tataricus

DESCRIPTION: Perennial. Clusters of purple, white, deep rose, or pink daisies with gold centers. Species and cultivars vary in height and flower size; tall types are best for cutting. *A. tataricus*, with large lilac-colored daisies, is tallest at 6 to 8 ft. For cutting, select 4-ft. cultivars of New England asters (*A. novae-angliae*) and 2- to 3-ft. cultivars of *A. novi-belgii* rather than dwarf strains. Asters bloom from summer into fall. Cut flowers last up to 1 week.

HARDINESS: Zones 4 to 8 for most species.

GROWING CONDITIONS: Prefers full sun and moist, rich, loamy soil; needs good drainage in winter. Plant 2 to 4 ft. apart.

PLANTING: Set out divisions in spring, acclimatized potted plants any time during growing season. Can be grown from seed sown ⅛ in. deep, 2 in. apart, indoors in winter or outdoors in summer; best at 65 to 75°F.

CARE: Use flower fertilizer through growing season. Thin seedlings if crowded. Divide in spring every 2 to 3 years. Pinch back tips for bushiness, except where growing season is short. Deadhead regularly. Stake tall types before flowers bloom.

HARVESTING AND CONDITIONING: Cut when flowers have begun to open. Remove lower leaves. Split and recut stems under water. Stand in deep water with sugar added for several hours.

USES: Filler or massed material.

ASTILBE
A. × arendsii, A. chinensis,
A. taquetii

DESCRIPTION: Perennial. Large, fluffy columnar or feathery plumes of small flowers, in pink, white, lilac, or red. Ferny leaves. Species and cultivars range in height from 6 in. to 4 ft. Blooms for 1 month in summer; longer in cool weather, more briefly above 90°F. Cut flowers last up to 1 week.

HARDINESS: Zones 4 to 8. Tolerates cold winters; killed by excessively hot, dry summers.

GROWING CONDITIONS: Prefers loamy soil enriched with compost, partial shade, and average to moist conditions. Space 2 to 3 ft. apart.

PLANTING: Plant bare-root divisions in early spring before new growth appears, acclimatized potted plants at any time during growing season. Slow to mature from seed (takes several years); sow ⅛ in. deep indoors or outdoors at about 65°F.

CARE: Apply 1 handful manure or compost to each established clump in fall or early spring. If necessary, divide in spring, every 3 years, while growth is small. Replant at same depth. Mulch around crowns winter and summer. Remove mulch if soil becomes soggy.

HARVESTING AND CONDITIONING: Cut in early morning or evening. Select spikes just beginning to bloom, immediately plunge into cool water up to lowest flowers, and soak several hours. Split stem ends; strip off leaves.

USES: Flowers as focal points or filler, leaves as filler. Take only one leaf per plant to avoid weakening it.

AVENA
ANIMATED OATS
A. sterilis

DESCRIPTION: Annual grass. Large, airy panicles of seedheads with twisting, long-bristled spikelets. Bristles curve and uncurve with changes in humidity. Decorative heads are pale green at maturity in summer, age to tan, have strawlike texture. Grassy leaves are green and linear. Height 3 ft. Grows in tufts. *A. fatua*, wild oats, is similar but a little less showy. Blooms summer and fall. When cut, stays fresh 1 week or more.

HARDINESS: Zones 2 to 11. Tolerates light frost and cool or warm climates.

GROWING CONDITIONS: Prefers average soil, fertility, and moisture; good drainage; full sun. Tolerates fairly dry conditions. Space 1½ ft. apart.

PLANTING: Sow seed ¼ in. deep, 4 in. apart, indoors in February or outdoors in spring about 4 weeks before the last expected frost. Set out plants grown indoors after the last expected frost.

CARE: Thin and transplant seedlings to desired locations when they are about 5 in. tall or are crowded. Side-dress growing plants with all-purpose fertilizer and compost in spring and early summer. Mulch in dry areas.

HARVESTING AND CONDITIONING: Cut when seedheads have matured but while still green. Strip off lower leaves. No conditioning needed.

USES: Filler or massed element, fresh or dried.

BEGONIA
TUBEROUS BEGONIA
B. × tuberhybrida

DESCRIPTION: Tuber. Waxy flowers up to 4 in. wide on bushy plants summer into fall. Single or double, white, yellow, orange, peach, pink, or red. Male flowers larger than females; each plant has both. Leaves broadly pointed. Plants upright or pendulous, 1½ to 2½ ft. tall or long. Lasts up to 7 days in vase.

HARDINESS: Zones 8 to 11; farther north with protection. Killed by frost and prolonged heat in upper 90s F.

GROWING CONDITIONS: Prefers loamy, fertile soil, excellent drainage, average moisture, and shade or partial shade. Space 12 in. apart.

PLANTING: Plant bowl-shaped tubers concave side up, 1 in. deep outdoors after frost, or nestled into soil surface indoors 6 weeks before last frost.

CARE: Water sparingly until leaves show, then increase. Use liquid fertilizer throughout growing. Stake upright types. Pinch off female flowers. Mulch. Dig in fall; let dry 2 weeks with soil and leaves attached. Trim tops back to 2 in. and dry further. Remove tops when they fall off; store tubers through winter in a paper bag containing peat moss, at 55°F.

HARVESTING AND CONDITIONING: Cut flowers when they have opened fully, leaves at any time. Split stem bases. Submerge in cool water briefly, then stand in deep water containing 1 tablespoon salt per gallon for several hours before arranging.

USES: Flowers focal, leaves as background element.

BELLIS
ENGLISH DAISY
B. perennis

DESCRIPTION: Perennial, often grown as biennial. Petite single or double white, pink, or red daisies up to 3 in. wide on single 6- to 8-in. tall stems above neat, matlike plants. Blooms spring to summer for about 8 weeks, longer if weather stays cool. Stays fresh 5 days when cut.

HARDINESS: Zones 3 to 9. Not suited to hot weather.

GROWING CONDITIONS: Rich, moist, loamy soil, full sun to partial shade; more shade in warm areas. Space 6 to 8 in. apart.

PLANTING: Set out blooming plants in midspring, divisions in early spring or fall. Sow seed for next year's blooms in early summer, 1/8 in. deep, 3 in. apart, at 70 to 80°F. Can be sown indoors or out in fertile, fine-textured soil.

CARE: Keep soil constantly moist. Mulch in dry areas. Harvest or deadhead often, but allow a few flowers to set seed for self-sown plants, if wanted. Divide in early spring, in summer after bloom ends, or in fall. Side-dress with compost or leaf mold in fall. Overwinter in cold frame in zones 3 to 5.

HARVESTING AND CONDITIONING: Cut when flowers have begun to open, in morning or evening. Stand up to flower heads in cool water for several hours.

USES: Focal material in tiny bouquets, or filler.

BERGENIA
B. cordifolia, B. crassifolia,
B. hybrids

DESCRIPTION: Perennial. Unusual round, leathery leaves 8 in. wide. Evergreen in most zones. Spikes of bell-like, white, pink, red, or purple flowers 8 to 18 in. tall late winter and early spring. Cut flowers last up to 1 week, leaves even longer. In hot areas, leaves burn around the edges in summer.

HARDINESS: Zones 3 to 8. Tolerates cold winters; killed by hot, dry summers.

GROWING CONDITIONS: Prefers moist, rich, loamy, well-drained soil; partial shade; also grows in dry or poor soil. Space 1 to 2 ft. apart.

PLANTING: Plant divisions in early spring, acclimatized potted plants at any time during growing seson. Sow seed 1/8 in. deep outdoors or in cold frame at 45 to 50°F. Germinates in 1 month to 1 year. Shift to larger pots or garden when crowded.

CARE: Apply 1 handful manure or compost to each established clump in fall. Protect from slugs. Divide crowded plants in late winter. Can be propagated from cuttings in winter by burying stems and leaf base of mature leaves; new roots form in spring. Deadhead regularly. Water during dry spells. Mulch around crowns winter and summer; remove mulch if soil becomes soggy.

HARVESTING AND CONDITIONING: Cut young flowers or leaves in early morning or evening. Stand in deep water for several hours.

USES: Flowers as linear element, leaves as accent or filler.

BRIZA
QUAKING GRASS
B. maxima, B. minor

DESCRIPTION: Hardy annual. Airy plumes of dangling green or tan seedheads on heavily branched, wiry stems. Straw-like texture. Leaves are light green, linear, and grassy. Height 1 to 1 1/2 ft. Grows in tufts. *B. maxima* (greater quaking grass) has larger seedheads and more height than *B. minor* (little quaking grass). Blooms summer and fall. When cut, stays fresh 1 week or more.

HARDINESS: Zones 2 to 11. Tolerates varied climates.

GROWING CONDITIONS: Prefers average soil, fertility, and moisture; good drainage; full sun. Tolerates dry conditions. Space 1 ft. apart.

PLANTING: Sow seed 1/4 in. deep, 3 in. apart, indoors in February or outdoors in spring about 3 weeks before the last expected frost. Set out plants grown indoors after the last expected frost.

CARE: Thin and transplant seedlings to desired locations when they are about 5 in. tall or are crowded. Side-dress growing plants with all-purpose fertilizer and compost in early summer. Mulch in dry areas.

HARVESTING AND CONDITIONING: Cut when seedheads have matured but are still green. Strip off lower leaves. No conditioning needed.

USES: Seedheads as filler or as massed element.

BRUNNERA
BUGLOSS
B. macrophylla

DESCRIPTION: Perennial. Sprays of tiny light or dark blue flowers with yellow eyes, 1 to 1 1/2 ft. tall, above forest-green, heart-shaped leaves. There is also a cultivar with variegated leaves. Deep-rooted. Blooms in midspring for several weeks. Cut flowers last up to 1 week.

HARDINESS: Zones 3 to 8. Tolerates cold winters; killed by excessively hot, dry summers.

GROWING CONDITIONS: Prefers loamy soil enriched with manure or flower fertilizer, partial shade, and moist conditions. Good among shrubs. Space 1 ft. apart.

PLANTING: Plant divisions in early spring before new growth begins, acclimatized potted plants at any time during growing season. Requires fresh seed for germination; sow 1/8 in. deep, 1 in. apart indoors or outdoors about 65 to 75°F in spring or summer.

CARE: Apply 1 handful manure or compost to each established clump in fall or early spring. If necessary, divide in early spring, while growth is small. Replant at same depth. Transplant seedlings from previous year in early spring. Mulch around crowns winter and summer. Deadhead regularly; remove browned leaves.

HARVESTING AND CONDITIONING: Cut flowers when sprays have begun to open, in early morning or evening. Slit and recut stems under water, remove lower leaves, and stand in deep water for several hours.

USES: Flowers and leaves as filler.

BUDDLEIA
BUTTERFLY BUSH
B. davidii

DESCRIPTION: Shrub. Densely filled, pointed plumes up to 10 in. long, with tiny fragrant flowers in shades of white, rose, violet, and purple. Narrow green leaves. Blooms prolifically, midsummer to frost. Arching deciduous shrubs 5 to 15 ft. tall depending on cultivar and climate. Freezes to ground in cold areas; treelike where winters are mild. Cut flowers last 3 days.

HARDINESS: Zones 5 to 9.

GROWING CONDITIONS: Prefers rich, loamy soil; full sun; average moisture. Will survive almost anywhere. Space 8 ft. apart in areas where plants freeze or are cut to the ground; 10 to 15 ft. apart (closer for dwarf types like 'Nanho') where winterkill is less likely.

PLANTING: Plant bare-root plants in early spring, acclimatized potted plants at any time during growing season. Easily transplanted. Take cuttings in summer. Sow seed indoors in late winter for bloom same year, or outdoors in summer for bloom next year.

CARE: Mulch with chopped leaves or compost, fertilize in spring and summer. Prune in spring to encourage new growth, which provides the flowers. Can be pruned to the ground each year. Harvest or deadhead regularly to promote bloom. Do not let canes get old.

HARVESTING AND CONDITIONING: Cut spikes which have begun to bloom, in early morning or evening. Slit; dip stem ends in boiling water. Remove foliage below water line. Stand in deep, warm water for several hours.

USES: Linear and filler material.

CALENDULA
POT MARIGOLD
C. hybrids, C. officinalis

DESCRIPTION: Hardy annual. Cream, orange, gold, or peach multipetaled single or double daisylike flowers 1½ to 4 in. wide on strong stems. Flowers close on cloudy days and at night. Fresh, pungent aroma. Branched plants with pointed green leaves, 1 to 3 ft. tall. Blooms spring through fall except during hottest weather; all year in mild zones. Cut flowers last 5 to 7 days.

HARDINESS: Zones 2 to 8 as annual, 9 to 11 as biennial. Tolerates frost down to 26°F; dislikes intense heat.

GROWING CONDITIONS: Prefers loose, light soil; average but steady fertility and moisture; good drainage; full sun or bright partial shade. Space 8 to 12 in. apart.

PLANTING: Set out bedding plants from spring through early fall. Sow seed outdoors ¼ in. deep, 4 in. apart in spring or, in mild areas, in autumn—in well-tilled, fertilized beds. Or sow indoors in individual pots 6 weeks before outdoor planting time.

CARE: Mulch in hot, dry areas. Harvest or deadhead often to promote bloom. Remove branched, spent plants. Prevent mildew by providing good air circulation.

HARVESTING AND CONDITIONING: Cut when flowers have nearly opened fully, in morning or evening. Remove lower leaves. Stand in deep water for several hours.

USES: Flowers as focal or accent material, petals in cooking.

CALLISTEPHUS
CHINA ASTER
C. chinensis

DESCRIPTION: Annual. Tissue-thin petals in all colors but orange, in pompon, single, or cactus form. Flowers 1 to 4 in. wide on bushy plants from 6 in. to 3 ft. tall; 2-ft. types need no staking and are tall enough for bouquets. Blooms 1 to 2 months in summer and fall. Cut flowers last 1 to 2 weeks.

HARDINESS: All zones. Best where summers are cool.

GROWING CONDITIONS: Prefers rich, loamy soil; full sun; plentiful moisture. Do not grow in the same site two years in a row. Space 6 to 18 in. apart.

PLANTING: Set out bedding plants in spring after danger of frost. Prefers well-tilled soil; incorporate flower fertilizer and compost. Sow indoors 8 weeks before frost-free date, ¼ in. deep in individual pots. Do not disturb roots. Sow ¼ in. deep, 4 in. apart outdoors after danger of frost.

CARE: Side-dress with compost or flower fertilizer in midsummer. Thin seedlings when 4 to 6 in. tall. Harvest or deadhead frequently. Remove and replace spent plants. Mulch to keep soil cool. Stake tall types.

HARVESTING AND CONDITIONING: Cut when flowers have opened halfway, in morning or evening. Recut stems under water. Wire stems of large flowers for support, if necessary. Remove all foliage; it wilts. Stand in deep water for several hours.

USES: Focal or accent element.

CAMELLIA
C. japonica, C. sasanqua

DESCRIPTION: Small tree. White, pink, or red flowers 3 to 5 in. wide in a wide variety of shapes; classed as single, semidouble, anemone-form, peony-form, roseform, formal double, or irregular double. Countless cultivars vary in bloom time from fall to spring; a few are sweetly scented. Evergreen leaves are glossy, pointed ovals, sometimes serrated. Trees, where hardy, reach over 15 ft. tall. Cut flowers and foliage last up to 1 week.

HARDINESS: Zones 7 to 9. Cultivars vary in cold tolerance. Open flowers are spoiled by light frost, leaves by hard frost. Plants may be killed by temperatures below 10°F.

GROWING CONDITIONS: Prefers moist, rich, loamy soil and a sheltered position in partial shade. Space 10 to 15 ft. apart (where hardy), or grow in large tubs.

PLANTING: Set out plants in mild weather, not too hot or cold.

CARE: Prune after flowering. Do not let plants become too dense. Mulch, especially if soil is sandy. Fertilize with rotted manure, compost, or acidic fertilizer several times a year. Treat for diseases, thrips, and scale. Bring potted plants indoors for winter in cold zones.

HARVESTING AND CONDITIONING: Cut in early morning or evening. Scrape, slit, and recut stems; stand in deep water several hours.

USES: Flowers used as focal points in bouquets or floating in low bowls; foliage used as filler.

CAMPANULA
BELLFLOWER
C. glomerata, C. medium,
C. persicifolia

DESCRIPTION: Perennial or biennial. Star- or bell-shaped flowers. Nearly 300 species vary in height and flower size; tall types are best for cutting. The prolific biennial *C. medium* (Canterbury bells) offers 2-ft. spires with 2-in. single or double white, pink, or violet bells throughout summer. *C. persicifolia*, a perennial, has 2-in. violet or white bells on 3-ft. spires in late spring. *C. glomerata*, another perennial, has dense, rounded clusters of purple bells on 3-ft. stems in early summer. Cut flowers last up to 5 days.

HARDINESS: Zones 4 to 8 for most perennials; all zones for *C. medium.*

GROWING CONDITIONS: Prefers partial shade where summer temperatures exceed 90°F, full sun elsewhere, and moist, rich, loamy soil. Plant 1½ to 3 ft. apart.

PLANTING: Set out divisions in spring, acclimatized potted plants at any time during growing season. Sow seed ⅛ in. deep, 2 in. apart, indoors in winter or spring; transplant outdoors after danger of frost.

CARE: Thin seedlings if crowded. Divide perennials in spring or fall every 3 years. Pinch back tips of *C. medium* for bushiness. Deadhead regularly. Stake if necessary. Protect from slugs.

HARVESTING AND CONDITIONING: Cut when flowers have begun to open. Remove lower leaves. Sear stem ends of *C. persicifolia*. Stand in deep water for several hours.

USES: Filler or focal material.

CAPSICUM
ORNAMENTAL PEPPER
C. annuum

DESCRIPTION: Annual. Inconspicuous white flowers followed by glossy, colorful round or tapered fruits in rich colors like gold, orange, plum, scarlet, and crimson. Bushy plants usually 1 to 2 ft. tall. Ready for cutting from summer's end to frost. Cut branches of fruit last 7 to 14 days.

HARDINESS: Zones 3 to 11. Needs heat; killed by frost. Tolerates high heat in upper 90s F.

GROWING CONDITIONS: Prefers light, fertile, well-drained, loamy soil; continuous moisture; full sun. Space 2 ft. apart.

PLANTING: Set out bedding plants in well-tilled, well-fertilized planting holes when the danger of frost ends. Slow to grow from seed; start indoors 10 weeks before danger of frost ends. Sow ¼ in. deep, 3 in. apart, in flats or cells. Germinate at 70 to 85°F, then grow a little cooler in very bright light. Move to larger pots if roots are cramped.

CARE: Side-dress growing plants with flower or tomato fertilizer and compost in midsummer. Mulch in dry regions. Pinch back for bushiness only where summers are long; fruits take a long time to ripen.

HARVESTING AND CONDITIONING: Harvest in morning or evening. Strip off lower leaves. Condition in deep water for several hours. Polish fruits if desired.

USES: Focal or accent element.

CATANANCHE
CUPID'S DART
C. caerulea

DESCRIPTION: Perennial. Dark-eyed double blue daisies 2 in. wide with short, squared-off petals, on branched, wiry 2-ft. stems all summer. Slender, whitened green leaves form a tidy rosette. Not long-lived but easy to grow. When cut, stays fresh 6 to 8 days.

HARDINESS: Zones 6 to 8.

GROWING CONDITIONS: Prefers well-drained sandy loam of average fertility, full sun, and good drainage, especially in winter. Does not like competition in root zone. Space 15 to 18 in. apart.

PLANTING: Set out plants in midspring, about 4 weeks before the last frost, or later. Set out divisions in early spring or at any time in fall. Sow seed ¼ in. deep, 2 in. apart, indoors in late winter for bloom the same year, or sow indoors or out in spring or summer for bloom the following year. Take cuttings from the roots in early fall.

CARE: Divide plants once a year in spring to prevent crowding. Harvest or deadhead frequently to promote new blooms. Mulch plants in dry areas and in winter. Side-dress with compost or leaf mold in fall.

HARVESTING AND CONDITIONING: Cut when flowers begin to open, in morning or evening. Dip stem ends in boiling water. Stand up to the flower heads in cool water for several hours.

USES: Filler or massed material.

CELOSIA
COCKSCOMB
C. cristata

DESCRIPTION: Annual. Plumelike or crested flowers of striking silkiness from 2 to more than 6 in. tall or wide, plant heights from 6 in. to 3 ft. Flower heads in every color but blue or white, leaves green or bronze and spear-shaped. Tall, branched types best for cutting. Blooms from midsummer to frost. Cut flowers stay fresh 1 week.

HARDINESS: Zones 2 to 11. Tolerates high heat; killed by frost.

GROWING CONDITIONS: Prefers rich, loamy, loose soil; steady moisture; full sun. Moisture important; if growth slows, bloom is delayed. Space 2 to 3 ft. apart.

PLANTING: Set out bedding plants in well-tilled soil in spring when the danger of frost ends. Sow seeds ⅛ in. deep, 4 in. apart, 6 weeks earlier indoors, or directly outdoors in warm weather, keeping very moist until germination.

CARE: Thin seedlings when 5 in. tall or crowded. Pinch back tips for branched plants, but leave unpinched for full-size, dramatic blooms—especially crested types. Side-dress growing plants with flower fertilizer and compost; keep plants steadily watered and fertilized for maximum productivity. Mulch. Stake plants as they grow, if needed. Pull and replace spent plants.

HARVESTING AND CONDITIONING: Cut newly opened flowers in morning or evening. Dip stem ends in boiling water. Stand in deep water for several hours.

USES: Versatile; focal or filler element, fresh or dried.

CENTAUREA
CORNFLOWER
C. cyanus, C. dealbata,
C. hypoleuca, and others

DESCRIPTION: Annual, biennial, or perennial. Fluffy round flowers 1 to 2 in. wide, on straight stems. Most types blue, white, pink, or red-purple; some yellow. Plants 1 to 4 ft. tall. *C. moschata* (annual or biennial) is fragrant. Species vary more in leaf shape than in appearance of flowers. Perennials bloom in spring and fall, biennials in summer, annuals in summer and fall. Cut flowers last 4 to 7 days.

HARDINESS: Most perennials, zones 4 to 8. Annuals tolerate frost, dislike heat. For larger plants, grow annuals as biennials in cold frames and outdoors in mild-winter areas.

GROWING CONDITIONS: Prefers average to rich, loamy soil; average moisture; full sun (or partial shade for perennials); excellent drainage. Plant 8 to 24 in. apart.

PLANTING: Set out acclimatized potted plants any time during growing season, especially spring. Can be grown from seed sown 1/4 in. deep, 2 in. apart, indoors in late winter or outdoors in summer.

CARE: Use flower fertilizer through growing season. Thin seedlings. If crowded, divide perennials in early spring. Do not let soil of annuals get dry. Pinch back tips for bushiness, except perennials. Propagate from seed or, for perennials, division. Deadhead regularly. Mulch in winter. Stake tall or top-heavy plants.

HARVESTING AND CONDITIONING: Cut unfaded flowers. Recut under water; split large stems. Stand in deep water for several hours.

USES: Versatile; usually used as filler, also attractive massed in bunches.

CENTRANTHUS
RED VALERIAN
C. ruber

DESCRIPTION: Perennial. Large, branching flowerheads made up of small rose-pink flowers in globular clusters. Plants are 2 to 3 ft. tall with fleshy stems and thick, spear-shaped leaves. Flowers appear from late spring to summer and, if harvested, again in autumn. When cut, flowers stay fresh about 5 days.

HARDINESS: Zones 5 to 9. Best in areas with relatively cool summers.

GROWING CONDITIONS: Prefers soil that is slightly alkaline and not too fertile or moist. Will grow in exposed conditions and during drought if temperatures are not too high. Space 1 1/2 to 2 ft. apart.

PLANTING: Sow seed 1/8 in. deep, 1 in. apart, in autumn or spring, outdoors, or spring indoors. Set out divisions, transplants, or basal cuttings in early spring.

CARE: Thin plentiful, self-sown volunteers in spring to keep plants from becoming overcrowded. Divide by digging up and replanting basal cuttings of main plants in spring if they are crowded. Harvest or deadhead regularly after first blooms appear, to promote new bloom. Side-dress with compost in fall.

HARVESTING AND CONDITIONING: Cut when flowers begin to open, in morning or evening. Dip stem ends in boiling water. Stand up to the lowest flower heads in cool water for several hours.

USES: Filler, focal, or massed material.

CHAENOMELES
FLOWERING QUINCE
C. japonica

DESCRIPTION: Shrub. Waxy 1-in. peach, pink, or red-orange flowers aligned on artfully angled stems several feet long. Attractive yellow or reddish fruits in fall. Rounded or weeping shrubs, depending on cultivar, blooming in late winter or early spring before deciduous leaves become prominent. Branches thorny, leaves pointed shiny green ovals or, in a few cases, bronze. Most types are 6 to 8 ft. tall and wide. Cut flowers last 6 to 10 days.

HARDINESS: Zones 5 to 9.

GROWING CONDITIONS: Prefers rich, loamy soil; full sun; average moisture. Space 8 to 12 ft. apart.

PLANTING: Set out bare-root plants in early spring, potted plants at any time during growing season. Can be purchased in bloom. Take softwood cuttings in summer. Plant seed in prepared beds or pots in fall for growth in spring.

CARE: Mulch with chopped leaves or compost; fertilize in spring, summer, and fall. Prune in spring after flowering. Do not let plants become too dense. If leaves yellow, add acidic fertilizer such as is used for hollies and azaleas. Remove and destroy branches affected by fireblight.

HARVESTING AND CONDITIONING: Cut long woody stems as blooms begin to open, in early morning or evening. Scrape and slit stems. Stand in deep water several hours.

USES: Flowers as linear elements, fruit as accents, branches can be forced.

CHEIRANTHUS
WALLFLOWER
C. cheiri

DESCRIPTION: Perennial, treated as a biennial. Fragrant clusters of small, four-petaled or double flowers in all colors but blue. Blooms in late spring and early summer for several weeks. Matlike plants have sword-shaped leaves and are 1 to 2 ft. tall when in bloom. Stays fresh 1 week when cut.

HARDINESS: Cool parts of zones 7 to 10 as a perennial. All zones as a hardy annual or biennial. Not suited to hot weather.

GROWING CONDITIONS: Prefers alkaline, moist, moderately rich soil in full sun. Space 1 ft. apart.

PLANTING: Set out plants in midspring, divisions in early spring or in fall. Sow seed 1/8 in. deep, 3 in. apart, indoors in late fall or early winter, at 60 to 70°F.

CARE: Keep soil moist. Mulch. Pinch back top bud for bushier plants. Harvest or deadhead often. Divide in early spring or in fall, where plants are hardy. If affected by clubroot, discard plants and do not replant in the same site for 2 years. Side-dress with bonemeal and compost in fall, flower fertilizer in spring. Overwinter in a cold frame in zones 4 to 6.

HARVESTING AND CONDITIONING: Cut when flowers begin to open, in morning or evening. Slit and recut stems. Stand in deep, cool water for several hours.

USES: Flowers as focal material in small bouquets, otherwise as filler.

CHRYSANTHEMUM
FLORIST'S CHRYSANTHEMUM
C. × morifolium hybrids

DESCRIPTION: Perennial. Strong-stemmed, bushy daisies with blossoms 1 to 6 in. wide, on branched, mainly fall-blooming plants 12 to 36 in. tall. Singles have gold centers, doubles can be dense or spidery, depending on petal length. Color range includes white, yellow, orange, rust, lilac, and wine red. Flowers classed as spider, football, pompon, reflexed, daisy, spoon, etc., according to flower size and petal shape. Cut flowers last up to 2 weeks.

HARDINESS: Zones 4 to 9 for most.

GROWING CONDITIONS: Prefers full sun and light, well-drained, moist, fertile soil. Plant 2 to 3 ft. apart.

PLANTING: Set out divisions in spring, acclimatized potted plants at any time throughout growing season. Spring and summer are best. Set out fall-purchased plants immediately, to allow them time to establish themselves; even so, they may fail to winter over. Sow seed indoors in February, 1/8 in. deep, 2 in. apart, or outdoors in summer at 65 to 80°F.

CARE: Use flower fertilizer through growing season. Thin seedlings if crowded. To maintain plant vigor, separate and replant offshoots from mature plants at correct spacing each spring when they are about 1 in. tall. Remove dead or unhealthy portions. Pinch back tips for bushiness several times, no later than July 1. Remove extra buds for larger flowers. Deadhead.

HARVESTING AND CONDITIONING: Cut when flowers open. Remove all leaves below water line. Split and recut stems under water. Stand in deep water for several hours.

USES: Focal or accent material.

CHRYSANTHEMUM
FEVERFEW, ANNUAL CHRYSANTHEMUM
C. carinatum, C. coronarium, C. parthenium

DESCRIPTION: Hardy annual or perennial. Strong-stemmed daisies with single or double blossoms 1 to 3 in. wide, on branched plants 1 to over 2 ft. tall. *C. carinatum* and *C. coronarium* are summer-blooming hardy annuals with solitary flowers on long stems. Flowers of *C. carinatum* such as 'Monarch Court Jesters' may be banded in combinations of white, red, orange, yellow, and black. *C. coronarium* (crown daisy) is yellow or yellow and white. Cluster-flowered *C. parthenium* (feverfew), a short-lived perennial, is single or double, yellow or white, with greenish gold centers. Leaves are divided. Cut flowers last 1 week.

HARDINESS: All zones. Prefers cool temperatures.

GROWING CONDITIONS: Prefers full sun and light, well-drained, moist, fertile soil. Plant 1 ft. apart.

PLANTING: Set out divisions of feverfew in spring, acclimatized bedding plants of all types in midspring to early summer. Sow seed indoors in February, barely covering, 2 in. apart, or outdoors as early as soil can be worked. In zones 9 to 11, treat all three as fall-planted biennials.

CARE: Use flower fertilizer through growing season. Thin seedlings if crowded. Divide feverfew in spring every 2 years. Deadhead.

HARVESTING AND CONDITIONING: Cut when flowers open. Remove lower leaves. Split and recut stems under water. Stand in deep water for several hours.

USES: Mainly as filler material.

CHRYSANTHEMUM
PYRETHRUM, PAINTED DAISY, SHASTA DAISY
C. coccineum (syn. *Tanacetum coccineum*), *C. × superbum* (syn. *C. maximum*)

DESCRIPTION: Perennial. Long-stemmed daisies 2 to 4 in. wide, 1 to 4 ft. tall, with gold centers. *C. × superbum* (shasta daisy) has snow-white petals and toothed leaves and forms an evergreen basal rosette from fall to spring. Single or double flowers, borne singly, bloom in late spring or early summer. *C. coccineum* (pyrethrum or painted daisy) has pink or red petals, gold centers; blooms in late spring. Threadlike, divided leaves form a basal rosette fall through spring. Cut flowers last 1 week.

HARDINESS: Zones 4 to 9.

GROWING CONDITIONS: Prefers full sun and light, well-drained, moist, fertile soil. Plant 2 to 3 ft. apart.

PLANTING: Set out divisions in spring, acclimatized potted plants at any time throughout growing season. Sow seed indoors late winter or spring, barely covering, 2 in. apart, or outdoors in summer at 65 to 80°F.

CARE: Use flower fertilizer through growing season. Thin seedlings if crowded. Divide in early spring or fall. Shasta daisies may need division each year; less vigorous painted daisies may remain undisturbed for several years. Stake tall types. Deadhead.

HARVESTING AND CONDITIONING: Cut when flowers have begun to open. Remove lower leaves. Split and recut stems under water. Stand in deep water for several hours.

USES: Focal or accent material.

CLARKIA
GODETIA
C. amoena

DESCRIPTION: Annual. Single or double five-petaled, cup-shaped flowers with satiny texture. Color may be white, cream, peach, rose, or violet. Clusters of flowers 2 to 3 in. wide on plants up to 3 ft. tall. Ordinary, lance-shaped leaves. Blooms for several weeks in early summer. Cut flowers last 5 days.

HARDINESS: Zones 2 to 11. Tolerates light frost; killed by high heat.

GROWING CONDITIONS: Prefers light, average to rich soil; average moisture; good drainage; full sun. Tolerates cool, dry conditions. Does not transplant well if roots are disturbed. Space 8 to 12 in. apart.

PLANTING: Sow seed indoors in February in individual pots or outdoors in spring about 3 weeks before the last expected frost, 1/8 in. deep, 2 in. apart. Set out plants grown indoors after the last expected frost. Sow outdoors in December in frost-free zones.

CARE: Thin and transplant seedlings to desired locations in well-prepared soil when they are about 6 in. tall or are crowded. Side-dress plants with all-purpose fertilizer and compost in late spring. Mulch in dry areas.

HARVESTING AND CONDITIONING: Cut when first few flowers in cluster have opened. Briefly dip stem ends in boiling water. Strip off lower leaves; stand in deep water for several hours.

USES: Versatile, focal or filler material.

CLEMATIS
C. × jackmanii, C. montana

DESCRIPTION: Perennial vine. Twining stems climb trellises or other shrubs, bearing large waterlily-like flowers up to 7 in. wide in late spring or summer. Most are white, pink, blue, or purple. Flower stems are short; leaves are pointed on one end and prominently veined. Some cultivars are repeat bloomers. *C. montana* has a springtime profusion of smaller flowers. Mature plants reach 12 ft. or more; can be pruned or trained to smaller size. Cut flowers last 3 days.

HARDINESS: Zones 3 to 8.

GROWING CONDITIONS: Prefers rich, loamy soil, moist shade for roots, but sun for foliage. *C. montana* prefers partial shade. Space 5 ft. apart. Provide support.

PLANTING: Plant bare-root plants in early spring, acclimatized potted plants at any time during growing season. Take cuttings a few inches long with a node between cuts, in summer.

CARE: Mulch with chopped leaves or compost, fertilize with manure or all-purpose fertilizer in early spring. Train on supports. Early bloomers flower on old wood, so prune after flowering. Late bloomers flower on new wood, so prune in spring to encourage new growth. Discard leaves affected by leaf miners.

HARVESTING AND CONDITIONING: Cut in early morning or evening. Select flowers just beginning to bloom, dip stem ends into boiling water, slit and recut stem bases, and stand in deep water for several hours.

USES: Focal, accent, or linear material, or floating in low bowls. Small-flowered types as filler.

CLEOME
SPIDER FLOWER
C. hasslerana

DESCRIPTION: Annual. Clusters of multi-petaled pink, deep rose, white, or lilac flowers. Elongated, spidery seedpods; palmate leaves, main stems spiny. Flower spikes lengthen dramatically as new blooms open near the top. Height from 3 to 6 ft., depending on growing conditions. Blooms all summer in most areas, earlier in warm zones. Flowers stay fresh indoors for a week or more.

HARDINESS: Zones 2 to 11. Tolerates high heat in upper 90s F.

GROWING CONDITIONS: Prefers rich to average soil, average moisture, full sun. Tolerates drought. Space 2 ft. apart.

PLANTING: Set out bedding plants (hard to find) in spring when the danger of frost ends. Or sow seeds indoors 6 weeks earlier for transplants, or directly outdoors in warm weather, ¼ in. deep, 3 in. apart.

CARE: Thin seedlings to correct spacing and desired sites when they have four true leaves or are crowded. Self sows; seeds germinate the following spring. Side-dress growing plants with flower fertilizer and compost. Mulch. Stake plants as they grow taller, if needed. Deadhead only if unsightly.

HARVESTING AND CONDITIONING: Cut long flower spikes in morning or evening. Strip off lower leaves and pods. Condition in deep, cool water for several hours.

USES: Large-scale linear element; also focal point.

COLEUS
C. blumei, C. hybrids

DESCRIPTION: Tender perennial, grown as annual. Small spikes of pale to deep blue flowers are incidental; main attraction is colorful foliage. Leaves are wide or narrow, lobed or pointed, usually toothed, in a wide range of banded or splotched color combinations. Colors include chartreuse, green, pink, red, rust, red-purple, cream, and bronze. Bedding plants may darken in color when set outdoors. Plants are bushy and well branched. Cultivars range from 1 to 3 ft. tall. Cut stems last over 1 week; may sprout roots in vase.

HARDINESS: Zones 10 and 11 as perennial. All zones as annual.

GROWING CONDITIONS: Prefers partial shade, plentiful moisture, and fertile, well-drained soil. Space 12 to 18 in. apart.

PLANTING: Set out plants in warm weather, after all danger of frost. Sow seed in winter at 75°F by pressing into moist growing medium; do not cover. Needs light to germinate. Root 3- to 5-in. tip cuttings in summer, in moist soil or water.

CARE: Apply high-nitrogen fertilizer lightly but steadily throughout growth. Pinch back for bushiness when 6 in. tall. Prune for compact shape. Pinch off buds before flowers bloom.

HARVESTING AND CONDITIONING: Cut stems of unspoiled leaves in morning or evening. Split stem ends and stand in deep, lukewarm water for several hours.

USES: Accent or filler.

CONSOLIDA
LARKSPUR
C. ambigua

DESCRIPTION: Annual. Many-petaled, purple, blue, violet, pink, or white flowers on densely filled, tall spires about 1 ft. long; threadlike, inconspicuous leaves. Plants 2 to 3 ft. tall. Blooms spring to summer for 6 weeks. Cut flowers last 5 to 8 days.

HARDINESS: All zones. Withstands light to heavy frost; suffers in hot weather.

GROWING CONDITIONS: Prefers rich, loose, loamy soil, not strongly acidic; full sun; plentiful moisture. Space 1 ft. apart.

PLANTING: Sow seed indoors or out, ¼ in. deep, 4 in. apart. Early sowing yields larger plants. Sow outdoors in early spring as early as soil can be worked or indoors in winter in 6-in. pots. In zones 6 to 8, self-sown seed which ripens in summer yields vigorous plants next spring. In mild-winter areas, sow outdoors in December.

CARE: Thin seedlings when 5 in. tall. Side-dress budded plants with compost and flower fertilizer in spring. Harvest or deadhead for new blooms, but allow some flowers to set seed for self-sown plants. Remove spent or diseased plants. Mulch to keep soil cool and moist. Treat mildew with fungicide.

HARVESTING AND CONDITIONING: Cut stems when one-third of flowers have opened, in morning or evening. If stems are hollow, fill with water and plug with cotton. Stand in deep water for several hours.

USES: Linear element.

CONVALLARIA
LILY OF THE VALLEY
C. majalis

DESCRIPTION: Perennial. Small white or pink bells lined up on one side of a slender 8-in. stalk. Tidy elliptical leaves. Blooms 2 weeks in midspring with strong, lovely fragrance, used in perfume. Plants up to 12 in. tall; rapidly form mats because of rhizomatous roots. Cut flowers last 5 to 9 days.

HARDINESS: Zones 3 to 9. Tolerates extreme weather.

GROWING CONDITIONS: Prefers loamy soil enriched with compost, bright partial shade, moist but well-drained conditions. Tolerates shade under deciduous trees. Space 1 ft. apart; plants fill in as they spread.

PLANTING: Set out plants or pips in early spring for blooms a few weeks later. Red-coated seed may be sown outdoors in fall ¹/₂ in. deep to germinate the following spring.

CARE: Mulch with a layer of rotted manure and compost in fall; do not remove. Keep very moist during growth in spring. Thin in fall or early in spring, if crowded. Rarely affected by pests or diseases. Deadheading is optional: seeds offer autumn color; however, they are toxic. Remove leaves in late autumn, for neatness.

HARVESTING AND CONDITIONING: Cut stems when top buds show color but before they have opened. Trim off white base of stem. Stand in deep water and condition for several hours.

USES: Small-scale linear or filler element.

COREOPSIS
TICKSEED
C. lanceolata, C. tinctoria,
C. verticillata

DESCRIPTION: Annual or perennial. Large or small daisies, some double, in shades of gold, orange, and rust. Each species includes short (under 18 in.) and tall (over 30 in.) cultivars. Shorter ones need no staking but are still good for cutting. *C. lanceolata* has lance-shaped foliage; others are threadlike. All bloom throughout summer. Cut flowers stay fresh 5 days.

HARDINESS: *C. tinctoria* (annual), all zones; tolerates light frost. *C. verticillata* (perennial), zones 3 to 10. *C. lanceolata* (perennial), zones 5 to 8.

GROWING CONDITIONS: Prefers rich to average soil, average moisture, full sun. Space 1¹/₂ to 3 ft. apart.

PLANTING: Set out plants in well-tilled soil in spring. Sow seeds ¹/₈ in. deep, 4 in. apart, annuals indoors in February, outdoors 3 weeks before last expected frost. Sow perennials indoors in spring, outdoors in spring or summer.

CARE: Divide *C. verticillata* in spring. Take softwood cuttings of *C. lanceolata* in summer. Thin seedlings if crowded. Pinch back tips of annuals once when plants are 6 in. tall. Side-dress with flower fertilizer and compost; keep steadily watered. Mulch. Stake tall types before buds open. Deadhead. Pull and replace spent annuals.

HARVESTING AND CONDITIONING: Cut newly opened flowers in morning or evening. Strip off lower leaves. Stand in deep water for several hours.

USES: Versatile, focal or filler.

CORNUS
FLOWERING DOGWOOD
C. florida

DESCRIPTION: Tree. Large white or pink blooms cover whole tree in midspring, before leaves appear. Button-shaped buds are attractive earlier. Graceful, horizontal branches bear numerous upward-facing blooms, each with four large petal-like bracts around small yellowish flowers. Deciduous leaves are broad, pointed ovals with parallel veining. Autumn leaf color is rich red or purple. Trees reach 20 to 40 ft. in height at maturity and spread even wider if grown in the open. Red fruits ripen in fall. Lasts 7 or more days in vase.

HARDINESS: Zones 5 to 9, most types.

GROWING CONDITIONS: Prefers rich, loamy, well-drained, acidic soil; average moisture; full sun to partial shade. An open, airy site helps prevent anthracnose fungus. Space 25 or more ft. apart.

PLANTING: Set out balled-and-burlapped or potted plants in spring. Can be grown from softwood cuttings in spring or seed planted outdoors in fall for spring germination; takes years to flower.

CARE: Prone to anthracnose. To increase resistance, remove deadwood and unhealthy branches; treat trees with fungicide. Fertilize in spring and summer. Prune after flowering, shaping trees to increase air circulation. Mulch. Water if soil dries. Treat for borers.

HARVESTING AND CONDITIONING: Cut flowers when buds have begun to open, or earlier to force indoors. Slit and peel bark of stem ends. Stand in deep, warm water for several hours.

USES: Flowers focal or massed, leaves and fruit as background or accent elements.

CORYLUS
HAZEL, FILBERT
C. avellana, C. maxima 'Purpurea'

DESCRIPTION: Shrub. Bushy, 10 to 20 ft. tall, offering branches of dangling green or bronze catkins (on male plants) in late winter. *C. avellana* 'Contorta', known as Harry Lauder's walking stick, yields fascinating, twisted bare branches in winter. *C. maxima* 'Purpurea' has purple leaves about 3 in. long and wide; others have yellowish green leaves. Frilled husks cover edible nuts. Cut catkins last up to 1 week, leaves 1 to 2 weeks, bare branches last indefinitely.

HARDINESS: Zones 4 to 9.

GROWING CONDITIONS: Prefers loamy soil enriched with compost, full sun to partial shade, and average to moist conditions. Space 10 ft. apart.

PLANTING: Plant bare-root plants in early spring, potted or balled-and-burlapped plants at any time during growing season. Take softwood cuttings, and treat with rooting hormone, in summer; percentage that root is low. Nuts planted outdoors in fall 3 in. deep will sprout in spring.

CARE: Mulch with chopped leaves or compost; fertilize with manure or all-purpose fertilizer in spring. Prune often, at any time of year. Cut down suckers and trim for shape.

HARVESTING AND CONDITIONING: Select branches with catkins just beginning to bloom, or with fresh, undamaged leaves. Stand in deep water several hours. Bare branches need no conditioning.

USES: Branches of catkins or twisted bare branches of 'Contorta' used as linear accents, leaves as filler in large bouquets.

COSMOS
C. bipinnatus, C. sulfureus

DESCRIPTION: Annual. Prolific daisies range in width from 2½ in. (*C. sulfureus*, in yellow, orange, or red) to over 6 in. (*C. bipinnatus*, in pink, lilac, magenta, or white). Blooms from midsummer to frost. Branching plants from 3 to 5 ft. tall. Dwarf types less suited for cutting. Cut flowers stay fresh 4 days.

HARDINESS: Zones 2 to 11. Tolerates high heat; killed by frost.

GROWING CONDITIONS: Prefers rich to average soil, average moisture, full sun. Tolerates drought. Space 2 to 3 ft. apart.

PLANTING: Set out bedding plants in well-tilled soil in spring when the danger of frost ends. Or sow seeds 6 weeks earlier indoors for transplants, or directly outdoors in warm weather, ½ in. deep, 4 in. apart.

CARE: Thin seedlings to correct spacing and transplant to desired sites when they are about 5 in. tall or are crowded. Pinch back tips once when plants are 8 in. tall, for bushiness. Side-dress growing plants with flower fertilizer and compost; keep plants steadily watered and fertilized for maximum productivity. Mulch. Stake plants as they grow taller, if needed. Harvest or deadhead regularly. Pull and replace spent plants.

HARVESTING AND CONDITIONING: Cut newly opened flowers with tight centers in morning or evening. Strip off lower leaves. Stand in deep water for several hours.

USES: Versatile, usually focal, also filler.

COTONEASTER
C. adpressus, C. apiculatus, C. divaricatus, C. horizontalis, and others

DESCRIPTION: Shrub. Many species; some, such as the popular *C. apiculatus* (cranberry cotoneaster) are deciduous, others evergreen. Wide range of shapes from prostrate to treelike. Up to 8 ft. tall or wide; can be pruned to desired size. Many branches of small white or pink flowers in spring; small, roundish leaves; red berries in fall. Cut flowers last nearly 1 week, cut foliage and berries up to 2 weeks.

HARDINESS: Zones 5 to 8 for most species.

GROWING CONDITIONS: Prefers well-drained soil of average to good fertility, full sun to bright partial shade (evergreens take more shade than deciduous types), and average moisture. Established plants tolerate drought. Space 4 to 8 ft. apart.

PLANTING: Set out plants in spring in well-prepared holes. Take softwood cuttings of deciduous plants in spring, or semihardwood cuttings of evergreen plants in summer.

CARE: Apply a 1-in. layer of manure and compost around each established plant in fall or early spring. Prune for shape and to eliminate crossed branches in spring or fall. Prostrate types may be trained as weeping standards.

HARVESTING AND CONDITIONING: Cut in early morning or evening. Trim off extra branches and leaves below water line. Stand in deep water for several hours.

USES: Flowers, leaves, or berries as linear or filler elements.

CROCUS
C. hybrids, C. species

DESCRIPTION: Corm. Egg-shaped flowers open out on sunny days to reveal six pointed petals and brilliant orange stigmata. Most hybrids bloom late winter in white, yellow, lilac, or purple, 8 in. tall. Species are 4 or 5 in. tall, same colors plus pink, blue, and cream; many bicolors. Species bloom earlier than hybrids, except fall bloomers like *C. sativus* and *C. kotschyanus*. Narrow, grasslike leaves elongate to 1 ft., persist until late spring. Cut flowers last 2 to 3 days.

HARDINESS: Zones 4 to 8. Needs chilling in winter.

GROWING CONDITIONS: Prefers well-drained, average soil with average moisture and full sun to part shade. Grow in places that will not be mowed before late spring. Grows well under deciduous trees. Plant 3 in. deep, 3 in. apart.

PLANTING: Plant corms in fall or immediately after dividing plants in late spring. Can be grown from saved seed sown ½ in. deep outdoors in late spring; takes 2 to 3 years to flower.

CARE: Fertilize at planting time and in spring after flowering. Mulch in winter; remove gradually as sprouts appear. Protect from rodents. Keep moist during growth, drier during dormancy. Allow foliage to ripen; then divide, every other year.

HARVESTING AND CONDITIONING: Cut newly opened flowers in morning. Arrange immediately or stand in cool water for several hours.

USES: Small-scale focal element.

CYTISUS
SCOTCH BROOM
C. scoparius

DESCRIPTION: Shrub. Flowers in early spring with profuse 1-in., pealike blossoms aligned on slender stems—a blast of color, like forsythia, but in shades of yellow, white, pink, red, or purple. Stems are densely bunched, with ridged bark. Deciduous leaves are small ovals; bushes lose their charm as summer wears on. Plants are up to 10 ft. tall (taller if crowded) and 10 ft. wide if allowed to spread. Cut flowers last up to 6 days.

HARDINESS: Zones 5 to 8. Not long-lived.

GROWING CONDITIONS: Prefers well-drained sandy soil, not too fertile, in full sun; average moisture. Space 10 ft. apart.

PLANTING: Plant bare-root plants in early spring, potted or balled-and-burlapped plants at any time during growing season. Take softwood cuttings and treat with rooting hormone in summer, using a light, loose medium such as perlite. Presoak seed overnight in hot water; then plant 1 in. deep, 3 in. apart at temperatures between 65 and 90°F.

CARE: Fertilize with compost in spring. Prune after flowering. Cut back older plants. Remove leaves affected by blight. Train to supports if necessary.

HARVESTING AND CONDITIONING: Select branches with freshly opened flowers. Cut in morning or evening. Slit and recut stems. Dip stem ends in boiling water; then stand in deep water for several hours.

USES: Flowers as linear accent or filler.

DAHLIA
D. hybrids

DESCRIPTION: Tuber. Flowers in many shapes and sizes, in every color but blue. Many bicolors. Plants 6 in. to over 5 ft. tall. Flowers classed as single, anemone, collarette, water lily, decorative, ball, pompon, and cactus. Blooms midsummer to frost on bushy plants. Cut flowers last 5 days.

HARDINESS: All zones, as annuals. Hardy where ground does not freeze; dormant in winter.

GROWING CONDITIONS: Prefers loose, light soil enriched with manure; plentiful moisture; good drainage; full sun. Set tubers 3 to 5 in. below soil surface, 1 to 4 ft. apart.

PLANTING: Set out bedding plants or tubers after danger of frost, or plant tubers indoors 6 weeks before danger of frost ends and transplant. Sow seeds of small, fast types such as 'Figaro' indoors for transplants, or outdoors in warm weather, ¼ in. deep, 3 in. apart.

CARE: Thin seedlings to correct spacing and desired sites when crowded. Stake large types when planting or before they are 2 ft. tall. Pinch back tips early in summer. Side-dress growing plants with rotted manure or flower fertilizer and compost. Mulch. Harvest or deadhead frequently. Dig tubers before frost and store in sand in a cool (not freezing) basement in winter.

HARVESTING AND CONDITIONING: Cut newly opened flowers in morning or evening. Strip off lower leaves. Stand in deep water for several hours.

USES: Focal point.

DELPHINIUM
D. belladonna, D. elatum hybrids

DESCRIPTION: Perennial. Tall spires from 2 to 7 ft. densely filled with multipetaled, open-faced flowers in purple, blue, yellow, violet, rose, or white. Ferny, rich green leaves. *D. elatum* is more widely grown than *D. belladonna*; there are numerous named cultivars and strains. Blooms 1 month in summer; reblooms if harvested early. Cut flowers last 5 to 8 days.

HARDINESS: Zones 3 to 8. Likes cool nights in summer. Tolerates cold winters; killed by heat and drought.

GROWING CONDITIONS: Prefers deep, rich, loamy soil, neutral or alkaline. Needs full sun, ample moisture, and shelter from strong wind. Space 2 to 3 ft. apart.

PLANTING: Plant divisions in early spring, acclimatized potted plants at any time during growing season. Add high phosphorus fertilizer to planting holes. After prechilling, plant seed ⅛ in. deep indoors or out at about 65°F. Germinates within 1 month; blooms second year.

CARE: Apply compost and bonemeal to each established clump in fall and spring. Side-dress with flower fertilizer in early summer. If crowded, divide in spring. Firmly tie each flower spire to a slim bamboo stake. Mulch around crowns winter and summer. Remove stalks after bloom. Protect from slugs.

HARVESTING AND CONDITIONING: Cut when two-thirds of flowers on spire have opened. Fill hollow stem with water and plug with cotton. Stand in deep water for several hours.

USES: Linear or filler element.

DEUTZIA
D. gracilis

DESCRIPTION: Shrub. Multitudes of single or double ¾-in. white, pink, or violet blossoms aligned on long stems cover plants in midspring for a 2-week show. Lance-shaped leaves follow. Can look ragged in summer; does not offer autumn color. Deciduous. Mature plants reach 4 to 6 ft. tall, 4 ft. wide; can be pruned lower. Cut flowers last up to 1 week.

HARDINESS: Zones 4 to 8.

GROWING CONDITIONS: Prefers loamy soil enriched with compost, full sun to partial shade, and average to moist conditions. Space 4 to 5 ft. apart.

PLANTING: Plant bare-root plants in early spring, acclimatized potted plants at any time during growing season. Add compost to planting holes. Take softwood cuttings in late spring or summer; keep moist and shaded. Sometimes volunteers root where branch tips touch the ground; cut free, dig, and replant in desired places.

CARE: Mulch with chopped leaves or compost, fertilize with manure or all-purpose fertilizer in early spring. Prune hard just after blooming, removing old wood. Trim for shape in summer. Remove and discard leaves affected by leaf miners. Treat for aphids if necessary.

HARVESTING AND CONDITIONING: Cut in early morning or evening. Select spikes which have just begun to bloom. Stand in deep water for several hours.

USES: Linear accents or filler.

DIANTHUS
SWEET WILLIAM, CARNATION, PINK
D. barbatus, D. caryophyllus, D. deltoides, D. hybrids

DESCRIPTION: Annual, biennial, or perennial. Round, spicily scented flowers, some in broad clusters, in every color but blue. Many bicolors. Petals smooth or fringed. Species and cultivars vary in flower width (1 to 4 in.), length of stem, branching, and height (4 in. to over 3 ft.). Some offer neat mounds of whitened, narrow-leaved foliage. Most perennials bloom once in spring, biennial *D. barbatus* blooms in spring and summer, annuals bloom in spring, summer, and fall. Cut flowers last 5 to 10 days.

HARDINESS: Types for all regions.

GROWING CONDITIONS: Prefers average to rich sandy loam soil, average moisture, full sun, and excellent drainage. Plant 8 to 15 in. apart.

PLANTING: Set out acclimatized potted plants at any time during growing season, especially spring. Can be grown from seed sown ⅛ in. deep, 2 in. apart, indoors in late winter or outdoors in summer; best at 65 to 70°F.

CARE: Use flower fertilizer throughout growing season. Thin seedlings. If crowded, divide perennials in early spring. Pinch back tips for bushiness. Propagate from tip cuttings and layers. Deadhead regularly. Mulch in winter. Protect from slugs.

HARVESTING AND CONDITIONING: Cut when flowers have begun to open. Recut under water on a slant above stem joint. Split large stems of carnations. Stand in deep water for several hours.

USES: Focal, accent, or filler material.

DICENTRA
BLEEDING HEART
D. spectabilis

DESCRIPTION: Perennial. Several 2-in. pink or white heart-shaped blooms like dangling lockets aligned on arched 10-in. stems; ferny leaves. *D. spectabilis* blooms in spring; *D. eximia* and *D. formosa*, less showy, from spring to fall. Species range from 1 to 3 ft. in height. Foliage of *D. spectabilis* yellows, then disappears in summer; grow with ferns to cover. Cut flowers last about 5 days.

HARDINESS: Zones 4 to 8.

GROWING CONDITIONS: Prefers loamy soil enriched with compost, bright partial shade, average to moist conditions. Space 2 to 3 ft. apart.

PLANTING: Plant divisions in early spring just as new growth begins, acclimatized potted plants at any time during growing season; overcast day preferred. Plant seeds ⅛ in. deep in shaded bed in summer. Also self-sows. Seedlings do not show until late the next spring.

CARE: Apply 1 handful manure or compost to each established plant in fall or early spring. Avoid moving mature plants if possible. In autumn or early in spring, thin or transplant volunteers crowding established plants. Mulch around crowns winter and summer; remove mulch if soil becomes soggy.

HARVESTING AND CONDITIONING: Cut stems when several lower flowers have opened, in early morning or evening. Immediately plunge into cool water up to lowest flowers. Submerge foliage. Condition for several hours.

USES: Flowers as linear element, leaves as filler.

DIGITALIS
FOXGLOVE
D. grandiflora, D. mertonensis,
D. purpurea

DESCRIPTION: Perennial or biennial. Tall spires from 2 to 6 ft., densely filled with nodding, tubular 3-in. flowers. Most are lilac, pink, or white; some pale yellow. Thick, hairy leaves in rosettes. *D. grandiflora* is hardiest; others are biennials or short-lived perennials. Blooms 1 month in late spring. Second bloom may follow. Cut flowers last 5 to 7 days.

HARDINESS: Zones 3 to 8. Short-lived. Tolerates cold winters; killed by heat and drought.

GROWING CONDITIONS: Prefers loamy soil enriched with compost and leaf mold, partial shade, and average to moist conditions. Space 2 to 3 ft. apart.

PLANTING: Plant divisions in early spring, potted plants at any time during growing season. Self-sows freely; plant seeds ⅛ in. deep indoors or out at about 70°F.

CARE: Apply 2 handfuls compost to each established clump in fall and spring. If in early spring rosettes are clumps of plantlets, divide and replant. Transplant volunteers to permanent places. Keep moist until established. Mulch around crowns winter and summer. Remove mulch if soil becomes soggy. Remove most stalks after bloom; allow some to remain to set seed.

HARVESTING AND CONDITIONING: Cut when first few flowers have opened. Dip stem ends in boiling water after removing larger leaves. Fill and plug stems; then stand in deep water for several hours.

USES: Large-scale linear element.

DORONICUM
LEOPARD'S BANE
D. pardalianches
(formerly *D. cordatum*)

DESCRIPTION: Perennial. Large, bright yellow daisies in early spring, up to 3 in. wide, stems about 12 in. long. Soft, heart-shaped, medium-green toothed leaves. Plants up to 2½ ft. tall. Plants bloom for up to 6 weeks. Cut flowers last 5 days. In hot areas leaves disappear in late summer.

HARDINESS: Zones 4 to 7. Easily killed by hot, dry summers.

GROWING CONDITIONS: Prefers moist, rich, loamy, well-drained soil, partial shade; also grows in full sun in cool areas. Good under deciduous trees if not too close to roots. Space 1 to 2 ft. apart.

PLANTING: Set out plants in early spring or late fall. Usually propagated by division; difficult from seed though it may self-sow under ideal conditions.

CARE: Apply 1 handful manure or compost to each established clump in fall or early spring. Divide in late fall or late winter. Harvest or deadhead frequently. Water steadily during dry spells. Do not discard if plant appears dead in summer; it is probably dormant. Continue watering. Mulch around crowns.

HARVESTING AND CONDITIONING: In early morning, cut long-stemmed young flowers before pollen is apparent. Remove foliage below water line of vase. Stand in deep water for several hours.

USES: Focal or accent material.

ECHINACEA
PURPLE CONEFLOWER
E. purpurea

DESCRIPTION: Perennial. Long-lasting flowers with spiky, prominent orange centers surrounded by lilac-pink or whitish green petals. Large hairy leaves. Flowers are about 4 in. wide; prolific plants are 3 to 4 ft. tall. Blooms all summer into fall. Cut flowers, which are used with or without the petals, last over 1 week.

HARDINESS: Zones 3 to 8. Tolerates cold and heat.

GROWING CONDITIONS: Provide average to fertile loamy soil and average moisture; full sun or bright partial shade. Space plants 2 feet apart.

PLANTING: Plant divisions in spring, acclimatized potted plants at any time during growing season. Not difficult from seed, but usually takes 2 years from seed to bloom; sow thinly ¼ in. deep in prepared beds in summer or start indoors in spring, at temperatures from 70 to 85°F.

CARE: Apply 2 handfuls manure or compost to each established clump in fall or early spring. If crowded, divide or respace mature plants in spring, every 4 years. Transplant seedlings to desired places in fall or the following spring. Mulch around crowns unless soil is soggy. Water during dry spells and harvest or deadhead flowers frequently.

HARVESTING AND CONDITIONING: Cut newly opened flowers in morning or evening. Recut and slit stem bases, remove lower leaves, and condition in deep, cool water for several hours.

USES: Flowers usually focal points; spiky cones with petals removed as accents.

ECHINOPS
GLOBE THISTLE
E. ritro

DESCRIPTION: Perennial. Large globular, metallic blue composite flowers on robust, branched plants from 2 to 5 ft. tall. Many long-stemmed flowers 2 in. wide appear in summer or fall. Green, divided leaves are spiny but not dangerous; they become neat rosettes in winter. Cut flowers last 7 to 10 days.

HARDINESS: Zones 3 to 9. Withstands heat and cold.

GROWING CONDITIONS: Prefers moderately rich, well-drained soil; average moisture; full sun. Space 2 to 3 ft. apart.

PLANTING: Set out divisions in spring, acclimatized potted plants at any time during growing season. Sow seed $1/4$ in. deep, 2 in. apart, indoors in spring or outdoors when temperatures will remain between 65 and 80°F for 4 weeks. Germination usually takes 3 weeks. Move seedlings outdoors when they have six leaves.

CARE: Mulch with 2 in. chopped leaves or compost in fall. Divide in early spring if crowded or to propagate plants. Transplant seedlings grown the previous year to permanent garden spots in spring. Keep moist during the growing season. Plants need no staking unless grown in rich soil or partial shade.

HARVESTING AND CONDITIONING: Cut before flowers develop fully, or they will shatter. Split stem ends and dip into boiling water. Stand in deep water for several hours.

USES: Filler or accent material.

ELAEAGNUS
RUSSIAN OLIVE
E. angustifolia

DESCRIPTION: Shrub. Rounded shape up to 20 ft. tall; an excellent small bushy tree for silver foliage. Young branches are silvery, too. Narrow and pointed deciduous leaves, not too dense or heavy. Yellowish flowers in spring, inconspicuous but very fragrant. Attractive yellow fruit $1/2$-in. long follows; *E. a.* 'Red King' has rust-red fruit. Cut flowers, foliage, or berries last about 1 week.

HARDINESS: Zones 2 to 9; does poorly in intense heat.

GROWING CONDITIONS: Grows in any well-drained soil in full sun. Best in light, sandy loam; tolerates dry soil and salt spray. Space plants 20 ft. apart.

PLANTING: Set out bare-root plants in early spring, acclimatized potted plants at any time during growing season; transplants fairly well. Fairly difficult to grow from seed; plant in fall for germination in spring $1^{1}/2$ years later, or take cuttings in summer.

CARE: Apply all-purpose fertilizer or compost in spring. Prune after flowering. Trim for shape in summer. Treat for aphids and scale if necessary. Shrub may have to be removed if affected by verticillium wilt.

HARVESTING AND CONDITIONING: Cut branches in early morning or evening. Scrape, slit, and recut stems; stand in deep water for several hours.

USES: Foliage and berries as linear, accent, or filler material.

EMILIA
TASSEL FLOWER
E. javanica (formerly *Cacalia*)

DESCRIPTION: Annual. Small-flowered but unusually bright in intense shades of orange, red-orange, and gold; $1/2$- to $3/4$-in. daisies in branching sprays. Soft-textured plants have greenish gray lance-shaped leaves. In bloom, plants are $1^{1}/2$ to 2 ft. tall and bloom summer through fall. Cut flowers last 5 days.

HARDINESS: All zones. Killed by temperatures below 30°F; withstands intense heat.

GROWING CONDITIONS: Prefers loose, light soil; low to moderate but steady fertility and moisture; good drainage; full sun. Space 8 in. apart.

PLANTING: Sow seed $1/8$ in. deep, 1 in. apart, indoors 6 to 8 weeks before the last frost or outdoors after the danger of frost passes. Germinates best in darkness at temperatures between 60 and 75°F; usually in less than 2 weeks. Transplant seedlings to larger containers or thin if crowded. Self-sows in places with mild winters.

CARE: Transplant or thin seedlings to permanent positions when several inches tall. Mulch in hot, dry areas. Harvest or deadhead often to promote bloom, but allow some seed to ripen for self-sown plants.

HARVESTING AND CONDITIONING: Cut when flowers are nearly fully open, in morning or evening. Stand in deep water several hours.

USES: Bright accent, filler, or massed material.

EREMURUS
FOXTAIL LILY
E. himalaicus, E. robustus,
E. spectabilis

DESCRIPTION: Perennial. Hundreds of small tubular white, yellow, peach, or pink flowers arranged on huge, pokerlike racemes. Height from 3 to 10 ft. Some types are fragrant. *E. spectabilis*, at 4 ft., is best for most gardens. *E. robustus* is tallest at 7 to 10 ft. Bent, straplike leaves form a large clump in spring but vanish in summer, leaving a bare spot. Blooms once a year for 2 weeks in late spring. Cut flowers last 4 to 8 days.

HARDINESS: Zones 5 to 8.

GROWING CONDITIONS: Prefers rich, sandy loam soil with average moisture, full sun, and excellent drainage. Plant 6 in. deep, 2 to 5 ft. apart, with a cushion of grit below each fleshy root.

PLANTING: Plant roots in fall or spring, but manure soil 3 to 6 months in advance. Set in stakes when planting to avoid root damage. Can be grown from seed sown $1/8$ in. deep indoors in spring, set out in summer; may take 5 years to flower.

CARE: Fertilize at planting time and mulch with compost. Divide in early spring if crowded, handling brittle roots with care. Shelter sprouting plants from late frosts. Stake.

HARVESTING AND CONDITIONING: Cut when first half of flowers have opened on spike. Stand in deep water for several hours.

USES: Large-scale linear element.

ERICA AND CALLUNA
HEATHER, HEATH
E. carnea and *C. vulgaris*

DESCRIPTION: Shrubs. Matlike, spreading plants with tiny green, bronze, or yellow leaves, densely packed with white, pink, or red flowers in linear clusters. *Erica* blooms winter and spring. *Calluna* may be taller; flowers in summer or fall. Cultivars of *E. carnea* range from 4 in. to 2 ft. tall; some very prostrate. Cut flowers last 4 or more days.

HARDINESS: Zones 4 to 7 for most cultivars, but varies. Dislikes hot summers. *Calluna* species are more widely suited.

GROWING CONDITIONS: Prefers sandy, well-drained soil of average fertility and moisture; full sun. Space plants 1½ to 2 ft. apart.

PLANTING: Plant bare-root plants in early spring, acclimatized potted plants at any time during growing season. Take cuttings in summer; keep moist in sandy peat. Sow indoors as soon as collected or received, ⅛ deep, 1 in. apart, in a 1:1 mix of sand and peat moss.

CARE: Fertilize lightly in fall, spring, and summer. Prune for shape after flowering. Do not let bushes become too thick. If branches root where they touch the soil, cut them free and plant in new places to propagate.

HARVESTING AND CONDITIONING: Cut spikes just beginning to bloom, in early morning or evening. Slit stem ends. Stand in deep water for several hours.

USES: Small-scale linear or filler element.

ERYNGIUM
SEA HOLLY
E. alpinum, E. giganteum

DESCRIPTION: Hardy biennial or perennial. Showiest is biennial *E. giganteum*, 2 to 4 ft. tall; 2-in. flowers have prominent cones surrounded by spiky bracts. 'Miss Willmot's Ghost' is the palest silver cultivar. Others are silvery blue or green. *E. alpinum*, which is metallic blue, large-flowered and 1½ to 2 ft. tall, is perennial. Bracts look spiky but are soft. *Eryngium* blooms in summer and autumn; leaves are silvery and lancelike. Species and cultivars vary in height, branching, and flower size. When cut, stays fresh over 1 week.

HARDINESS: Perennials, zones 5 to 8; biennials, zones 5 to 10.

GROWING CONDITIONS: Prefers rich, loamy soil, fairly dry and well drained. *E. giganteum* prefers full sun; *E. alpinum*, sun or partial shade. Space 1 to 3 ft. apart.

PLANTING: Set out plants in spring. Sow biennials in summer, ⅛ in. deep, 2 in. apart, at 70 to 80°F, indoors or out. In cold frames and hot climates, sow in autumn. Sow perennials outdoors in autumn.

CARE: Divide perennials in spring if crowded. Thin self-sown plants in spring. Use flower fertilizer in spring and summer. Deadhead regularly, but allow some flowers to set seed. Side-dress with compost in fall.

HARVESTING AND CONDITIONING: Cut while centers are tight and after blue color has developed. Stand in deep water for several hours.

USES: Focal or filler material.

ESCHSCHOLZIA
CALIFORNIA POPPY
E. californica

DESCRIPTION: Hardy annual. Silky orange, gold, or rose cup-shaped poppies up to 3 in. wide on slender stems. Pointed green caps pop off to reveal four-petaled or frilly double flowers. Foliage bluish green, threadlike. Height 1 to 2 ft. Blooms spring or summer for about 6 weeks. When cut, stays fresh 2 days; worth growing in spite of short vase life.

HARDINESS: Zones 2 to 11. Tolerates light frost and heat.

GROWING CONDITIONS: Prefers loose, light soil; average fertility and moisture; good drainage; full sun. Unusually drought-tolerant for a garden flower, also withstands salt spray near ocean. Space 1 ft. apart.

PLANTING: Sow seed outdoors, ⅛ in. deep, 3 in. apart, in spring or, in mild areas, autumn, in well-tilled, fertilized beds. Or start indoors in individual pots 6 weeks before outdoor planting time.

CARE: Water young plants until well established. Mulch in hot, dry areas. Harvest or deadhead often to promote bloom, but allow a few flowers to set seed for self-sown plants, if wanted. Remove branched, spent plants if they become unsightly. Prevent mildew and root rot by providing good drainage and good air circulation.

HARVESTING AND CONDITIONING: Cut when flowers begin to unfold, in morning just after caps have popped off. Stand in deep water for several hours.

USES: Focal or accent material.

EUONYMUS
WINTERCREEPER
E. fortunei

DESCRIPTION: Vine. Grows like ivy, climbing more than 40 ft. up supports or scrambling over the ground up to 6 in. deep. Evergreen leaves of about 1 in. long vary in shape, size, and coloration. Attractive new growth in late spring. Cultivars in dark forest green, plummy purple, green and gold, and green and white. Green types turn red in autumn. Cut foliage lasts over 2 weeks if water is changed and may root in the vase.

HARDINESS: Zones 4 to 9.

GROWING CONDITIONS: Grows in any soil that is not waterlogged, does well on slopes because of good drainage. Grows best in partial shade but also in full sun or deep shade. Space large plants 5 ft. apart, rooted cuttings 2 ft.

PLANTING: Plant bare-root plants in early spring, acclimatized potted plants at any time throughout the growing season. Take cuttings in late spring or summer; keep moist and shaded. Sometimes roots where branch tips touch the ground; cut free, dig, and replant in desired places.

CARE: Mulch with chopped leaves or compost in winter, apply all-purpose fertilizer in spring. Trim for shape in summer. Treat also for mildew and scale if necessary.

HARVESTING AND CONDITIONING: Cut in early morning or evening. Scrape, slit, and recut stems; stand in deep water for several hours.

USES: Foliage as linear or filler material.

EUPHORBIA

SPURGE, POINSETTIA

E. amygdaloides, E. heterophylla,
E. marginata, E. pulcherrima

DESCRIPTION: Annual, perennial, or
shrub. Colorful leaves or bracts; small
flowers. Huge genus; nonwoody types
best for cutting. *E. marginata* (snow-on-
the-mountain), a 2-ft. hardy annual, has
striped green-and-white leaves, small
white flowers. *E. heterophylla* (fire-on-the-
mountain, or annual poinsettia) is a 3-ft.
tender annual with red bracts near flowers. *E. amygdaloides* (woodspurge) is a 1-ft.
hardy perennial with greenish yellow
leaves and flowers. All bloom in summer.
E. pulcherrima (poinsettia), a tender shrub,
blooms in winter; red, pink, or greenish
white bracts surround small flowers, forming 5-in. heads. Cut flowers last 5 days.

HARDINESS: Hardy perennials, zones 4 to
8; tender perennials, zones 9 to 11 (wider
range indoors); annuals, all zones; hardy
annuals need cool weather.

GROWING CONDITIONS: Full sun; relatively dry, poor to average soil, good
drainage. Plant 1 to 3 ft. apart.

PLANTING: Set out divisions in spring,
acclimatized potted plants at any time
during growing season. Sow seed ⅛ in.
deep, 2 in. apart, indoors in winter or
spring; set out after danger of frost. Sow
seed of *E. marginata* where it will grow
outdoors, 6 weeks before last frost.

CARE: Thin seedlings if crowded. Divide
perennials in spring or fall every 3 years.
Deadhead regularly.

HARVESTING AND CONDITIONING: Sear
stem ends (except fire-on-the-mountain).
Stand in deep water for several hours.

USES: Poinsettia used as focal material,
others as filler.

EUSTOMA

LISIANTHUS, PRAIRIE
GENTIAN

E. grandiflorum

DESCRIPTION: Hardy annual. Large,
graceful, cup-shaped flowers up to 3 in.
wide, single or double. Buds resemble
rosebuds. Colors range through white,
peach, rose, lilac, and purple. Slender
stems, silvery green lance-shaped leaves.
Height 1½ to 3 ft. Blooms summer until
hard frost. When cut, stays fresh up to
3 weeks.

HARDINESS: Zones 2 to 11. Tolerates
erratic climates; tolerates light frost and
high heat.

GROWING CONDITIONS: Prefers loose,
light soil; average fertility and moisture;
good drainage; full sun. Mature plants tolerate dry conditions. Space 1 ft. apart.

PLANTING: Set out bedding plants in
well-prepared sites after the last expected
frost. Most gardeners buy plants. Sow
seeds indoors in early winter less than ⅛
in. deep in sterile soil; cover with glass or
plastic until seeds sprout; keep at 70°F.
Germination may take 3 to 6 weeks. Seed
to bloom takes at least 5 months. Transplant if crowded.

CARE: Water young plants until well
established outdoors. Keep plants steadily
but not heavily fertilized during the long
flowering period. Mulch in hot, dry areas.
Harvest or deadhead often and stake if
necessary.

HARVESTING AND CONDITIONING: Cut
when flowers have begun to unfold, in
morning or evening. Dip stem ends in
boiling water, then stand in deep water
for several hours.

USES: Focal or accent material.

FERNS

Many genera and species

DESCRIPTION: Perennials. Ferns for
flower arrangers range in shade of green,
leaf shape, size, and season. Heights range
from 1 to over 4 ft. Most have fine-textured, filigreed foliage; some are evergreen,
and some have attractive spore cases on
separate stems. *Adiantum pedatum* (maiden-
hair fern) is delicate looking, with small
leaflets loosely arrayed on wiry 18-in.
stems. *Athyrium felix-femina* (lady fern) has
medium green fronds 3 ft. tall. *Osmunda
regalis* (royal fern) is 5 ft. tall and stately.
Rumohra adiantiformis (leather fern) is used
by florists, as is *Dryopteris dilatata* (formerly *D. spinulosa*), usually 3 or 4 ft. tall,
with broad fronds. Most ferns look best in
spring and early summer. When cut, most
last 3 to 5 days, leather fern over 1 week.

HARDINESS: Zones 3 to 8 for most;
Rumohra, zones 9 and 10 only; types for
all zones.

GROWING CONDITIONS: Most prefer
rich, moist, loamy soil and partial shade.
Space 1 to 3 ft. apart.

PLANTING: Set out dormant plants in
early spring, potted plants in spring
or fall.

CARE: Keep soil constantly moist. Mulch.
Divide in early spring as new growth
begins, or in fall. Side-dress with compost
or leaf mold in fall.

HARVESTING AND CONDITIONING: For
most, dip ends of stems into boiling
water; then submerge whole fronds in cool
water 4 to 8 hours. If fronds wilt, try
other fronds without treating the ends.

USES: Fronds as filler material; spore
cases as accents.

FILIPENDULA

QUEEN-OF-THE-PRAIRIE

F. rubra

DESCRIPTION: Perennial. Spectacular
broad, feathery plumes of pale to bright
pink florets, up to 1 ft. wide, on branching plants 5 to 8 ft. tall. Leaves are large
and almost star-shaped, with six points.
'Venusta' is a frequently recommended
bright pink cultivar. Blooms for several
weeks in midsummer. When cut, stays
fresh about 5 days.

HARDINESS: Zones 3 to 8. Dislikes
intense heat.

GROWING CONDITIONS: Prefers deep,
moist, rich, loamy soil and bright partial
shade. Space 4 ft. apart.

PLANTING: Set out divisions in early
spring or fall, acclimatized potted plants
at any time during growing season. Rarely
grown from seed.

CARE: Divide in early spring if necessary,
usually every 2 years. Make sure that soil
is continuously moist and fertile. Mulch in
dry areas. May become mildewed if grown
in unfavorably dry conditions. Deadhead
regularly. Treat for spider mites if necessary, or remove affected portions of
plants. Side-dress with compost and rotted manure in fall.

HARVESTING AND CONDITIONING: Cut
when half the flowers on the stalk are
open, in morning or evening. Split bases
of stems and stand in lukewarm water up
to the lowest flowers for several hours.

USES: Large-scale filler, focal, or massed
material.

FOENICULUM
FENNEL
F. vulgare, F. v. 'Purpureum'

DESCRIPTION: Perennial or biennial herb. Misty plumes of threadlike foliage on strong stems. Wide, flat umbels of yellow flowers in summer. Green or bronze leaves—*F. v.* 'Purpureum' is a wonderful shade of purplish brown. Upright, branching habit; 4 to 6 ft. tall when well grown. Foliage of overwintered plants looks best in late spring, and spring-sown plants look best in late summer and early autumn. Plants die back in winter. Cut flowers last 4 days, foliage up to 1 week.

HARDINESS: Zones 5 to 9 as perennial (hardy strains). Zones 1 to 11 as annual. Tolerates heat.

GROWING CONDITIONS: Prefers non-acidic, loamy, well-drained soil enriched with compost and leaf mold; full sun; average moisture. Space 1 to 1½ ft. apart.

PLANTING: Sow seed ¼ in. deep indoors in individual pots 6 weeks before last frost or outdoors after frost. Needs darkness to germinate. Set out plants after frost. Dislikes root disturbance.

CARE: Apply 3 handfuls compost per plant in fall. Apply all-purpose fertilizer in spring and summer. Transplant seedlings in spring. Cut off flowers to promote foliage growth. Deadhead to prevent self-sown seedlings. Cut off tops of plants in late autumn; mulch around crowns.

HARVESTING AND CONDITIONING: Cut newly opened flowers or ferny foliage in morning. Stand in deep water for several hours.

USES: Filler element or edible, anise-flavored garnish.

FORSYTHIA
F. × intermedia

DESCRIPTION: Shrub. A multitude of star-shaped yellow blossoms aligned on long stems. A less vigorous type has white flowers. Deciduous, toothed, lance-shaped leaves appear after flowers fade. Blooms for 3 weeks in late winter, on last summer's growth. Mature plants reach 10 ft. or more; can be pruned to smaller size. Cut flowers last up to 1 week.

HARDINESS: Zones 5 to 8. Flower buds may freeze some years in zone 5.

GROWING CONDITIONS: Prefers loamy soil enriched with compost, full sun to partial shade, and average to moist conditions. Space 10 ft. apart, 5 ft. for hedges.

PLANTING: Plant bare-root plants in early spring, acclimatized potted plants at any time during growing season. Take softwood cuttings in late spring or dig up volunteers which root where branch tips touch the ground.

CARE: Mulch with chopped leaves or compost; fertilize with manure or all-purpose fertilizer in early spring. Prune just after blooming by removing old canes at ground level. Trim for shape in early summer. Do not let canes stand for more than 3 years; make room for the new, floriferous canes which grow each year. Can be pruned to the ground each year immediately after bloom.

HARVESTING AND CONDITIONING: Cut in early morning or evening. Select spikes which have begun to bloom. Stand in deep water for several hours.

USES: Flowers used as linear accents or filler. Often forced.

FREESIA
F. alba, F. hybrids

DESCRIPTION: Corm. Sweetly fragrant, tubular flowers mainly in pastel shades of all colors but blue, on slender, branched stems. Swordlike leaves form basal fans; vanish in summer. Each flower is about 2 in. long; stems 1 to 1½ ft. tall—varies with cultivar. Blooms once a year for 2 weeks, in late winter or spring in mild zones, spring or summer elsewhere. Cut flowers last 5 to 12 days.

HARDINESS: Zones 9 to 10 (without protection); all zones if kept from freezing. Prefers cool weather; dormant during hot weather.

GROWING CONDITIONS: Prefers average to rich, sandy loam soil with average moisture, full sun, and excellent drainage. Plant 4 in. deep, 6 in. apart.

PLANTING: Plant corms in fall indoors or, where hardy, blooming plants in cool weather at any time, especially spring. Plant specially treated corms outdoors in spring. Can be grown from seed, ⅛ in. deep indoors in spring; may take 2 years to flower.

CARE: Fertilize at planting time, mulch with compost. Keep cool and moist while growing. Stake with bamboo. Where ground freezes in winter, dig, dry, and store corms after foliage yellows.

HARVESTING AND CONDITIONING: Cut when first few flowers on spike have opened. Add sugar to water. Stand in deep water for several hours. Change water often.

USES: Versatile; focal or linear material or as single specimens.

FRITILLARIA
CROWN IMPERIAL, FRITILLARY
F. imperialis, F. meleagris

DESCRIPTION: Bulb. Both species mentioned bloom with bell-shaped flowers and narrow leaves each spring, but are otherwise dissimilar. *F. imperialis* has stout, stiff stems 3 to 4 ft. tall bearing up to a dozen large, pendent yellow, orange, or red flowers in a ring near the top. Plants tend to have a rank smell but are stately in appearance. *F. meleagris*, 1 ft. tall, has slender stems each bearing a checkered red-purple or violet flower. There is also a white strain, with checkered petal texture. Cut flowers last 4 to 7 days.

HARDINESS: *F. imperialis*, zones 5 to 9; *F. meleagris*, zones 3 to 8.

GROWING CONDITIONS: Prefers full sun, average moisture, and fertile, well-drained soil. Space *F. imperialis* 12 in. apart, 8 in. deep; *F. meleagris*, 4 in. apart, 3 to 4 in. deep.

PLANTING: Set out bulbs in fall or as soon as received. Can be difficult to establish. Growing from seed is impractical for seedlings take many years to reach blooming size; may be sown outdoors ¼ in. deep in summer when ripe, however.

CARE: Apply an inch of rotted manure and compost over beds in fall. Divide every 3 years, if crowded.

HARVESTING AND CONDITIONING: Cut newly opened flowers in morning or evening. Stand in deep, cool water for several hours.

USES: Focal or filler element.

GAILLARDIA
BLANKET FLOWER
G. aristata, G. x grandiflora,
G. pulchella

DESCRIPTION: Annual or perennial. Masses of daisies, often bicolored, up to 4 in. wide on strong stems, in red, yellow, and orange. Plants are up to 3 ft. tall; leaves are fuzzy. *G. pulchella* is annual and often double. Other species are perennials grown as biennials. Blooms summer and fall. Cut flowers last up to 1 week.

HARDINESS: Zones 3 to 11. Tolerates high heat.

GROWING CONDITIONS: Prefers well-drained soil, not too fertile; full sun; average moisture. Grows well in sandy soil. Becomes leggy in rich soil or partial shade. Roots rot if soil is wet in winter. Plant 1 to 3 ft. apart.

PLANTING: Plant divisions in early spring, acclimatized potted plants at any time during growing season. Sow seed ¼ in. deep indoors or outdoors at 65 to 70°F. Start annuals indoors where summers are short. Transplant when crowded.

CARE: Apply 1 handful compost to each plant in fall or spring. Divide old plants in fall, discarding unhealthy portions. Harvest or deadhead frequently. Cut back stems in midsummer to encourage new growth. Mulch around crowns in winter and summer.

HARVESTING AND CONDITIONING: Cut in early morning or evening. Select flowers with tight centers. Recut and split stems. Strip off lower leaves and stand for several hours in deep water with sugar added.

USES: Focal point or filler.

GALANTHUS
SNOWDROP
G. elwesii, G. nivalis

DESCRIPTION: Bulb. Cuplike, multi-petaled ½ in. white blossoms with spots of lime green dangle from slim stalks. *G. nivalis,* 4 to 6 in. tall, spreads rapidly into broad patches; blooms late winter. *G. elwesii,* 10 in. tall, blooms in early spring, spreads slowly. Flowers open on sunny days. Gray-green straplike leaves vanish in summer. Cut flowers last 4 days.

HARDINESS: Zones 3 to 8. Withstands heat and cold.

GROWING CONDITIONS: Prefers sandy loam but grows in any soil. Likes average fertility and moisture, good drainage, and full sun or partial shade. Good under deciduous trees. Space 2 in. apart, 3 in. deep.

PLANTING: Set out bulbs in fall, mixing bonemeal and compost into soil. Set out divisions in spring, before, during, or after bloom.

CARE: Mulch with 1 in. of chopped leaves or compost in fall. Divide if so crowded that plants blossom poorly (every 5 years or so), or to propagate plants. Dig up clumps in early spring, separate with your hands to prevent injuring bulbs, and replant at same depth immediately. Or divide in autumn (mark location in spring).

HARVESTING AND CONDITIONING: Cut when flowers have opened in morning. Discard white portion of stem. Stand in deep water for several hours.

USES: Small-scale focal or accent element. Also planted in moss-topped baskets.

GAZANIA
TREASURE FLOWER
G. hybrids, G. pinnata

DESCRIPTION: Tender perennial, grown as annual. Multicolored daisies, in cream, gold, orange, rust, or bronze, up to 4 in. wide. Distinctive dotted or barred markings. Flowers close on cloudy days and at night. Unbranched plants with swordlike green leaves, silver below, in basal rosettes; 8 to 12 in. tall. Blooms summer through fall. Cut flowers last 5 days.

HARDINESS: Zones 2 to 7 as an annual, 9 to 11 as a perennial. Tolerates light frost; withstands intense heat.

GROWING CONDITIONS: Prefers loose, light soil; average but steady fertility and moisture; good drainage; full sun. Space 10 to 12 in. apart.

PLANTING: Set out plants after danger of frost passes. Sow seed ¼ in. deep, 1 in. apart, in late winter at temperatures between 60 and 75°F. Transplant to larger containers if crowded. In mild-winter zones, take cuttings from near the crown in summer for bloom next year.

CARE: Mulch in hot, dry areas. Remove flowers affected by mildew. Harvest or deadhead often to promote bloom. To overwinter in mild-winter areas, protect plants with mulch or temporary covers. Overwinter in greenhouse elsewhere, if desired.

HARVESTING AND CONDITIONING: Cut when flowers have nearly opened fully, before pollen is apparent, in morning or evening. Stand in deep water several hours.

USES: Focal or accent material. Use in brightly lit areas or blossoms may close.

GENISTA
BROOM, WOAD
G. tinctoria

DESCRIPTION: Shrub. Bears dense spires of small yellow flowers on arching branches in late spring or early summer. Spreading plants are 2 or 3 ft. tall and somewhat wider; some types more prostrate than others. Many are fragrant. Oval leaves 1 in. long are rich green; stems grooved. Cut flowers last 5 or more days.

HARDINESS: Zones 3 to 8.

GROWING CONDITIONS: Prefers an alkaline soil but will grow in any soil which has a nearly neutral pH and is not too rich. Requires good drainage. Best in sunny, dry sites. Space 3 to 5 ft. apart.

PLANTING: Plant bare-root plants in early spring, acclimatized potted plants at any time during growing season. Difficult to transplant once established. Take cuttings in summer; keep moist in sandy peat. Grows from seeds if soaked overnight in a solution of ⅓ vinegar, ⅔ water; however, germination may still be irregular. Sow outdoors in summer or indoors any time, ½ in. deep in sandy soil.

CARE: Fertilize lightly in fall, spring, and summer. Prune in early summer after flowering; may flower again on new growth. Do not let bushes become too dense.

HARVESTING AND CONDITIONING: Cut spikes beginning to bloom, in early morning or evening. Slit stem ends. Stand in deep water for several hours.

USES: Linear or filler material.

GERANIUM
CRANESBILL
G. endressii, G. hybrids,
G. pratense, G. sanguineum

DESCRIPTION: Perennial. Neat, matlike plants dotted with five-petaled flowers from 1 to 3 in. wide in pink, white, magenta, lilac, or violet. Divided, veined leaves are about 2 in. wide, changing from green to red in autumn. Height ranges from 8 to 30 in.; taller types like *G. pratense* (30 in.) are better for cutting. Blooms prolifically in late spring and sporadically throughout summer. Cut flowers last up to 3 days, foliage 1 week.

HARDINESS: Zones 4 to 8.

GROWING CONDITIONS: Prefers loamy soil moderately enriched with manure or flower fertilizer, full sun to partial shade, and moist but well-drained conditions. Space 8 to 12 in. apart.

PLANTING: Plant divisions in early spring before new growth begins, acclimatized potted plants at any time during growing season. Sow ¼ in. deep, 1 in. apart indoors or outdoors at 65 to 75°F in spring or summer.

CARE: Apply 1 handful rotted manure or compost to each established clump in fall. If necessary, divide in spring, while growth is small. Mulch around crowns winter and summer. Deadhead regularly.

HARVESTING AND CONDITIONING: Cut newly opened flowers in early morning or evening. Remove lower leaves and stand in deep water for several hours.

USES: Flowers and leaves used mainly as filler material.

GERBERA
AFRICAN DAISY
G. jamesonii

DESCRIPTION: Tender perennial, often grown as annual. Large daisies on unbranched stems. Deep and pastel shades include white, cream, yellow, orange, coral, red, and pink. Dwarf or tall plants are 10 to 24 in. tall, with flowers usually 6 in. wide. Fuzzy-leaved plants form a neat rosette with a deep taproot. Blooms all year in frost-free climates, summer elsewhere. Cut flowers last 2 weeks.

HARDINESS: All zones as annual. Zones 8 to 11 as perennial. Likes heat. Grows anywhere if protected from frost.

GROWING CONDITIONS: Prefers rich, sandy loam soil with average moisture, full sun, and excellent drainage. Plant 1 to 2 ft. apart.

PLANTING: Set out divisions in spring after frost, acclimatized potted plants at any time during warm weather. Sow seed ⅛ in. deep in individual pots indoors in January at 70°F, 12 hours of light per day, for flowers in summer. Root heel cuttings from side shoots in late summer.

CARE: Fertilize at planting time and throughout growing season; mulch with compost. Where hardy, divide in spring only if there are multiple crowns; dig carefully to avoid cutting taproots. Shelter new growth from late frosts. Deadhead regularly.

HARVESTING AND CONDITIONING: Cut when central discs first show a ring of pollen. Split stem ends and dip in boiling water; stand in deep water containing sugar for several hours.

USES: Large-scale focal element or single specimen.

GEUM
AVENS
G. × borisii, G. hybrids

DESCRIPTION: Perennial. Round single or double flowers with oval petals on slender, branching stems. Clumps of bright yellow, orange, or red flowers with prominent yellow stamens bloom in late spring and summer. Bushy plants, sometimes drooping under weight of flowers, 18 to 24 in. tall. Plants may take several years to become established in sizable clumps. Leaves are broadly lobed, round, evergreen in southern end of range. Cut flowers last 4 to 7 days.

HARDINESS: Zones 5 to 8. Some strains less hardy. Dislikes hot weather.

GROWING CONDITIONS: Prefers rich, moist but well-drained, loamy soil in full sun. Space 15 in. apart.

PLANTING: Set out divisions in early spring or late fall, acclimatized potted plants in late spring. Sow seed indoors in February or March, ⅛ in. deep. Germinates in 12 to 15 days. Or sow outdoors in summer; germinates in 20 to 30 days.

CARE: Apply 1 handful manure or compost to each established clump in fall or early spring. Divide in early spring if crowded, every 3 or 4 years. Harvest or deadhead regularly. Water steadily during dry spells.

HARVESTING AND CONDITIONING: Cut when flowers have nearly opened, in morning or evening. Briefly dip stem ends in boiling water and stand in deep water for several hours.

USES: Focal or accent element.

GLADIOLUS
G. callianthus, G. hybrids

DESCRIPTION: Corm. Hybrids offer funnel-shaped flowers in every shade but blue, aligned on unbranched stems. Striking variations in ruffling and marking. Bold, swordlike leaves. Stem and leaf height from 2 to 4 ft. Most flowers 2 in. long. *G. callianthus* (formerly *Acidanthera*), 2½ ft. tall with fragrant white flowers blotched with purple. *Gladiolus* blooms once a year for 1 to 2 weeks, usually in summer. Cut flowers last 7 to 14 days.

HARDINESS: Zones 9 to 11 without protection; all zones if kept from freezing. Some cultivars are hardier than the zones given.

GROWING CONDITIONS: Prefers rich, sandy loam soil with average moisture, full sun, and excellent drainage. Plant 4 to 6 in. deep, 6 in. apart. Dislikes inadequately aged manure.

PLANTING: Plant corms after danger of frost passes. Make successive plantings 2 weeks apart for extended bloom. Prestart indoors and transplant where summers are short. Can be grown from seed sown ⅛ in. deep; takes years to flower.

CARE: Fertilize at planting time. Mulch. Keep moist during growth, dry during dormancy. Where ground freezes in winter, dig, dry, and store corms and cormlets after foliage yellows. Divide in spring where hardy.

HARVESTING AND CONDITIONING: Cut when first few flowers have opened. Strip 3-in. portions of bases of large spikes. Stand in deep water with sugar added for several hours.

USES: Linear element or single specimen.

GOMPHRENA
GLOBE AMARANTH
G. globosa

DESCRIPTION: Annual. Rounded, multi-flowered 1-in. heads with strawlike texture resembling clover are borne prolifically on branched, stiff stems. Colors include white, ivory, peach, orange, pink, and magenta. Small leaves are fuzzy, pointed ovals. Blooms from midsummer to frost on dwarf or tall plants from 6 in. to 2 ft.; tall types are best for cutting. Cut flowers stay fresh 5 to 7 days.

HARDINESS: Zones 2 to 11. Tolerates high heat; killed by frost.

GROWING CONDITIONS: Prefers rich to average soil, average moisture, full sun. Tolerates drought once established. Space 10 to 16 in. apart.

PLANTING: Set out bedding plants in spring after danger of frost. Or sow seed 8 weeks earlier indoors in small pots for transplants, or directly outdoors after danger of frost, 1/8 in. deep, 3 in. apart.

CARE: Thin or transplant when seedlings are 4 in. tall or are crowded. Pinch back tips once for bushiness. Side-dress plants with flower fertilizer and compost during growth. Mulch in hot or dry areas. Stake if necessary. Harvest or deadhead regularly. Pull and replace spent plants.

HARVESTING AND CONDITIONING: Cut when half the florets in flowerheads have opened, in morning or evening. Strip off lower leaves. Stand in deep water for several hours.

USES: Filler element, fresh or dried.

GYPSOPHILA
BABY'S BREATH
G. elegans, G. paniculata

DESCRIPTION: Annual or perennial. Cloudlike bunches of small white or rose flowers on finely branched stems. *G. paniculata*, perennial, 3 ft. tall and wide, blooms in summer. Look for doubles. *G. elegans*, hardy annual 1½ to 2 ft. tall, blooms late spring through fall except in hottest weather. In both species, leaves are grayish, pointed, and inconspicuous during bloom; stems wiry. Cut flowers last 5 to 8 days.

HARDINESS: *G. elegans*, all zones. Prefers cool temperatures; killed by high heat. Seedlings withstand light frost. *G. paniculata*, zones 3 to 9.

GROWING CONDITIONS: Prefers sandy, neutral to alkaline, well-drained soil; average fertility and moisture; full sun. Space annuals 1 ft. apart, perennials 3 ft.

PLANTING: Set out plants in spring after danger of frost, divisions of perennials earlier. Sow seed indoors 6 weeks before last frost. Or sow annuals outdoors 3 weeks before last frost, 1/8 in. deep, 2 in. apart.

CARE: Thin or transplant when 3 in. tall or crowded. Pinch back tips of annuals. Stake with pea brush (slim, branched sticks) if necessary. Protect from slugs, sowbugs, and leaf miners. Fertilize during growth. Mulch in hot or dry areas. Deadhead regularly.

HARVESTING AND CONDITIONING: Cut when one-third of flowers on stem have opened, in morning or evening. Strip off lower leaves. Stand in cool water for several hours.

USES: Filler element, fresh or dried.

HAMAMELIS
WITCH HAZEL
H. × intermedia,
H. japonica, H. mollis,
H. virginiana

DESCRIPTION: Shrub or tree. Species vary in height from 10 to 25 ft. Frost-resistant, spidery flowers with four crinkled petals, resembling forsythia, appear in mid to late winter or early spring. Most species and cultivars have yellow flowers, but *H. × intermedia* 'Arnold Promise' has rusty red flowers with unusually long petals. *H. mollis* is very fragrant. Leaves are prominently veined, glossy, pointed green ovals, turning rich yellow or orange in autumn before dropping. Cut flowers stay fresh 5 to 7 days.

HARDINESS: Zones 5 to 8 for most; 3 to 8 for native *H. virginiana.*

GROWING CONDITIONS: Prefers fertile, loamy, acid soil; average moisture; full sun to partial shade. *H. virginiana* often found near streams. Space 12 ft. apart.

PLANTING: Set out bare-root plants in late winter before leaves appear, balled-and-burlapped plants at any time during growing season. Can be grown from seed sown outdoors in fall for spring germination, or grown from softwood cuttings in summer.

CARE: Surround each plant with a broad mulch of compost or chopped leaves. Prune after flowering. Side-dress with all-purpose fertilizer in spring. Water during drought.

HARVESTING AND CONDITIONING: Cut at midday when some flowers on branch have opened. Slit and recut stem ends, and stand in deep water for several hours.

USES: Filler or as forced branches.

HEDERA
IVY
H. helix

DESCRIPTION: Perennial vine. Waxy, evergreen leaves patterned with strong veining. Plants trail in thick mats or climb walls and trees up to 90 ft. Cultivars vary in leaf shape, size, and color. Hardiest, most common types are glossy, blackish green with 5-in. triangular leaves with three to five lobes and whitened undersides. Cultivars may be variegated or veined with cream, yellow, silver, bronze, purple, or light green. Stems last 2 weeks in water and may root in vase.

HARDINESS: Zones 4 to 9 for dark cultivars; variegated types are less hardy.

GROWING CONDITIONS: Prefers loamy, well-drained soil in partial to deep shade; average moisture. Types variegated with cream or yellow prefer more light. Spacing variable: for groundcover, 1 ft. apart.

PLANTING: Set out plants spring through fall. Start beds by inserting 14-in. stem or tip cuttings 7 in. deep in moist, well-prepared soil. Take tip or stem cuttings spring through fall.

CARE: Mulch with compost and aged manure at planting time and each spring. Trim for shape throughout growing season. Treat for scale, aphids, mites, and mealybugs if necessary. Protect from sun and wind in winter to prevent winterkill.

HARVESTING AND CONDITIONING: Cut 1- to 3-ft. stems with new growth at tip. Slit and recut stem ends; stand in deep water for several hours.

USES: Linear or filler element.

HELENIUM
SNEEZEWEED
H. autumnale, H. hybrids

DESCRIPTION: Perennial. Large clusters of daisies on branched, strong, upright stems. Petals are cream, yellow, gold, orange, rust, or peach, and cone-shaped centers tend to be dark. Height ranges from 3 to 5 ft. Shorter types are neater and need less staking. Plants are bushy, leaves long and pointed, roots fibrous. Blooms for a month or more in late summer. Cut flowers last about 5 days.

HARDINESS: Zones 4 to 8.

GROWING CONDITIONS: Prefers moist but well-drained, fertile soil in full sun. Space 2 ft. apart.

PLANTING: Plant divisions in early spring or fall, acclimatized potted plants at any time during growing season. Sow seeds ⅛ in. deep indoors 6 weeks before last frost or outdoors at about 70°F. 'Redgold Hybrids', 2 to 4 ft., are dependable from seed.

CARE: Apply several handfuls of compost to each established clump in fall and spring. Divide annually in spring or fall (after flowering). Transplant seedlings to permanent places when crowded. Mulch around crowns winter and summer. Side-dress with light applications of flower fertilizer during growth. Water to keep soil moist at all times. Stake before flowers open.

HARVESTING AND CONDITIONING: Cut when first few flowers have opened. Slit and recut stems. Stand in deep water for several hours.

USES: Filler or massed material.

HELIANTHUS
SUNFLOWER
H. annuus, H. × multiflorus

DESCRIPTION: Annual or perennial. Tall, branched, stiff stems bear large disc and ray flowers throughout summer. Plants are 3 to 8 ft. tall. *H. × multiflorus* is a gold-flowered perennial, either single or double, with 2½ to 3 in. blooms. *H. annuus* is an annual available in cream, gold, rust, rose, and brown, sometimes banded. Small-flowered types such as 4-ft. 'Sunburst Mixed' are better for cutting than 10 ft. 'Russian Giant'. Leaves hairy, sometimes drooping, nearly heart-shaped. Cut flowers last up to 7 days.

HARDINESS: Zones 4 to 8, perennials; all zones, annuals.

GROWING CONDITIONS: Prefers rich, loamy soil; full sun; average to moist conditions. Tolerates but is dwarfed by drought. Space 2 to 3 ft. apart.

PLANTING: Perennials: plant divisions in early spring, acclimatized potted plants at any time during growing season. Annuals: sow seed indoors 4 weeks before last frost, ¼ in. deep in 4-in. pots, or outdoors after frost.

CARE: Perennials: divide or thin every spring. Mulch all year. Remove stalks after bloom. Annuals: Pinch back for bushiness. Mulch in hot, dry weather. Discard spent plants. Both: protect from squirrels, deer, caterpillars, and mildew. Apply flower fertilizer or manure during growing season. Deadhead regularly. Stake.

HARVESTING AND CONDITIONING: Cut newly opened flowers. Scald stem ends; stand in deep water for several hours.

USES: Focal, accent, or massed material.

HELICHRYSUM
STRAWFLOWER, IMMORTELLE
H. bracteatum

DESCRIPTION: Annual. Round flowerheads with central discs surrounded by layers of glossy, colorful, pointed bracts; strawlike texture. Plants range from 1 to 4 ft. tall, flower size from 1 to 3 in. wide, depending on cultivar. Tall types best for cutting. Prolific crops borne on branched, stiff stems. Colors include white, yellow, cream, ivory, peach, orange, red, rust, pink, and magenta. Leaves are lance-shaped and downy. Blooms midsummer to frost. Cut flowers last 7 days.

HARDINESS: Zones 3 to 11. Tolerates high heat and light frost.

GROWING CONDITIONS: Prefers rich to average soil, average moisture, full sun. Space 1 to 2 ft. apart.

PLANTING: Set out bedding plants in spring after danger of frost. Sow seed 8 weeks earlier indoors for transplants, or directly outdoors after danger of frost, ⅛ in. deep, 3 in. apart.

CARE: Thin seedlings to correct spacing and desired sites when they are 4 in. tall or are crowded. Pinch back tips for bushiness. Side-dress plants with flower fertilizer and compost during growth. Mulch in hot or dry areas. Stake if necessary. Harvest or deadhead regularly. Discard spent plants.

HARVESTING AND CONDITIONING: Cut before central discs show pollen, in morning or evening. Strip off lower leaves. Stand in deep water for several hours.

USES: Filler, accent, or focal element, fresh or dried.

HELIOPSIS
FALSE SUNFLOWER
H. helianthoides

DESCRIPTION: Perennial. Large, bushy plants resemble sunflowers in flower and leaf. Flowers freely for many weeks in late summer with orange or golden, single or double frilled disc and ray flowers 3 to 4 in. wide. Centers are gold or green. Plants are 3 to 5 ft. tall. 'Light of Loddon' is a popular, reliable double cultivar, 5 ft. tall. Leaves are deep green, toothed, hairy, pointed ovals. Cut flowers will last up to 7 days.

HARDINESS: Zones 4 to 9.

GROWING CONDITIONS: Prefers rich, loamy soil; full sun to part shade; average moisture. Space 2 to 3 ft. apart.

PLANTING: Plant divisions in fall or early spring, acclimatized potted plants at any time during growing season. Sow seed indoors 4 weeks before last frost, 1/4 in. deep in pots or flats, or outdoors after frost.

CARE: Divide or thin in spring or fall, after bloom, if plants have diminished in size or quantity of flowers. Mulch in winter and during hot, dry weather. Remove stalks after bloom. Protect from deer, caterpillars, and mildew. Apply flower fertilizer or manure during growing season. Deadhead regularly. Stake.

HARVESTING AND CONDITIONING: Cut newly opened flowers in morning or evening. Stand in deep water for several hours.

USES: Focal or massed material.

HELIOTROPIUM
HELIOTROPE
H. arborescens

DESCRIPTION: Tropical shrub, grown as an annual. Large flat clusters of small purple, lavender, or white flowers on bushy plants. Reaches 18 in. tall and blooms first year; becomes shrublike the next. Scent is similar to cherry pie, its nickname. Glossy, deep green, wrinkled leaves. Blooms summer to frost; longer in mild climates. Cut flowers last 1 week.

HARDINESS: Zones 10 to 11 as perennial; farther north with protection. All zones as annual. Killed by frost.

GROWING CONDITIONS: Prefers rich, sandy loam soil with plentiful moisture, full sun, and excellent drainage. Plant 1 to 1½ ft. apart.

PLANTING: Set out plants during warm weather. Sow seed ⅛ in. deep in individual pots indoors in March at 70 to 85°F for flowers in summer. Needs light to germinate; germination takes 7 to 21 days. Take cuttings in summer or fall.

CARE: Fertilize at planting time and throughout growth. Mulch. Avoid disturbing roots. Shelter from late frosts. Deadhead regularly. Protect from whitefly, scale, spider mites, and aphids. Tip-prune in spring for bushiness. Cut back leggy plants in summer. Where protected in winter, can be trained as woody shrub or standard.

HARVESTING AND CONDITIONING: Cut when half of flower cluster has opened. Split and scald stem ends, and stand in warm water (100°F) for several hours.

USES: Accent or filler.

HELIPTERUM
ACROCLINIUM, RHODANTHE
H. manglesii, H. roseum

DESCRIPTION: Annual. Round flowerheads with rows of delicate, petal-like, pointed bracts with a silky sheen and papery texture, pale to deep rose or white. Central discs gold or black. Grayish, pointed leaves; wiry stems. Branched plants are 1 ft. tall; flower size from 1 to 2 in., depending on cultivar. *H. roseum* 'Giganteum' is largest. Blooms early summer; longer in cool temperatures. Cut flowers last 7 days.

HARDINESS: Zones 3 to 11. Prefers cool temperatures. Seedlings withstand light frost. Killed by prolonged heat in 90s F.

GROWING CONDITIONS: Prefers sandy, nonacidic, well-drained soil; average fertility and moisture; full sun. Space 10 in. apart.

PLANTING: Set out bedding plants in spring after danger of frost. Sow seed 6 weeks earlier indoors or in cold frame for transplants, or outdoors 3 weeks before the last expected frost, ⅛ in. deep, 2 in. apart.

CARE: Thin seedlings or transplant to desired sites when 3 in. tall or crowded. Pinch back tips once for bushiness. Provide flower fertilizer during growth. Mulch in hot or dry areas. Harvest or deadhead regularly. Discard spent plants.

HARVESTING AND CONDITIONING: Cut before central discs show pollen, in morning or evening. Strip off lower leaves. Stand in deep water for several hours.

USES: Filler or focal, fresh or dried.

HELLEBORUS
HELLEBORE, CHRISTMAS OR LENTEN ROSE
H. niger, H. orientalis,
H. viridis, and others

DESCRIPTION: Perennial. Many-petaled, waxy, 2- to 3-in. blossoms for 4 to 8 weeks in late winter and early spring. Colors are white, soft rose, purple, and brownish green; some types speckled. *H. niger* (Christmas rose) with white flowers resembling waterlilies, blooms in winter, fades to pink. *H. orientalis* (Lenten rose) has nodding pink blooms in spring. Plants 12 to 24 in. tall, tend to be evergreen, with divided, leathery leaves. Lasts 7 to 14 days in vase.

HARDINESS: Zones 5 to 8 for most species; moderately to very hardy.

GROWING CONDITIONS: Prefers rich, loamy, moist but well-drained soil under deciduous trees for sun in winter, shade in summer. Space 1 to 1½ ft. apart.

PLANTING: Plant divisions in fall or spring, acclimatized potted plants at any time during growing season.

CARE: Apply 3 handfuls compost to each established clump in fall. Cut off badly damaged leaves in early spring as buds develop. Keep moist until established (takes several years). Do not move or divide unless necessary. Flowers may be left on for self-sown seedlings, easily moved while small.

HARVESTING AND CONDITIONING: Cut when new flowers have opened. Scald stem ends. Stand in deep water for several hours.

USES: Small-scale accent or focal element.

HEMEROCALLIS
DAYLILY
H. asphodelus (syn. *H. flava*),
H. fulva, H. hybrids

DESCRIPTION: Perennial. Branched stems of large single or double lilies up to 6 in. wide. Some are fragrant. Blooms throughout summer if early-, middle-, and late-season hybrids are selected. Standard types are 4 ft. tall, but cultivars range from under 1 to more than 6 ft. Colors include peach, orange, yellow, cream, lilac, pink, and green. Many bicolors. *H. asphodelus* is yellow, known as lemon lily. Orange *H. fulva* grows wild. Leaves green, arched and straplike. Flowers close at night, last one day in vase. A stem with multiple buds blooms progressively for over a week.

HARDINESS: Zones 3 to 9. Tolerates cold and heat.

GROWING CONDITIONS: Prefers good soil, full sun to partial shade, and moist conditions. Tolerates drought, bad drainage, and poor soil. Space 1 to 3 ft. apart.

PLANTING: Plant divisions in spring or fall; plant acclimatized potted or deeply dug plants during growing season.

CARE: Apply 3 handfuls compost and aged manure to each established clump in fall. Divide every 2 to 3 years in spring or after bloom. Keep moist until established and during blooming period. Protect from slugs. Mulch around crowns winter and summer. Remove stalks after bloom for neatness.

HARVESTING AND CONDITIONING: Cut newly opened flowers in morning. Arrange in deep water immediately, or refrigerate (in water) several hours so that blooms will stay open at night.

USES: Focal element or specimen.

HESPERIS
SWEET ROCKET
H. matronalis

DESCRIPTION: Perennial or biennial. Fluffy, abundant heads of white, rose, lilac, or purple flowers on plants 2½ to 4 ft. tall. Individual flowers have four petals, are fragrant in evening. Hairy, pointed leaves form an evergreen rosette in winter. Blooms generously 1 month in late spring or early summer. Second bloom follows but looks a bit ragged. Cut flowers last 4 days; petals drop.

HARDINESS: Zones 4 to 9. Short-lived after seed sets.

GROWING CONDITION: Prefers loamy soil enriched with compost and leaf mold, full sun to partial shade, and average to moist conditions. Tolerates poor soil and lightly wooded areas. Space 2 ft. apart.

PLANTING: Plant divisions in early spring, acclimatized potted plants at any time during growing season. Plant seeds ⅛ in. deep indoors or out at about 70°F. Self-sows freely. Grows from stem cuttings in late summer where small plantlets form at nodes.

CARE: Apply 1 handful compost to each established clump in fall and spring. Divide crowded rosettes in spring. Transplant volunteers to permanent places. Keep moist until established. Mulch around crowns winter and summer. Remove mulch if soil becomes soggy. Remove stalks after bloom, or leave a few for seed but remove by autumn.

HARVESTING AND CONDITIONING: Cut when first few flowers have opened. Stand in deep water for several hours.

USES: Filler, accent, or massed material.

HEUCHERA
CORAL BELLS
H. × brizoides, *H.* hybrids (mostly from *H. sanguinea*)

DESCRIPTION: Perennial. Slender, wiry, airy plumes of small flowers rising 1 to 2 ft. above 2-in., rounded, scalloped leaves in trim rosettes. Blooms repeatedly mid-spring to summer in shades of red, pink, coral, or greenish white. Showiest flower plumes found on *H. × brizoides* cultivars such as 'Pluie de Feu'. Leaves green, sometimes bronzed. *H.* 'Palace Purple' has large purple leaves, inconspicuous white flowers. Cut flowers, dainty-looking but rugged, last 5 to 8 days.

HARDINESS: Zones 4 to 8.

GROWING CONDITIONS: Prefers rich, loamy, well-drained soil in partial shade; average moisture. Space 1 ft. apart.

PLANTING: Plant divisions in early spring, acclimatized potted plants at any time during growing season. Can be grown from seed. Prechill one month in refrigerator, and plant ⅛ in. deep; grow at 70°F.

CARE: Apply 1 handful compost and aged manure to each established clump in early spring, before buds form. Divide every 2 to 3 years in spring or fall, but do not replant too deeply. Discard older portions. Keep moist until established; then allow to remain drier, but water during drought. Treat for mealybugs if necessary. Discard portions affected by stem rot. Remove stalks after bloom.

HARVESTING AND CONDITIONING: Cut spikes when half the flowers have opened. Stand in deep water for several hours.

USES: Linear or filler element.

HOSTA
PLANTAIN LILY
H. species and cultivars

DESCRIPTION: Perennial. Grown for long-lived rosettes of large, deeply veined, puckered, or ridged leaves in shades of green, gray-blue, gold, and white. Leaf texture, shape, and variegation vary; most are heart-shaped and 2 to 3 ft. tall, others dwarf or lance-shaped. Deciduous leaves mature in late spring, followed in summer by spikes of tubular white or lilac flowers. White flowers of *H. plantaginea* are extraordinarily fragrant. Leaves and flowers last 4 to 6 days in vase.

HARDINESS: Zones 4 to 9.

GROWING CONDITIONS: Prefers rich, loamy, neutral soil; partial shade; moist conditions. Space 1 to 3 ft. apart.

PLANTING: Plant divisions in early spring, acclimatized potted plants at any time during growing season. Can be grown from seed planted ¼ in. deep in summer.

CARE: Apply 3 handfuls compost and aged manure to each established clump in fall and spring. Divide rosettes every 2 to 3 years in spring. Keep moist until established and during blooming period. Protect from slugs. Mulch around crowns winter and summer. Remove mulch if soil becomes soggy. Remove stalks after bloom.

HARVESTING AND CONDITIONING: Cut unscarred leaves and flower spikes when the first few flowers have opened, in morning or evening. Submerge leaves and stand flowers in deep water for several hours.

USES: Leaves as filler, flowers as linear element.

HYACINTHOIDES
WOOD HYACINTH
H. hispanica (formerly *Endymion*)

DESCRIPTION: Bulb. Numerous bell-shaped flowers dangle from 18-in. spires. Colors include blue, violet, pink, and white. Blooms once a year for 2 weeks in late spring. Multiplies rapidly. Straplike leaves can be a problem: they collapse, turn yellow, then vanish in summer. Cut flowers last up to 1 week.

HARDINESS: Zones 4 to 8.

GROWING CONDITIONS: Prefers rich, sandy loam soil with average moisture, excellent drainage, and partial shade, but grows in any soil, even clay. Plant 4 to 6 in. deep, 5 in. apart. Naturalizes well in lightly wooded areas.

PLANTING: Plant bulbs in fall (replant immediately if they turn up during cultivation of garden), green plants at any time during growing season, especially spring. Do not let bulbs dry in storage. Can be grown from seed sown ⅛ in. deep outdoors in summer; takes at least 3 years to flower. Self-sows.

CARE: Mulch bulbs with 1 in. of compost in fall. Plants quickly become crowded; dig and divide after blooms fade and foliage yellows; replant immediately. Bulbs pull themselves deeply down into soil, with new bulbs above them. Mark locations to avoid stabbing bulbs. Mulch in winter. Deadhead.

HARVESTING AND CONDITIONING: Cut when flowers have begun to open. Stand in deep water for several hours. Change water often.

USES: Linear or filler element.

HYACINTHUS
HYACINTH
H. hybrids

DESCRIPTION: Bulb. Fat spikes crammed with flaring, star-shaped flowers in late winter or early spring, 8 to 12 in. tall and about 5 in. in diameter while in bloom. Plants usually lose size but gain grace after a few years in the garden. Sweet, heavy fragrance. Colors include rich shades of red, rose, blue, purple, peach, yellow, cream, and white. Straplike leaves elongate to 1½ ft. and persist until late spring. Cut flowers last 5 to 7 days.

HARDINESS: Zones 6 to 8. Farther north under thick mulch. Needs chilling in winter.

GROWING CONDITIONS: Prefers rich, loamy soil with average moisture, full sun, and excellent drainage. Plant 4 to 6 in. deep, 6 in. apart.

PLANTING: Plant bulbs in fall, divisions in late spring.

CARE: Fertilize at planting time and each fall with bonemeal, and in spring before and after flowering with all-purpose fertilizer. Mulch in winter; remove gradually in spring as sprouts appear. Keep moist during growth, drier during dormancy. Allow foliage to yellow; then divide if crowded, about every 3 years.

HARVESTING AND CONDITIONING: Cut when half of flowers on stalk have opened. Discard white portion at base of stem. Stand in deep, cool water separately from other flowers for several hours. If necessary, support stem with an inner wire.

USES: Focal element or single specimen.

HYDRANGEA
HORTENSIA
H. macrophylla

DESCRIPTION: Shrub. Huge white, pink, purple, and blue flowerheads 4 to 8 in. wide cover 3- to 6-ft. deciduous shrubs all summer. Includes two types: hortensias, with rounded bunches of large, papery flowers (actually sterile sepals), and lacecaps, clusters of tiny flowers with an outer ring of papery large ones. Flowers fade to green, then tan, by fall. Leaves are 8-in. pointed ovals with serrated edges. Cut flowers last 6 to 12 days.

HARDINESS: Zones 6 to 9. Some cultivars less hardy.

GROWING CONDITIONS: Prefers full sun to partial shade, plentiful moisture, and fertile, well-drained soil. Space as far apart as they are tall (e.g., 3-ft. types 3 ft. apart).

PLANTING: Set out acclimatized plants in spring or fall. Take softwood cuttings in summer or hardwood cuttings in late winter.

CARE: Apply 1 in. of rotted manure and compost over beds in fall. Color is affected by pH: make soil more acid to get blue flowers (pH below 5.5), more alkaline for pink (pH above 6.0). Whites unaffected by pH. Prune in late winter, cutting oldest canes to ground, leaving newer growth 2 to 3 ft. tall. Flowers from old wood. Treat for mildew. Remove spent flowers.

HARVESTING AND CONDITIONING: Cut when flowers reach full color, or later, while green. Sear stem ends and stand in cool water for several hours.

USES: Focal or filler, fresh or dried.

HYPERICUM
ST. JOHN'S WORT
H. calycinum, H. hybrids,
H. × inodorum

DESCRIPTION: Shrub. Covered from midsummer into fall with 2- to 3-in. golden yellow round flowers with prominent stamens. Dense bushy plants have narrowly oval leaves of deep, glossy green. Species and cultivars vary in height and hardiness. *H. calycinum* is usually 1 ft. tall, several feet wide. *H. × inodorum* and *H.* 'Hidcote' are about 5 ft. tall and wide. Cut flowers last 4 days.

HARDINESS: *H. calycinum*, zones 7 to 9. *H. × inodorum*, zones 6 to 9. Hybrids vary.

GROWING CONDITIONS: Prefers full sun, average fertility, excellent drainage, and moderate moisture. Does best if roots are not too wet in winter. Space 3 to 4 ft. apart.

PLANTING: Set out acclimatized container plants in spring. Sow seed ⅛ in. deep, 2 in. apart, indoors in winter or outdoors in spring at about 55°F. May take 3 months to germinate. Root semiripe tip cuttings in summer.

CARE: Fertilize lightly throughout growth. Transplant seedlings when crowded. Prune mature plants hard in early spring, before flowering, for compact shape. Mulch lightly in winter. May be short-lived in excessive heat or if wilt strikes.

HARVESTING AND CONDITIONING: Cut branches bearing newly opened flowers. Split stem ends and stand in deep water for several hours. Recut stems before arranging.

USES: Accent or filler material.

IBERIS
CANDYTUFT
I. amara, I. sempervirens,
I. umbellata

DESCRIPTION: Annual or perennial. Domed or flat umbels of small, four-petaled flowers. Annuals *I. amara* and *I. umbellata* may be pink, white, lilac, rose, or wine red. The 12- to 18-in. branched plants with lancelike leaves bloom in early summer. Perennial *I. sempervirens* is white, blooming 1 month in late spring on evergreen plants 6 to 12 in. tall, 2 ft. wide. Small, linear, deep green leaves; slender stems. Lasts 5 days in vase.

HARDINESS: Annuals, all zones, *I. amara* hardier. *I. sempervirens*, zones 5 to 9.

GROWING CONDITIONS: Annuals prefer full sun; well-drained, nonacidic sandy loam; plentiful moisture and fertility. Space 1 ft. apart. *I. sempervirens* takes full sun or part shade, any well-drained soil, and average moisture and fertility. Space 2 ft. apart.

PLANTING: Set out divisions in early spring, acclimatized potted plants after frost. Sow seed of annuals indoors 8 weeks before last frost, ⅛ in. deep, 2 in. apart, or outdoors 2 to 4 weeks before last frost. Sow *I. sempervirens* indoors or out at 55 to 65°F, same spacing. Take cuttings after flowers fade.

CARE: Transplant seedlings when crowded. Divide established perennials in early spring, if crowded. Protect from slugs. Mulch if dry. Deadhead regularly. *I. umbellata* tends to self-sow.

HARVESTING AND CONDITIONING: Cut when half of florets have opened, in morning or evening. Split woody stem ends. Stand in deep water for several hours.

USES: Filler element.

ILEX
HOLLY
I. species and hybrids

DESCRIPTION: Tree or shrub. Most are broad-leaved evergreens with spiky, glossy leaves and red berries. Typical is cone-shaped *I. opaca* (American holly), over 40 ft. tall. There are numerous other species, many smaller and rounded, some deciduous. *I.* 'Sparkleberry' loses its leaves and has huge, tight bunches of scarlet berries in winter. Others have smooth or prickly leaves and red, yellow, black, or blue berries. Cultivars with variegated green-and-white leaves are popular. Plant both a male and a female for berries. Cut branches last 14 days.

HARDINESS: Most, zones 4 to 8; varies with species.

GROWING CONDITIONS: Needs vary with species. American holly grows in full sun to deep shade. Prefers acidic, fertile, well-drained soil and average moisture. Deciduous hollies need full sun or partial shade. Space plants 5 to 25 ft. apart.

PLANTING: Set out plants in spring. Take cuttings in late summer; wound stem ends to promote rooting. Berries planted outdoors ½ in. deep in spring may germinate next year; plants take years to mature.

CARE: Fertilize in spring and summer with holly fertilizer and compost. Mulch beds with pine needles. Prune hard in early spring. Protect from holly leafminer; remove and burn affected leaves.

HARVESTING AND CONDITIONING: Cut berried or leafy stems at midday. Scrape off bark near base of stem and slit. Stand in deep water for several hours.

USES: Background or filler element.

IMPATIENS
I. wallerana

DESCRIPTION: Perennial, grown as annual. Iridescent flowers with reflective texture on everblooming plants. Can be flat or double, white, pink, peach, orange, red, red-purple, or lilac, sometimes starred with white. Plants are bushy and succulent, between 6 in. and 2 ft. tall; taller in second year. Leaves glossy, green, pointed; some variegated with white or touched with bronze. New Guinea hybrids have large flowers and leaves variegated with yellow, white, and bronze. Blooms summer to frost. Cut flowers last 4 days; petals drop.

HARDINESS: Zones 10 to 11 as perennial. All zones as annual. Killed by frost.

GROWING CONDITIONS: Prefers rich, loamy, light soil with plentiful moisture, partial shade, and good drainage. Plant 6 to 18 in. apart.

PLANTING: Set out plants after danger of frost. Great pot plant. Sow seed ⅛ in. deep indoors in March or outdoors at 65 to 85°F; takes 2 months to flower. Take tip cuttings in summer or fall and root in moist, shaded soil or a glass of water.

CARE: Fertilize throughout growth. Mulch. Shelter from frost. Keep moist. Protect from whitefly, scale, and spider mites. Cut back leggy plants. In hot weather, spray with water at midday to prevent wilting.

HARVESTING AND CONDITIONING: Cut stems of newly opened flowers in morning or evening. Slit stem ends. Stand in deep water for several hours.

USES: Accent or filler material.

IRIS
BEARDED IRIS, FLAG
I. germanica and related species, hybrids, and cultivars

DESCRIPTION: Perennial. Flowers six-petaled in two groups of three, in all colors, often multicolored and patterned. Arching standards (upper petals) and drooping falls (lower petals) with a "beard," or row of short, dense, hairs, at the midline. Strong stems bear several 2- to 6-in. flowers. Hundreds of named cultivars on plants from 8 in. to more than 3 ft. tall, classed as miniature dwarf, standard dwarf, intermediate, miniature tall, border, and standard tall. We recommend miniature talls and border hybrids, for they are long-stemmed, prolific, and relatively weatherproof; all types are useful. Leaves straplike, some variegated with white or yellow. Blooms for 1 to 3 weeks, with types for late spring through midsummer. Lasts 3 to 6 days in vase.

HARDINESS: Zones 4 to 9.

GROWING CONDITIONS: Prefers full sun; fertile, loamy soil; excellent drainage; average moisture. Tolerates drought. Space 8 to 12 in. apart.

PLANTING: Set out divisions, partly but not completely covering the thick rhizomatous root, in summer or fall. Set out acclimatized potted plants at any time, preferably selecting while in bloom.

CARE: Apply flower fertilizer and compost throughout growth. Divide every 3 years, if necessary, after bloom or in early fall.

HARVESTING AND CONDITIONING: Cut buds showing color in morning or evening. Split stem bases. Stand in deep water for several hours.

USES: Focal or accent element.

IRIS
DUTCH, ENGLISH, OR SPANISH IRIS
I. xiphium and similar bulbous species and hybrids

DESCRIPTION: Bulb. Flowers six-petaled in two groups of three, in all colors but red and pink. Many are multicolored with contrasting blotches and veining. Stems stiff and straight, usually bear one or several 3- to 4-in. flowers on 2-ft. plants. Leaves linear, arched, graceful, from underground, bulbous root. Plants bloom for 1 to 2 weeks, with types for late spring and early summer. Lasts 3 to 6 days in vase.

HARDINESS: Zones 5 to 8. Can be harmed by repeated freezing and thawing in winter.

GROWING CONDITIONS: Prefers full sun; sheltered location; loamy, fertile soil; excellent drainage; average moisture. Set bulbs 3 in. below soil surface, 6 in. apart.

PLANTING: Set out bulbs in fall. Plant divisions in late summer or fall.

CARE: Apply flower fertilizer and compost throughout growth. Mulch deeply with salt hay, chopped leaves, or other lightweight mulch in winter to protect bulbs from freezing and thawing. Deadhead. Allow foliage to yellow before removing it. Replant beds with new bulbs as needed; in some areas, blooms well only the first year, though foliage is reliable.

HARVESTING AND CONDITIONING: Cut fully developed buds showing good color in morning or evening. Split stem bases. Stand in deep water for several hours.

USES: Focal or accent element.

IRIS
JAPANESE AND
SIBERIAN IRIS
I. ensata, I. sibirica

DESCRIPTION: Perennial. Flowers six-petaled in two groups of three, in all colors, often multicolored. Blooms are nearly flat. Many cultivars of Japanese iris (*I. ensata*) have wide petals, giving a circular appearance. Most Siberians (*I. sibirica*) have narrower petals, as do some of the Japanese iris. Strong, straight stems bear one or several 3- to 6-in. flowers on 3-ft. plants. Leaves are linear, narrower for Siberian types, forming huge, thick, round clumps. Foliage stays neat and attractive after blooms fade, though the Siberian foliage droops toward the end of summer. Blooms for 1 to 3 weeks, with types for early and midsummer. Lasts 3 to 4 days in vase; longer if second buds on stems unfold.

HARDINESS: Siberian, zones 4 to 9; Japanese, zones 5 to 9.

GROWING CONDITIONS: Prefers full sun and moist, rich, loamy soil. Tolerates wet or boggy soil; grows well by waterside. Set clumps 2 ft. apart.

PLANTING: Set out divisions in spring while growth is small or in early fall. Set out acclimatized potted plants at any time during growing season.

CARE: Apply flower fertilizer and compost throughout growth. Divide every 3 years, in spring or fall.

HARVESTING AND CONDITIONING: Cut buds showing color in morning or evening. Split stem bases. Stand in deep water for several hours.

USES: Focal or accent element.

KNIPHOFIA
TORCH LILY,
RED-HOT POKER
K. hybrids, *K. uvaria*
(formerly *Tritoma*)

DESCRIPTION: Perennial. Stiff spikes composed of overlapping, drooping, tubular flowers in shades of gold, red, coral, orange, and ivory. Most have gold florets at bottom of spike overlaid with red ones at the top. Plants have multiple bloomstalks above straplike leaves and bloom in late summer or fall. Height from 2 to 6 ft.; most garden types about 3 ft. Cut flowers last 6 to 8 days.

HARDINESS: Zones 6 to 9.

GROWING CONDITIONS: Prefers rich, sandy loam soil with average moisture; full sun; excellent drainage. Cannot withstand waterlogged soil in winter; plant at the top of a slope. Space clumps 2 to 4 ft. apart.

PLANTING: Set plants out in spring in holes wide enough for whole spread of roots. Can be grown from seed sown 1/8 in. deep indoors 4 weeks before last frost, later transplanted outdoors; takes years to flower.

CARE: Fertilize with several handfuls of manure per clump at planting time. Keep moist during growth, dry during dormancy. Divide in spring only if necessary; plants dislike disturbance. Protect from slugs. Mulch lightly in summer, deeply in winter; tie leaves together over centers to protect plants. Uncover in spring.

HARVESTING AND CONDITIONING: Cut when 1/3 of flowers on stalk have opened, in morning or evening. Slit stem bases. Stand in cool water for several hours.

USES: Linear element or single specimen.

LAGURUS
HARE'S TAIL GRASS
L. ovata

DESCRIPTION: Annual. Grass with soft, furlike, silky, oval seedheads about 1 in. long, on strong, slender stems. Grows green, turns pale ivory when ripe. Seedheads form in summer and persist well into autumn. Leaves are narrow, long, and green, fading to ivory in autumn. Plants are 18 in. tall. Lasts indefinitely when cut.

HARDINESS: Zones 3 to 11. Tolerates heat and light frost.

GROWING CONDITIONS: Prefers rich to average soil, average moisture, good drainage, and full sun. Space 6 in. apart.

PLANTING: Set out bedding plants in spring after danger of frost. Sow seed 8 weeks earlier indoors for transplants, or directly outdoors 4 weeks before danger of frost ends, 1/8 in. deep, 3 in. apart.

CARE: Thin seedlings to correct spacing and desired sites when they are 4 in. tall or are crowded. Protect small plants from slugs. Side-dress with flower fertilizer and compost during growth. Mulch in hot or dry areas. Harvest regularly or leave heads on for garden decoration. Discard spent plants.

HARVESTING AND CONDITIONING: Cut before seedheads have entirely lost green color, to prevent their shattering, but after they have developed fully with strawlike texture. Strip off lower leaves if you wish. No conditioning necessary.

USES: Linear filler or massed element, fresh or dried.

LANTANA
L. camara

DESCRIPTION: Shrublike perennial, grown as an annual. Bushy plants 3 to 6 ft. tall are covered with 3-in. slightly domed, dense, round flowerheads. Each head has rings of tubular florets of several different shades; those opening yellow turn orange, then red, and those opening white turn pink, then lilac. Blooms continuously in warm weather. Pest plant in Florida. Seeds toxic. Leaves deep green, oval, wrinkled. Cut flowers last 4 to 6 days; petals drop.

HARDINESS: Zones 9 to 11. Grown elsewhere as annual or greenhouse plant. Killed by hard frost.

GROWING CONDITIONS: Prefers full sun and fertile, well-drained soil. Needs moist soil during flowering, moderate moisture at other times. Tolerates poor, sandy soil. Space 2 to 6 ft. apart.

PLANTING: Plant divisions or acclimatized potted plants at any time after frost. Plant seed 1/2 in. deep indoors or out at 75 to 85°F. Take semiripe stem cuttings in summer.

CARE: Apply 6 handfuls manure and compost to each established plant in fall (where hardy) and spring. Pinch back young plants for bushiness. Divide mature plants if crowded. Keep moist until established. Trim for shape as needed. Withstands heavy pruning or harvesting. Treat for whitefly and red spider mites if necessary.

HARVESTING AND CONDITIONING: Cut when first few flowers have opened. Stand in deep water for several hours.

USES: Filler or accent material.

LATHYRUS
SWEET PEA
L. latifolius, L. odorata

DESCRIPTION: Annual or perennial. Several 1-in. or larger flowers per stem on 8-ft. vines. Blooms late spring and summer. Dwarf, bush, and tall cultivars of *L. odorata*, sweet-scented annual, available in all colors. *L. latifolius*, perennial, more vigorous, similar flowers in white, pink, and magenta. Paired oval leaves and twining tendrils. Cut flowers last to 6 days.

HARDINESS: *L. odoratus*, all zones. Prefers cool temperatures; withstands frost. *L. latifolius*, zones 5 to 9. Thrives in high heat.

GROWING CONDITIONS: Prefers rich, deep, loamy, well-drained soil; plentiful moisture; full sun. Space annuals 1 ft. apart, perennials 3 ft.

PLANTING: Set out plants in spring. Presoak overnight and sow seed ½ in. deep. Indoors, sow annuals in individual pots in winter. Outdoors, sow 3 in. apart in shallow trench where wanted, 6 weeks before last frost. Sow perennials during warm weather.

CARE: Transplant when 6 in. tall or crowded. Pinch back tips of annuals once. Gradually fill trench with soil around seedlings to keep roots cool. Keep steadily watered and fertilized. Protect from slugs and sowbugs. Train on trellises or 6-ft. stakes. Deadhead regularly. Cut back perennials in late autumn.

HARVESTING AND CONDITIONING: Cut when two flowers on stem have opened, in morning or evening. Stand in cool water containing sugar for several hours.

USES: Accent or massed element in small bouquets.

LAVANDULA
LAVENDER
L. angustifolia, L. stoechas

DESCRIPTION: Shrub. Slender spikes of tiny purple or lavender flowers on bushy, mounded plants. Both foliage and flowers are sharply fragrant. Leaves are evergreen, silver gray, needle-shaped. *L. angustifolia*, (English lavender) grows 2 ft. tall, densely covered with elongated flower spikes. *L. stoechas* (Spanish or French lavender) is slightly smaller with numerous shorter spikes. Blooms in early summer. Cut flowers last 1 week.

HARDINESS: *L. angustifolia*, zones 6 to 9. *L. stoechas*, zones 7 to 11, farther north with protection.

GROWING CONDITIONS: Prefers non-acidic soil in full sun with average fertility, excellent drainage, and moderate moisture. Does best if roots are kept dry in winter. Space 12 in. apart.

PLANTING: Set out acclimatized plants in spring or early summer. Difficult to grow from seed. Can be sown ¼ in. deep, 2 in. apart, indoors in winter or spring after refrigeration for 6 weeks. Sow seed outdoors in fall for germination in spring. Root semiripe tip cuttings in summer.

CARE: Fertilize lightly but steadily throughout growth. Prune for compact shape after flowering, and touch up early the next spring. Cover lightly in winter with loose straw or evergreen boughs; remove when ground thaws. Divide large plants in early spring if necessary.

HARVESTING AND CONDITIONING: Cut when half of flower cluster has opened. Split stem ends and stand in deep water for several hours.

USES: Accent or filler, fresh or dried.

LAVATERA
MALLOW
L. cachemiriana, L. trimestris

DESCRIPTION: Annual or perennial. Lustrous, cup-shaped flowers. *L. cachemiriana* is a 7-ft.-tall, branching perennial that is covered with 3-in. lilac-pink flowers with heart-shaped petals all summer. Established plants are 3 or 4 ft. wide. In winter, retains small basal rosette of leaves. *L. trimestris* is a branched, shrub-like annual 2 to 4 ft. tall bearing 4-in. white, pink, or ruby red flowers all summer. Leaves lobed. Lasts 4 days in vase.

HARDINESS: *L. trimestris*, all zones; *L. cachemiriana*, zones 6 to 8.

GROWING CONDITIONS: Prefers full sun, well-drained loam, plentiful moisture and fertility. Space annuals 2 ft. apart, perennials 3 ft.

PLANTING: Set out divisions in early spring, acclimatized potted plants after frost. Soak seed overnight. Sow annuals indoors in individual pots 8 weeks before last frost, ⅛ in. deep, or outdoors after last frost; sow in fall in mild areas. Sow perennials indoors or out at 70 to 80°F.

CARE: Transplant seedlings when crowded. Divide perennials in early spring, if crowded, and stake before blooms open. Protect from slugs. Mulch if dry and in winter. Deadhead regularly. Remove tall stems of *L. cachemiriana* in early fall; allow basal rosette to form. Spray to protect against rust disease.

HARVESTING AND CONDITIONING: Cut when several flowers have opened in morning or evening. Remove lower foliage. Stand in cold water for several hours.

USES: Focal or accent element.

LEUCOTHOE
FETTERBUSH
L. fontanesiana

DESCRIPTION: Shrub. Broad-leaved evergreen with graceful, 3-in. clusters of small white bell-like flowers at nodes along stems in spring. Sometimes called lily-of-the-valley bush. Clumps of arched stems with few side branches. Leaves glossy, pointed, green, bronze, or variegated green, cream, and bronze. Bronze and purple colors intensify in winter. Dwarf to tall types range from 2 to 6 ft. tall and wide. Cut flowers and leaves last 7 days.

HARDINESS: Zones 5 to 8.

GROWING CONDITIONS: Prefers partial to deep shade, plentiful moisture, and humus-rich, fertile, well-drained, acidic soil. Space plants as far apart as they are tall.

PLANTING: Set out plants in spring. Take softwood tip cuttings in summer or hardwood cuttings in winter.

CARE: Mulch beds with compost; do not permit soil to become dry. Prune after flowering, cutting older canes down to the base and leaving younger ones. Plants are clumps of suckers and may be divided or thinned in early spring. To rejuvenate an old, misshapen plant, cut all canes down to the ground after bloom ends. Leaf spot can damage or kill plants; remove affected portions promptly.

HARVESTING AND CONDITIONING: Cut flowers when three-quarters of raceme has opened, in morning or evening. Cut branches of unspoiled foliage at any time. Slit stem ends. Stand in deep water for several hours.

USES: Background or filler element.

LIATRIS
BLAZING STAR, GAYFEATHER
L. spicata

DESCRIPTION: Perennial. Stiff spikes of small magenta or white flowers, 2 ft. tall and ½ in. wide, above tufts of linear green leaves in summer. Flowers open from top to bottom. Most types 2 ft. tall. Cut flowers last 6 to 10 days.

HARDINESS: Zones 4 to 9. Dislikes dry or hot and humid climates.

GROWING CONDITIONS: Grows in full sun or partial shade, more shade in hot regions. Prefers rich, moist, sandy loam soil with good drainage. Tolerates occasional drought. Space 12 in. apart.

PLANTING: Set out acclimatized plants in spring or early summer. Sow seed indoors in spring or outdoors late spring or summer, after prechilling 6 weeks in refrigerator. Plant ⅛ in. deep, 3 in. apart. Seedlings germinate in 3 to 4 weeks.

CARE: Divide in spring when new growth begins, if crowded. Transplant seedlings in spring or summer. Mulch beds with compost summer through winter. Protect with several inches of evergreen boughs in winter; remove mulch and boughs gradually in early spring. Apply flower fertilizer each spring. Water to prevent soil from drying out. Deadhead by cutting spikes at base.

HARVESTING AND CONDITIONING: Cut when half of flowers on spike have opened, in morning or evening. Slit stem ends. Stand in deep water for several hours.

USES: Linear accent.

LILIUM
LILY
L. species and hybrids

DESCRIPTION: Bulb. Flowers flaring, six-petaled, sometimes recurved, some strongly fragrant. All shades except blue; some speckled. Several 3- to 6-in. flowers and numerous small, linear leaves along tall stems from 2 to more than 6 ft. tall. Plants bloom for 1 to 3 weeks, with types for early summer to early fall. Lasts 6 to 8 days in vase.

HARDINESS: Most, zones 5 to 8. *L. candidum* (Madonna lily), zones 6 to 10; Aurelian and Asiatic hybrids, zones 4 to 7; *L. regale*, zones 4 to 9.

GROWING CONDITIONS: Prefers loamy, light, fertile soil; excellent drainage; average moisture; partial shade or full sun. Set bulbs 3 to 6 in. below soil surface, 8 to 15 in. apart. *L. candidum* prefers sandy, neutral to alkaline soil and planting 1 in. below surface.

PLANTING: Set out bulbs when received in fall or spring. Scales from bulbs and bulbils from leaf axils can be sown. Plants grown from seed take many years to reach flowering size; however *L. regale* germinates in 30 days and blooms in 3 years.

CARE: Thin or divide when crowded, in fall or spring. Apply flower fertilizer and compost throughout growth. Stake if necessary. Mulch. Deadhead.

HARVESTING AND CONDITIONING: Cut top third of stems with several fresh flowers in morning or evening. Remove anthers to prevent pollen stains. Strip off lower leaves, and split stems. Stand in deep water for several hours.

USES: Focal element.

LIMONIUM
STATICE, SEA LAVENDER
L. sinuatum

DESCRIPTION: Semihardy perennial, grown as annual. Loose clusters of small, paper-textured, cuplike blossoms in bright colors of every shade. About a dozen stiff, flower-bearing stems rise in summer from a flat basal rosette of linear leaves with lobed edges; 1½ to 2 ft. tall. Cut flowers last 2 weeks.

HARDINESS: All zones, as annual. Mild areas as perennial or biennial. Prefers cool temperatures but killed by hard frost.

GROWING CONDITIONS: Prefers well-drained, rich, loamy soil; full sun; average moisture. Likes raised beds. Space 1½ ft. apart.

PLANTING: Set out plants after last frost. Sow seed ¼ in. deep indoors in individual pots in late winter or 12 weeks before last expected frost. Can be sown in cool greenhouse or outdoors in mild-winter areas in fall for bloom in spring.

CARE: Apply flower fertilizer throughout growth. Divide in early spring (where hardy). Deadhead or harvest by cutting off stems at base. Mulch around crowns during hot, dry weather. Keep plants fairly dry to protect from leaf spot, blight, and crown rot. Protect from mealybugs and aphids.

HARVESTING AND CONDITIONING: Cut during dry weather when nearly all flowers (calyces) show color. Stand in deep water for several hours. Can be stored refrigerated in water for several weeks.

USES: Filler element, fresh or dried.

LINARIA
TOADFLAX
L. maroccana

DESCRIPTION: Annual. Masses of small, spurred, tubular flowers with two lips. Branched plants bloom on linear spires in spring, summer, fall, or, in areas with little or no frost, winter. May be red, yellow, white, purple, lilac, or pink, with contrasting veining or splotches. Height ranges from 8 to 24 in.; 'Northern Lights' at 24 in. is productive for cutting. Stems slender; leaves soft, needle-shaped. Cut flowers last for more than 7 days.

HARDINESS: All zones. Withstands light frost.

GROWING CONDITIONS: Prefers well-drained, rich, sandy soil in full sun with average moisture. Grows in meadows or beds. Space 6 to 12 in. apart.

PLANTING: Set out acclimatized bedding plants after danger of temperatures below 28°F. Prechill seed in refrigerator for 4 days, thinly sow by pressing into surface of soil, barely covering. Indoors, sow in small pots in winter for plants to set out in spring, in summer for fall plants. Outdoors, sow in spring as early as soil can be worked. In zones 9 to 11, sow in fall for late winter bloom.

CARE: Thin seedlings before they become crowded. Keep transplants moist until established. Apply flower fertilizer throughout growth. Remove flowerstalks after bloom, or leave for self-sown plants.

HARVESTING AND CONDITIONING: Cut when lower third of flowers on stem have opened. Stand in deep water for several hours.

USES: Filler or massed material.

LOBELIA
CARDINAL FLOWER
L. cardinalis, L. siphilitica

DESCRIPTION: Perennial. Tubular flowers with two lips aligned on tall columns. Blooms late summer into fall, in clumps. *L. cardinalis* (cardinal flower) has cherry red blooms, narrow green or bronze leaves; grows 3 to 4 ft. tall. *L. siphilitica* has blue or white blooms in 3-ft. spires, rounded green leaves. Lasts 4 to 7 days in vase.

HARDINESS: *L. cardinalis*, zones 3 to 9; short-lived. *L. siphilitica*, zones 4 to 9; withstands heat and cold.

GROWING CONDITIONS: *L. cardinalis* prefers full sun and rich, loamy, well-drained, acidic soil; plentiful moisture. *L. siphilitica* prefers partial shade and moist to wet, rich loamy soil; any pH. Space 1 ft. apart.

PLANTING: Set out divisions in early spring, acclimatized potted plants any time during growing season. Sow seed indoors after prechilling in refrigerator for 6 weeks; barely press into soil; keep moist. Sow seed outdoors or in cold frame in fall for germination in spring.

CARE: Transplant seedlings when crowded. Divide plants in early spring, to separate bunched rosettes. Cut off tall stems after bloom to promote development of basal rosettes.

HARVESTING AND CONDITIONING: Cut when a fourth to a half of the flowers on the spike have opened. Remove lower foliage. Dip stem ends of *L. cardinalis* in boiling water and stand in warm water for several hours. Stand *L. siphilitica* in cool water overnight.

USES: Linear element.

LOBULARIA
SWEET ALYSSUM
L. maritima

DESCRIPTION: Annual. Small, rounded heads of lacy flowers with four petals make a snowy layer above matlike plants. Fragrant flowers are most often white, also rose, purple, or lilac. Blooms spring through fall; all year in mild climates. Leaves are grayish green, lancelike. Plants are 4 to 6 in. tall, up to 12 in. wide. Cut flowers last 4 days; petals drop.

HARDINESS: All zones. Leaves and flowers tolerate light frost. Dislikes intense heat.

GROWING CONDITIONS: Prefers average soil enriched with flower fertilizer, full sun to partial shade, and average to moist conditions. Tolerates brief periods of drought. Space 6 to 12 in. apart.

PLANTING: Set out plants midspring through summer; winter in frost-free zones. Plant seeds 1/8 in. deep, 2 in. apart, indoors or out at 60 to 75°F. Self-sows freely.

CARE: Fertilize steadily throughout growth. Thin or transplant seedlings to permanent places when they are 2 in. tall. Mulch if weather is hot and dry; remove if soil becomes very soggy. Shear tops if plants look straggly. Let some seed ripen for self-sown plants, if wanted.

HARVESTING AND CONDITIONING: Cut stems before lower flowers have formed seedpods, while tops are tightly filled with flowers and buds. Stand in deep, cool water for several hours.

USES: In tussy mussies and as small-scale filler material.

LUNARIA
MONEY PLANT, HONESTY
L. annua, L. rediviva

DESCRIPTION: Biennial or perennial. Grown for flat seedpods the size and shape of quarters. When dried, prized for the banded circles of silver formed by inner membranes. Showy heads of four-petalled pink or purple blossoms in summer. Leaves are scalloped, pointed ovals. Variety with white-edged foliage is attractive. Plants 2½ ft. tall. *L. annua* is usually a biennial, *L. rediviva* a short-lived perennial. Cut flowers last 5 days, pods over a week.

HARDINESS: *L. annua*, zones 5 to 8; *L. rediviva*, zones 6 to 8.

GROWING CONDITIONS: Prefers average soil, not too rich; good drainage; average moisture. Grows well in full sun or partial shade. Space 1 ft. apart.

PLANTING: Set out bedding plants in spring for bloom in summer. Sow seed indoors in spring or outdoors in summer (autumn in zones 8 and 9), 1/8 in. deep, 4 in. apart. Plants self-sow freely.

CARE: Thin and transplant seedlings when 3 or 4 in. tall or when crowded. Divide perennials in early spring. Side-dress with compost in spring. Water if plants wilt. Do not deadhead; allow coin-like pods to ripen. Remove spent or diseased plants.

HARVESTING AND CONDITIONING: Cut stems when half the flowers have opened, in morning or evening, or several weeks later when seedpods are mature but still bright green. Stand in deep water for several hours. Allow pods for drying to ripen fully and to turn brown or tan before picking. Remove husks when dried.

USES: Filler or accent material.

LUPINUS
LUPINE
*L. luteus, L. polyphyllus,
L. Russell Hybrids*

DESCRIPTION: Perennial. Many species. Russell Hybrids are popular, grown for densely filled 3-ft. spires of large, fragrant flowers in late spring and summer. Colors include white, yellow, orange, red, pink, and violet, with many bicolors. *L. luteus* is a similar yellow species, sometimes grown as cover crop to enrich soil and also in garden. Palmate leaves. Lasts 5 to 7 days in vase.

HARDINESS: Zones 5 to 8.

GROWING CONDITIONS: Prefers full sun; well-drained, sandy loam; average moisture and fertility. Space 1 to 2 ft. apart.

PLANTING: Plant divisions in early spring, acclimatized potted plants at any time during growing season. Sow seed indoors in spring or outdoors in summer at 70 to 80°F, 1/4 in. deep, 2 to 4 in. apart. Presoak seed overnight and, if you wish, treat with legume inoculant (nitrogen-fixing bacteria), as for garden peas.

CARE: Transplant seedlings when crowded. Divide plants in early spring, if crowded. Fertilize steadily throughout growth. Stake. Protect from slugs. Mulch if soil is hot and dry. Deadhead by cutting off spent flower stalks near base of plant.

HARVESTING AND CONDITIONING: Cut spikes when half of flowers have opened, in morning or evening. Remove foliage below water line. Split stem ends. Stand in deep water for several hours. Some arrangers prefer to fill stem ends with water and plug with cotton.

USES: Bold linear element.

LYCHNIS
MALTESE CROSS, ROSE CAMPION
L. chalcedonica, L. coronaria

DESCRIPTION: Perennial. *L. chalcedonica* (Maltese cross) has flat heads composed of many cross-shaped, brilliant red-orange or white flowers. Leaves are deep green, stems long, plants 2 to 4 ft. tall. *L. coronaria* (rose campion) blooms with numerous individual 1-in. round flowers on sturdy, much-branched 3-ft. stems in magenta, cherry, pink, and white. White feltlike covering on leaves and stems. Lasts 1 week in vase.

HARDINESS: Zones 4 to 8.

GROWING CONDITIONS: Prefers full sun; rich, well-drained soil; average to plentiful moisture. Maltese cross also does well in partial shade. Space 1½ to 2 ft. apart.

PLANTING: Set out divisions in early spring, acclimatized potted plants after frost. Sow seed indoors or out at 60 to 75°F, ⅛ in. deep, 2 in. apart. Take stem cuttings of *L. coronaria* where clumps of leaves form on stems, in summer after bloom.

CARE: Transplant seedlings when crowded. Divide clumps in early spring, if crowded. Also divide *L. coronaria* after bloom; each clump divides into several and needs respacing. Cut back tops after bloom. Mulch if dry. Rarely needs staking.

HARVESTING AND CONDITIONING: Cut when half of florets in cluster or on branched stem have opened in morning or evening. Split woody stem ends. Stand in deep water containing sugar for several hours.

USES: Focal or accent element.

LYCORIS
MAGIC LILY, RESURRECTION LILY
L. squamigera

DESCRIPTION: Bulb. Huge pink lilies suddenly appear in August on strong, leafless 2- to 3-ft. stems. Sweet-scented, long-petaled flowers several inches wide in round heads with six or more blooms. Broad, straplike leaves come up from hefty underground bulbs in late spring, quickly ripen, and fade. This species leaves a bare spot unless interplanted with ferns or other plants. Plants slow to increase but long-lived. Flowers last up to 2 weeks in garden, more than 1 week when cut.

HARDINESS: Zones 6 to 11.

GROWING CONDITIONS: Prefers rich, well-drained, loamy soil; average moisture; full sun to partial shade; more shade in hot areas. Plant 6 in. apart and 6 in. deep.

PLANTING: Plant bulbs when received. Best planted in early summer while dormant, also in fall or, if in pots, in spring. Not practical to grow from seed.

CARE: Apply several handfuls bonemeal, rotted manure, and compost per plant in fall. Divide in early summer after leaves fade, only if necessary—very rarely. Try not to disturb once planted. Mark plants carefully to prevent damaging them when cultivating soil during their dormancy.

HARVESTING AND CONDITIONING: Cut when half the flowers on the stem have opened, in evening. Split stem ends and stand in deep water overnight. After arranging, remove faded flowers from clusters; buds continue to open.

USES: Focal element.

LYSIMACHIA
GOOSENECK LOOSE-STRIFE, YELLOW LOOSESTRIFE
L. clethroides, L. punctata

DESCRIPTION: Perennial. Tall columns of small flowers on vigorous, clump-forming plants, slightly scorned for their invasiveness. *L. clethroides* (gooseneck loosestrife) has graceful, arched cones of small white flowers on 3-ft. stems from mid to late summer. Leaves are rich green, pointed, 3 in. long. *L. punctata* (yellow loosestrife), 2 ft. tall, is also called circle flower for its circle of brown in the throat of star-shaped yellow flowers. Cut flowers last 1 week.

HARDINESS: Zones 4 to 8.

GROWING CONDITIONS: Prefers partial shade, damp to well-drained loamy soil, and plentiful moisture and fertility. Yellow loosestrife also grows in sun, while white grows in deep shade. Space clumps 3 ft. apart; they fill in quickly.

PLANTING: Set out divisions in early spring, acclimatized potted plants at any time during growing season. Individual plants can be dug in fall and cut back, and the cluster of roots transplanted for a good clump the next year.

CARE: Divide or thin at least once per year, in spring or fall. Top-dress beds in fall or spring with 1 in. of compost and rotted manure. Water in hot, dry weather. Deadhead. Cut down stems in fall or winter, for neatness.

HARVESTING AND CONDITIONING: Cut when lower flowers on spike have begun to open, in morning or evening. Remove lower foliage. Stand in deep water for several hours.

USES: Linear element.

LYTHRUM
PURPLE LOOSESTRIFE
L. hybrids

DESCRIPTION: Perennial. Tall, bushy plants bear dense, pointed plumes of small bright purple, rose, or magenta flowers. Prohibited in California and Minnesota because it displaces native plants from wetlands. Control invasiveness by planting nonseeding forms such as 'Morden's Pink'. Height ranges from 3 to 8 ft.; most named cultivars are under 5 ft. Stems strong; leaves deep green, lance-shaped. Blooms for 8 weeks in late summer. Cut flowers last 5 days; florets drop.

HARDINESS: Zones 3 to 9.

GROWING CONDITIONS: Prefers average to fertile, moist to marshy soil in full sun or light shade. Space 2 to 3 ft. apart.

PLANTING: Plant divisions in spring, acclimatized potted plants at any time during growing season. Take stem cuttings in summer. Sow seeds ⅛ in. deep indoors or outdoors at 70°F. Do not grow from seed or plant seed-bearing types near wetlands.

CARE: Apply several handfuls compost to each established clump in fall and spring. Divide every 3 or 4 years in spring. Transplant seedlings when crowded. Mulch around crowns winter and summer. Side-dress lightly with flower fertilizer during growth. Water to keep soil moist. Protect from Japanese beetles.

HARVESTING AND CONDITIONING: Cut when a third of flowers on spike have opened. Slit and recut stems. Stand in deep water for several hours.

USES: Linear element or massed material.

MALUS
CRABAPPLE
M. species and hybrids

DESCRIPTION: Tree. Profuse, showy, single or double 1-in. flowers cover the plant for several weeks in spring. Colors are peachy, rose, purplish pink, red, or white. Deciduous leaves are pale to dark green or bronze, and fall fruits may be red, orange, yellow, or green, from 1/2 to 2 in. wide. Hundreds of species and cultivars, spreading, upright, or weeping, with most between 15 and 25 ft. tall at maturity. Lasts for more than 7 days in vase.

HARDINESS: Zones 4 to 8.

GROWING CONDITIONS: Prefers rich, heavy, loamy, acidic, well-drained soil; average moisture; full sun. Space 12 or more ft. apart.

PLANTING: Set out plants in spring. If possible, purchase in bloom. Can be grown from seed planted outdoors in fall for spring germination; takes 5 or more years to flower, and resulting plants vary in appearance.

CARE: Use acidic fertilizer such as is used for hollies and rhododendrons, in neutral to limy soils. Prune in early to midspring. Water if soil becomes dry. Remove limbs affected by fireblight or scab. Protect from aphids, scale, and leaf spot.

HARVESTING AND CONDITIONING: Cut foliage and fruit when desired. Cut flowers when buds have begun to open, or a little earlier to force indoors. Slit stem ends. Stand in deep water for several hours.

USES: Flowers, leaves, and fruit as background, filler, or massed elements.

MATTHIOLA
STOCK, GILLYFLOWER
M. hybrids, M. incana

DESCRIPTION: Hardy annual or biennial. Long spikes of large, spicily fragrant single or double flowers are borne for several weeks in late spring, longer where summers stay cool. Colors include white, cream, peach, rose, red, lilac, and purple. Whitened leaves form a bushy clump. Height ranges from 8 to 30 in. 'Brompton' stocks are excellent tall biennials. Where summers are hot, try 'Trysomic Seven Week' or 'Dwarf Stockpot' for a quick crop. Cut flowers last 6 to 8 days.

HARDINESS: All zones. Dislikes heat over 90°F; thrives at 55°F. Withstands light frost; biennial types are hardiest.

GROWING CONDITIONS: Prefers fertile, nonacidic, well-drained soil in full sun; steady moisture. Space 6 to 12 in. apart.

PLANTING: Sow seed 1/8 in. deep indoors 10 weeks before or outdoors 4 weeks before last frost at about 55°F. Transplant when crowded. Set out plants grown indoors 2 to 4 weeks before last frost.

CARE: Mulch if weather is dry or hot. Side-dress with flower fertilizer during growth. Water often. Protect from slugs and caterpillars. For taller plants, do not pinch.

HARVESTING AND CONDITIONING: Cut when half of flowers on spike have opened. Slit stems deeply. Remove leaves below water level. Stand in deep, cool water containing sugar for several hours.

USES: Linear element or massed material.

MENTHA
MINT
M. × piperita, M. spicata,
M. suaveolens

DESCRIPTION: Perennial. Herb grown for scented, flavorful foliage. *M. × piperita* is peppermint; *M. spicata*, common spearmint. Orange mint, *M. suaveolens*, has a perfumelike scent used in potpourri. Most mints have rounded or pointed green leaves on branched stems up to 3 ft. tall. Hybrids may be curled, variegated, or bronzed. Inconspicuous flower spikes are violet or white. Underground runners are strong, fleshy, and invasive. Lasts 1 week in bouquets.

HARDINESS: Most, zones 4 to 11. Varies with species.

GROWING CONDITIONS: Grows well in full sun or partial shade. Prefers well-drained soil with average fertility and moisture. Space 1 to 2 ft. apart or grow in large containers.

PLANTING: Set out plants from early spring through summer. Take 4- to 6-in. cuttings from runners from spring through summer, and plant horizontally 1/2 in. deep; easier to grow than stem cuttings. Does not come true from seed.

CARE: Control invasiveness by thinning and dividing often, or by growing within a barrier or container. Apply all-purpose fertilizer and compost lightly throughout growth. Water during drought. Cut back plants if they become too tall or leggy.

HARVESTING AND CONDITIONING: Cut fresh, leafy stems in morning. Stand in deep water for several hours. Or refrigerate moistened leaves in a jar for later use.

USES: Leaves as scented filler or edible garnish.

MERTENSIA
VIRGINIA BLUEBELL
M. virginica

DESCRIPTION: Perennial. Large clusters of tubular, fragile-looking 2-in. blossoms dangle from tall, arched stems. Short shoots showing lilac flowerbuds in late winter elongate rapidly in spring. Blooms for several weeks with midseason narcissus. Most are sky blue, a few white or pink. Plants 12 to 30 in. tall. Large, oval, whitened leaves yellow and vanish as summer approaches. Woody taproots remain dormant until the next year. Lasts 3 to 5 days in vase.

HARDINESS: Zones 3 to 8.

GROWING CONDITIONS: Prefers rich, loamy, moist but well-drained soil under deciduous trees for sun in winter, shade in summer. Combines well with ferns. Space 1 to 1 1/2 ft. apart.

PLANTING: Plant divisions in spring, acclimatized potted plants at any time during growing season. Allow seed to ripen on plants and sow immediately in moist, shaded beds for germination next year. Transplant seedlings if crowded. Takes years to flower.

CARE: Apply 3 handfuls compost to each established clump in fall. Transplant seedlings in spring when they are large enough to handle. Divide mature plants in early spring with sharp tools only if necessary or to propagate. Remove and discard yellowed foliage. Mark plants to prevent damaging them during dormancy.

HARVESTING AND CONDITIONING: Cut when new flowers have opened, in morning. Stand in deep, cold water for several hours.

USES: Filler, accent, or massed element.

MISCANTHUS
CHINESE SILVER GRASS
M. sinensis

DESCRIPTION: Perennial. Clump-forming grass grown for graceful foliage and dramatic flowerheads. Blooms from late summer through fall. Roots are thick, hairy rhizomes. Plants emerge from dormancy with low, thin shoots in early spring; progress to slender, waving fronds over 4 ft. tall by summer; in fall are topped by plumelike, fan-shaped, brownish, shiny seedheads on straight stems 6 to 10 ft. tall. Seedheads curve as they age. Foliage and seedheads turn ivory, remain handsome most of winter. Gold or white variegated cultivars such as 'Zebrina' available. Seedheads last indefinitely when cut.

HARDINESS: Zones 4 to 9.

GROWING CONDITIONS: Prefers full sun, well-drained soil with average fertility and moisture; also grows in part shade. Space 5 ft. apart.

PLANTING: Set out acclimatized plants in spring. Take cuttings from rhizomes in spring. Cultivars do not come true from seed; species can be sown indoors or outdoors, ¼ in. deep at around 70°F.

CARE: Divide every few years if clumps become overcrowded. Apply all-purpose fertilizer and compost in early spring and, in poor soil, throughout growth. Water during drought. Stake plants (especially in shade or rich soil) if necessary. Cut off last year's dormant growth in early spring before new growth begins.

HARVESTING AND CONDITIONING: Cut seedheads either green or dried. No conditioning is needed.

USES: Linear, filler or massed element, fresh or dried.

MOLUCELLA
BELLS OF IRELAND
M. laevis

DESCRIPTION: Annual. Pale green, paper-textured, 2-in. bell-shaped calyces around small white, fragrant flowers, aligned on upright stalks. Branched plants 2 to 3 ft. tall bloom from late summer until frost. Small leaves are oddly interspersed along bloom spires; larger leaves found near base. Cut flowers last 7 to 14 days.

HARDINESS: All zones.

GROWING CONDITIONS: Prefers rich to average, light, loamy or sandy soil; average moisture; full sun. Space 10 in. apart.

PLANTING: Set out bedding plants in spring when the danger of frost ends. Or sow seed 8 weeks earlier indoors for transplants, or directly outdoors after frost. Germinates best between 70 and 85°F. Presoak the hard-coated seeds in warm water overnight and plant ¼ in. deep, 2 in. apart, or in individual pots.

CARE: Thin seedlings to correct spacing or transplant to desired sites when they are 4 in. tall or are crowded. Side-dress plants with flower fertilizer and compost during growth. Protect from slugs. Do not let soil dry out; mulch in hot or dry areas. Harvest regularly to promote bloom from side shoots. Allow to self-sow, if wanted. Pull and replace spent plants.

HARVESTING AND CONDITIONING: Cut when calyces have become papery. Strip off all leaves. Scald stem ends and stand in deep water for several hours.

USES: Linear accent or filler.

MONARDA
BEE BALM, BERGAMOT
M. didyma

DESCRIPTION: Perennial herb. Clusters of curved, hooded, tubular flowers and colorful bracts form tufts at intervals on tall stems. Fragrant leaves and flowers used to flavor Earl Grey tea. Species is brilliant red; cultivars white, pink, salmon, lilac, and purple. Branched plants with stiff stems and toothed, hairy leaves are 2 to 4 ft. tall. Blooms for 2 months in summer. Cut flowers last 5 to 7 days.

HARDINESS: Zones 4 to 9. Resists cold and heat.

GROWING CONDITIONS: Prefers moist but well-drained, loamy soil in partial shade or full sun. Tolerates drought and poor soil once established. Space clumps 2 ft. apart.

PLANTING: Plant divisions in early spring or fall, acclimatized potted plants at any time during growing season. Sow seed ⅛ in. deep indoors at 55°F in spring or outdoors as early as soil can be worked.

CARE: Apply several handfuls of compost to each established clump in fall and spring. Divide or thin annually in spring or fall to control invasiveness. Transplant seedlings to permanent places when crowded. In poor soil, side-dress with light applications of flower fertilizer during growth.

HARVESTING AND CONDITIONING: Cut when first few flowers have opened. Remove lower leaves. Stand in deep water for several hours.

USES: Versatile; focal, filler, accent, or massed material for arrangements or edible garnish.

MUSCARI
GRAPE HYACINTH
M. armeniacum

DESCRIPTION: Bulb. Leafless, upright flower stems bear trim, grapelike clusters of little round blue or white flowers. A constriction at the tip of each flower creates a rounded shape. Blooms for several weeks, with tulips. Plants are 8 to 10 in. tall in bloom. Pale green leaves are strap-like and floppy, lingering long after flowers fade before yellowing. Cut flowers last 3 to 7 days.

HARDINESS: Zones 5 to 8.

GROWING CONDITIONS: Prefers rich, loamy, moist but well-drained soil in full sun in spring. Will grow under deciduous trees and in average or poor, well-drained soil. Space 3 in. apart, 3 in. deep.

PLANTING: Plant bulbs in fall or as soon as received. If you wish, allow seed to ripen on plants and sprinkle where you would like plants to grow; cover ⅛ in. deep and keep moist. Takes several years to flower.

CARE: Little or no fertilizer needed in rich soil. If necessary, apply bulb or flower fertilizer during growing season. Divide crowded clumps in early summer when leaves yellow; replant immediately. Hide aging foliage with other plants. Remove and discard yellowed foliage. Mark plants to prevent damage during dormancy.

HARVESTING AND CONDITIONING: Cut when bottom flowers have opened, in morning or evening. Discard pale green bases of stems. Stand in deep, cold water for several hours.

USES: Filler or linear element.

MYOSOTIS
FORGET-ME-NOT
M. alpestris, M. scorpioides,
M. sylvatica

DESCRIPTION: Biennial or perennial. Sprays of ¼-in. blue, pink, or white flowers with yellow eyes and linear, fuzzy leaves. *M. sylvatica*, biennial, 1 to 2 ft. tall, long-stemmed, blooms profusely in spring for 4 weeks. *M. s.* 'Azur' is a tetraploid, a cultivar whose flowers are twice as large as the rest of the species. *M. s.* 'Blue Bird' is bright and reliable. *M. alpestris* is similar with shorter stems. *M. scorpioides* (water forget-me-not), perennial, blooms all summer. Cut flowers last 3 to 5 days.

HARDINESS: Biennials, zones 5 to 8. *M. scorpioides*, zones 4 to 11.

GROWING CONDITIONS: Prefers rich, loamy well-drained soil; average moisture; partial shade to full sun. *M. scorpioides* prefers moist to wet soil. Space 8 in. apart.

PLANTING: Sow seed of biennials outdoors in summer where they will grow, for bloom the next spring. Sow seed of *M. scorpioides* indoors or out at about 70°F; divide in spring or take cuttings in summer.

CARE: Thin or transplant seedlings when they are 2 in. tall or are crowded. Fertilize during growth. Protect from slugs. Water often. Allow biennials to self-sow: pull spent plants in summer and rub off seeds where plants are wanted. Trim *M. scorpioides* often.

HARVESTING AND CONDITIONING: Cut when flowers have begun to bloom. Stand in cool water for several hours.

USES: Filler.

NARCISSUS
DAFFODIL
N. hybrids and species

DESCRIPTION: Bulb. Winter- or spring-flowering. Many hybrids of mixed heritage. Best-known types have 3-in. golden flowers composed of a perianth of six petals around a long, tubular trumpet, one per 2-ft. stem. Also short, wide, or split trumpets, double or flared petals, and up to eight flowers per stem. Size ranges from 6 in. to 2½ ft. Colors also include white, orange, peach, and red, including many bicolors and a few tricolors. Cut flowers last 4 to 7 days.

HARDINESS: Most, zones 4 to 8; paper-whites, zones 9 to 11.

GROWING CONDITIONS: Prefers full sun to light, dappled shade; average moisture; fertile, well-drained soil. Space 3 to 6 in. apart and deep; the larger the bulb, the deeper it is planted.

PLANTING: Set out bulbs in fall or as soon as received. Growing from seed is impractical for bloom takes many years; may be sown outdoors ¼ in. deep in summer when ripe, however.

CARE: Apply 1 in. of rotted manure and compost over beds in fall. Divide every 3 years, if crowded.

HARVESTING AND CONDITIONING: Cut flowers in "gooseneck" phase—when color begins to show at tip of bud. Split stem ends. Stand in deep, cool water containing sugar for several hours.

USES: Focal or massed element.

NICOTIANA
FLOWERING TOBACCO
N. alata

DESCRIPTION: Tender perennial, grown as an annual. Bushy plants with large, fuzzy leaves bear sprays of narrow, tubular 3-in. flowers, star-shaped at ends. Colors include soft shades of white, red, pink, purple, and green. Newer cultivars stay open all day. Some types sweetly scented, especially at night. Cultivars range from 1 to over 3 ft. tall. Blooms summer to frost; all year in frost-free climates. Cut flowers last 3 to 7 days.

HARDINESS: Zones 10 to 11 as perennial. All zones as annual. Killed by frost.

GROWING CONDITIONS: Prefers full sun or bright partial shade, rich soil, average moisture, and excellent drainage. Tolerates dry spells. Plant 1 ft. apart.

PLANTING: Set out plants during warm weather. Press seed into surface of soil of individual pots indoors in February at 70 to 80°F. Sow outdoors 2 in. apart during warm weather, zones 7 to 11. Needs light to germinate, in 5 to 12 days.

CARE: Thin or transplant seedlings to their correct spacing. Fertilize at planting time and steadily throughout growth. Mulch. Avoid disturbing roots. Deadhead. Protect from cucumber, flea, and potato beetles. Tip-prune in spring for bushiness. Cut back leggy plants in summer.

HARVESTING AND CONDITIONING: Cut when several flowers in cluster have opened. Split stem ends. Stand in warm water (80 to 100°F) for several hours.

USES: Accent or filler.

NIGELLA
LOVE-IN-A-MIST
N. damascena, N. hispanica

DESCRIPTION: Annual. Delicate, spurred, round 2-in. flowers with a "mist" of lacy bracts below and filigreed stamens above layers of petals. *N. damascena* flowers blue, violet, white, or pink. Balloonlike green seedpods striped with purple. 'Miss Jekyll' is cornflower blue. *N. hispanica* has purple or white flowers with reddish stigmata. Leaves are finely divided and threadlike. Blooms late spring or summer. Plants 1 to 2 ft. tall. Cut flowers and pods stay fresh 7 days.

HARDINESS: Zones 2 to 11. Tolerates light frost; killed by high heat.

GROWING CONDITIONS: Prefers fertile, moist, loamy soil with good drainage and full sun. Space 10 in. apart.

PLANTING: Set out bedding plants in spring after danger of frost. Sow seed 8 weeks earlier indoors in individual pots, or outdoors 4 weeks before danger of frost ends, ⅛ in. deep, 2 in. apart. Self-sows; sprinkle ripe seed in summer for plants next spring. In mild-winter areas, sow in fall.

CARE: Thin seedlings to their correct spacing and desired sites when they become crowded. Fertilize throughout growth. Mulch. Deadhead if pods and seeds are not wanted. Protect from caterpillars.

HARVESTING AND CONDITIONING: Cut newly opened flowers and mature pods in evening. Stand overnight in deep water containing sugar.

USES: Flowers and pods as filler.

ORNITHOGALUM
STAR-OF-BETHLEHEM, CHINCHERINCHEE
O. arabicum, O. thyrsoides,
O. umbellatum

DESCRIPTION: Bulb. White, star-shaped flowers. Two 1½-ft. types bloom in early summer: *O. arabicum* (Arabian starflower), with flat clusters of cream-colored flowers with black centers, and *O. thyrsoides* (chincherinchee), with greenish white, cone-shaped flower spikes. *O. umbellatum* (star-of-Bethlehem) has clusters of small, fragrant white and green flowers 8 to 12 in. tall in spring. Flowers close for part of the day. This species is widely naturalized and sometimes considered a pest. Ornithogalums have straight stems and linear leaves. Cut flowers last 6 to 8 days.

HARDINESS: *O. arabicum* and *O. thyrsoides*, zones 8 to 10; *O. umbellatum*, zones 5 to 9.

GROWING CONDITIONS: Full sun for most; light shade for *O. umbellatum*. Average moisture and fertile, well-drained soil. Space 4 to 6 in. apart, 4 in. deep.

PLANTING: Set out bulbs in fall, or in spring if growing tender types in a northern zone. *O. umbellatum* self-sows; scatter ripe seed where desired.

CARE: Apply 1 in. of rotted manure and compost over beds in fall. Allow foliage to ripen (turn yellow) before removing it in summer. Dig and store indoors for winter if not hardy. Divide every 3 years or when crowded.

HARVESTING AND CONDITIONING: Cut newly opened flowers. Trim white portion from base of stem. Stand in cool water for several hours.

USES: Filler or massed element.

PAEONIA
PEONY
P. hybrids, P. lactiflora,
P. suffruticosa

DESCRIPTION: Perennial or small shrub. Perennials (*P. lactiflora* and hybrids) have round flowers 4 to 6 in. wide, on long stems late spring and early summer; single, semidouble, double, or anemone-form. Colors include white, pink, cream, deep rose, red, lilac, and magenta. Leaves 3 to 4 ft. tall, divided. Roots fleshy, several feet deep. Tree peonies, *P. suffruticosa* and hybrids, branched, deciduous shrubs 4 to 7 ft. tall, have similar flowers in same colors plus yellow. Cut flowers last 4 to 7 days.

HARDINESS: Perennials, zones 4 to 8; shrubs, zones 5 to 8.

GROWING CONDITIONS: Prefers rich, moist, well-drained loamy soil; full sun. Tree peonies like partial shade. Space 3 to 6 ft. apart.

PLANTING: Set out in early spring or late fall. Plant perennials so that top of root is 1 in. below soil surface. If set too deeply, plants will not bloom. Plant tree peonies at the same depth at which they grew.

CARE: Apply several handfuls of bonemeal, rotted manure, and compost per plant in fall. Divide perennials in fall every 4 years only if crowded. Stake large-flowered cultivars with hoops.

HARVESTING AND CONDITIONING: Cut when buds have split to show flower color, in early morning or evening. Split stem ends and stand in deep, cool water containing sugar for several hours. Stems in bud can be stored in water in the refrigerator for several weeks before being arranged.

USES: Focal element.

PANICUM
SWITCH GRASS
P. virgatum

DESCRIPTION: Perennial. Tall, clump-forming grass bearing silky, long plumes from summer into winter. The 20-in. arching tassel-like panicles are purplish brown when they begin to bloom. Along with the long, green leaf blades and stalks, they turn golden orange in autumn, paler in winter. Roots rhizomatous, spreading. Height from 5 to over 7 ft. Plumes last over 7 days in vase.

HARDINESS: Zones 5 to 10.

GROWING CONDITIONS: Prefers well-drained, fertile, loamy or sandy soil in full sun to partial shade, with average moisture. Grows well at the seaside. Space clumps 4 ft. or more apart.

PLANTING: Set out divisions in early spring, acclimatized potted plants at any time throughout growing season. Sow seed indoors or out in spring at 50 to 70°F, covered by ⅛ in. of soil. Indoors, sow in small pots for easier handling. In zones 9 to 10, sow in late fall.

CARE: Thin seedlings before they become crowded. Apply flower fertilizer throughout growth. Divide clumps in early spring if they lost some of their upright growth habit the previous year. Leave plumes on plants in winter for decoration, then cut down plants at base in early spring.

HARVESTING AND CONDITIONING: Cut plumes in summer when they have developed fully, or whenever their appearance suits you. No conditioning needed.

USES: Large-scale filler or massed material, fresh or dried.

PAPAVER
POPPY (ANNUAL AND BIENNIAL TYPES)
P. commutatum, P. nudicaule,
P. rhoeas

DESCRIPTION: Annual or biennial. Cup-shaped flowers have silky, tissue-thin petals. Stems long and wiry; single or double flowers 1 to more than 4 in. wide, all shades but blue. Hairy, divided leaves, sometimes gray or blue, in evergreen rosettes. Branched plants bloom 6 weeks, spring to summer. *P. nudicaule* (Iceland poppy), *P. commutatum*, and *P. rhoeas* (Shirley poppy) usually under 2 ft. tall. *P. commutatum* is Flanders poppy, single, deep red with black blotches. Cut flowers last 2 to 5 days.

HARDINESS: Zones 4 to 10.

GROWING CONDITIONS: Prefers light, fertile, sandy or loamy soil; full sun to partial shade; average moisture. Space most 1 ft. apart.

PLANTING: Set out acclimatized bedding plants in spring. Sow seed outdoors on soil surface where plants will grow in fall or early spring; fall-sown plants are larger and earlier. Sow seed indoors, thinly on surface, in flats or small pots in winter or spring.

CARE: Transplant crowded rosettes carefully in spring taking care not to disturb roots, during cool, moist weather. Fertilize lightly throughout growth. Mulch. Deadhead, but leave a few seedpods for self-sown plants.

HARVESTING AND CONDITIONING: Cut when buds are ready to open in morning. Sear stem ends. Stand in cold water for several hours. Add sugar to water in arrangement.

USES: Focal or massed material.

PAPAVER
ORIENTAL POPPY
P. orientalis

DESCRIPTION: Perennial. Large, silky, frilled flowers with a black blotch at the base of each petal. Flower width 4 to 6 in., red, orange, pink, white, or violet. Showy blooms on strong stems last a few days in early summer. Clump-forming plants, 3 ft. tall, have deep taproots. Hairy, divided green leaves vanish shortly after plants bloom, reappear as nearly evergreen rosettes in fall. Cut flowers last 3 to 4 days.

HARDINESS: Zones 3 to 8.

GROWING CONDITIONS: Prefers deep, fairly dense, fertile soil; excellent drainage; full sun; average moisture. Space 18 in. apart.

PLANTING: Set out acclimatized potted plants in spring, divisions in late summer. Sow seed thinly on soil surface, barely pressing in. Outdoors, sow in late summer or fall. Indoors or in cold frame, sow in fall or spring. May bloom in 1½ years. Take root cuttings in late summer or early fall.

CARE: Transplant seedlings carefully in spring, if crowded, taking care not to disturb roots, during cool, moist weather. Divide clustered plantlets in late summer after blooms and leaves fade, once every 4 or 5 years if necessary. Mark locations well and fill vacant spots with annuals. Fertilize lightly throughout growth. Mulch. Deadhead.

HARVESTING AND CONDITIONING: Cut when buds are ready to open in morning. Sear stem ends. Stand in cold water for several hours. Add sugar to water in arrangement.

USES: Focal or massed material.

PELARGONIUM
GERANIUM
P. species and hybrids

DESCRIPTION: Tender perennial or shrub, grown as annual. Bushy or trailing plants with tight, round clusters of small flowers during warm weather. Leaves round or lobed, sometimes variegated. Flowers red, white, pink, rose, peach, violet, or magenta. Types include zonal: bushy, 2 ft. tall, large flowering heads; Martha Washington or regal: large, bicolored flowers on 3-ft. bushy plants; ivy-leaved or trailing: fine-textured blossoms, 3 ft. wide; and scented-leaved, such as lemon: bushy plants 2 to 4 ft. tall with small flowers. Lasts 5 to 7 days in vase.

HARDINESS: Zones 9 to 11 as perennial. All zones, as annual.

GROWING CONDITIONS: Prefers full sun, average moisture, and fertile, well-drained soil. Space 12 in. apart.

PLANTING: Set out plants after danger of frost. Sow seed indoors in winter or spring at 75°F, ¼ in. deep in pots or flats. Takes 14 weeks to bloom. Root 4-in. stem or tip cuttings all year, especially in late summer.

CARE: Apply flower fertilizer throughout growth. Cut back if leggy. Deadhead frequently, and remove yellowed leaves. In cold zones, bring plants indoors for winter: repot, cut back tops, and grow in sun. Prevent viruses with fresh plants and clean soil.

HARVESTING AND CONDITIONING: Select flowers which have begun to bloom or stems with fresh leaves. Remove lower leaves. Condition in warm water for several hours.

USES: Flowers and leaves as accent or filler. Scented types as garnish.

PENSTEMON
BEARD TONGUE
P. species and hybrids

DESCRIPTION: Perennial or shrub, often grown as annual or biennial. Long, tubular, sometimes fringed flowers aligned in columns or heads. Colors include red, blue, violet, white, pink, salmon, and yellow. Most bloom in summer. Countless species, many native to western mountain regions of U.S., some difficult to grow at low altitude. Recommended for cutting are tall types (1½ to 3 ft.) such as *P. gloxinoides* (treat as annual except where hardy), *P. barbatus*, and *P. hartwegii*; also hybrids such as 'Hyacinth Flowered'. Cut flowers last 4 to 6 days.

HARDINESS: Most species, zones 5 to 9; however, varies with species. Dislikes hot, humid summers.

GROWING CONDITIONS: Requires well-drained soil. Prefers alkaline or sweet, moderately fertile soil with average moisture in full sun. Space 1 to 3 ft. apart.

PLANTING: Plant divisions in spring, acclimatized potted plants at any time during growing season. Prechill seed for several weeks to break dormancy; germination irregular. Sow seed on surface of soil indoors in late winter or outdoors at 55 to 60°F.

CARE: Divide perennials in spring if necessary, or to propagate. Thin seedlings. Mulch. Deadhead, or leave a few flowers for seed.

HARVESTING AND CONDITIONING: Cut stems when half of flowers have opened, in morning or evening. Remove lower foliage and split stem ends. Stand in deep water several hours.

USES: Linear or accent material.

PERILLA
BEEFSTEAK PLANT
P. frutescens

DESCRIPTION: Annual herb. Grown for foliage more than for flowers. Large, branched plants have large glossy purple or green leaves with a metallic sheen in summer. 'Crispa' has crimped edges; 'Atropurpurea' is deeply purple. Narrow spikes of white or lavender bloom from September until frost on plants 2 to more than 3 ft. tall. Stays fresh 7 or more days in vase.

HARDINESS: All zones. Tolerates high heat; killed by frost.

GROWING CONDITIONS: Prefers light, loamy soil; average moisture; good drainage; full sun. Space 1 to 2 ft. apart.

PLANTING: Set out bedding plants in spring when danger of frost ends. Sow seed indoors 6 weeks before last expected frost in flats or individual cells for transplants, or directly outdoors after danger of frost ends. Barely cover seeds, which germinate best in light.

CARE: Thin seedlings when they are 5 in. tall or are crowded. Pinch back plants once when they are 6 to 8 in. tall. Side-dress with flower fertilizer in poor soil. Mulch in hot or dry areas. Allow seeds to form for self-sown plants, if desired.

HARVESTING AND CONDITIONING: Cut attractive branches with or without flowers in morning or evening. Strip off lower leaves and side branches. Stand in deep, warm water for several hours.

USES: Dramatic background element, especially with pink flowers. Also filler material or edible garnish.

PETUNIA
P. hybrids

DESCRIPTION: Tender perennial, grown as annual. Tubular flowers flare into broad circles, late spring through frost. Some double or densely ruffled. Grandiflora types 3 to 7 in. wide; multifloras 2 to 3 in. Upright bedding types best for cutting. Leaves oval, fuzzy; pick up dirt in dusty places. Stems relatively weak; plants 1 to 2½ ft. tall and wide. Flowers white, blue, purple, pink, red, salmon, or yellow; may be starred, veined, or frosted with second color. Cut flowers last up to 1 week in vase.

HARDINESS: All zones. Killed by hard frost; blossoming suppressed when nighttime temperatures regularly exceed 85°F.

GROWING CONDITIONS: Prefers full sun to partial shade, plentiful moisture, and fertile, well-drained soil. Shelter from wind. Space 12 in. apart.

PLANTING: Set out plants after danger of frost passes. Sow seed indoors 10 weeks before last frost at 70 to 75°F. Press into moist growing medium, uncovered.

CARE: Apply low-nitrogen fertilizer throughout growth. Pinch back for bushiness when 6 in. tall. Mulch. Deadhead. Protect from tobacco mosaic virus, slugs, and aphids. Harvest flowers from above an outward-facing bud or branch, for well-shaped plants.

HARVESTING AND CONDITIONING: Cut with several inches of stem just before or after buds open, in morning or evening; cut grandifloras and doubles in bud. Remove lower leaves. Stand in deep water containing sugar for several hours.

USES: Focal or accent element.

PHILADELPHUS
MOCK ORANGE
P. coronarius, P. species

DESCRIPTION: Shrub. Numerous 1- to 2-in. fragrant white flowers aligned on arching branches. Single flowers in late spring have four petals and prominent golden stamens; some types are double. Cultivars vary in fragrance, flower size and shape, and bloom time. 'Belle Etoile' is a large-flowered, scented single with spots of pink in centers. Leaves are broad 2- to 4-in. ovals. Large, rounded shrubs up to 12 ft. tall, straggly if unpruned. Cut flowers last 6 to 8 days.

HARDINESS: Zones 4 to 8.

GROWING CONDITIONS: Grows well in full sun or light shade; rich, loamy, well-drained soil; average moisture. Space plants 10 ft. apart.

PLANTING: Set out bare-root plants in late winter, balled-and-burlapped or acclimatized container-grown plants in spring. Dig and transplant suckers in late winter.

CARE: Mulch beds with compost or chopped leaves. Prune after flowering. Remove old wood, cutting damaged canes to ground and leaving younger ones to flower next year. Overgrown shrubs may be cut to ground in spring; will regrow immediately. Treat for mildew, leaf miner, and aphids, if necessary.

HARVESTING AND CONDITIONING: Cut when half of flowers on branch have opened, in morning or evening. Remove lower foliage. Peel an inch of bark from base and slit stem ends. Stand in deep water for several hours.

USES: Filler, linear, or massed element.

PHLOX
DRUMMOND PHLOX, GARDEN PHLOX
P. drummondii, P. paniculata

DESCRIPTION: Annual or perennial. Dense heads of tubular flowers with five flaring lobes. Linear leaves. Flowers white, pink, salmon, violet, or red-purple. *P. drummondii*, annual, also yellow, 6 to 15 in. tall, branched, blooms summer into fall. *P. paniculata*, perennial, blooms late summer, 3 to 4 ft. tall; stiff stems. Cut flowers last 5 days.

HARDINESS: *P. drummondii*, all zones; tolerates frost and heat. *P. paniculata*, zones 4 to 8.

GROWING CONDITIONS: Prefers rich, loamy soil; full sun; average to moist conditions; good air circulation. Space annuals 1 ft. apart, *P. paniculata* 3 ft.

PLANTING: Plant perennial divisions in early spring as new growth begins, acclimatized potted plants during growing season. Perennials may self-sow but do not come true from seed. Sow seed ⅛ in. deep in cold frame in fall for germination in spring. Set annuals out in spring. Sow seed (prefers darkness) ⅛ in. deep outdoors as early as soil can be worked, several weeks earlier indoors. Prechill 2 weeks.

CARE: Apply 1 handful manure or compost to each plant in spring. Divide or thin perennials annually in spring. Thin or transplant seedlings if crowded. Mulch. Deadhead. Protect from mildew.

HARVESTING AND CONDITIONING: Cut when half of flowers have opened, in early morning or evening. Stand in cool water up to heads for several hours.

USES: Focal, filler, or massed element.

PHLOX
WOODLAND PHLOX
P. divaricata, P. stolonifera

DESCRIPTION: Perennial. Matlike, rapidly spreading, semievergreen plants bear dense, round heads of tubular flowers with five lobes. Blooms on upright stems 1 ft. tall for several weeks in spring. Linear to oval leaves. Flowers mainly blue, but also white, pink, or violet. *P. stolonifera* produces many runners. Cut flowers last 5 to 7 days.

HARDINESS: Zones 4 to 8.

GROWING CONDITIONS: Prefers rich, loamy soil; partial shade; moist but well-drained conditions; good air circulation. Space clumps 1 ft. or more apart.

PLANTING: Plant divisions in early spring as new growth begins, or in late summer. Set out acclimatized potted plants at any time during growing season. May self-sow. Sow seed ⅛ in. deep in beds in summer, or in cold frame in fall for germination in spring, or indoors after prechilling for 4 weeks.

CARE: Apply 1 in. of compost to beds in fall. Thin or divide plants in spring or late summer if crowded. Offshoots of *P. stolonifera* are easily separated and transplanted to permanent places in late summer. Thin or transplant seedlings if crowded. Mulch. Deadhead, also removing flower stems. Trim back foliage if necessary. Protect from mildew.

HARVESTING AND CONDITIONING: Cut stems when half of flowers have opened, in early morning or evening. Stand in cool water up to heads for several hours.

USES: Filler or massed element.

PHYSALIS
CHINESE LANTERN, GROUND CHERRY
P. alkekengi

DESCRIPTION: Perennial. Numerous inflated, papery husks up to 3 in. long enclose round fruits from late summer into fall, on branched plants. Midsummer flowers are round, yellowish, inconspicuous, followed by green husks which eventually turn bright red or orange. Toothed green leaves are wedge-shaped; plants about 2 ft. tall. Roots are underground runners, making plants invasive. Cut, the lanternlike pods last over 7 days.

HARDINESS: Zones 5 to 8. Grow as a biennial in zones 9 and 10.

GROWING CONDITIONS: Prefers moderately rich, sweet, well-drained soil; average moisture; full sun to partial shade. Space 1½ to 2 ft. apart.

PLANTING: Set out divisions in spring, acclimatized potted plants at any time during growing season. Barely cover and sow seed thinly indoors 8 weeks before last expected frost, or outdoors after frost. Germination usually takes 3 to 4 weeks. Take softwood cuttings in late spring.

CARE: Divide in spring if crowded or to propagate. Remove roots where plants are not wanted. Transplant seedlings when crowded; protect from cutworms. Apply all-purpose fertilizer in midsummer. Water if soil becomes dry.

HARVESTING AND CONDITIONING: Cut pods when red or orange color has developed, in morning or evening. For green lanterns, cut earlier. Stand in deep water for several hours.

USES: Accent material, fresh or dried, or as garnish for food.

PHYSOSTEGIA
OBEDIENT PLANT, FALSE DRAGONHEAD
P. virginiana

DESCRIPTION: Perennial. Spikes of long, tubular, pink, red-purple, or white flowers usually aligned in four patchy rows on square-stemmed plants. Blooms in wide clumps late summer into fall. Leaves linear, toothed, deep green. 'Variegata' has green-and-white leaves, pink flowers. Deep roots and spreading rhizomes make physostegia invasive, but productive where there is room for it. Height from 1½ to 4 ft. Cut flowers last about 1 week.

HARDINESS: Zones 4 to 9.

GROWING CONDITIONS: Prefers rich, moist, loamy soil; full sun. Tolerates partial shade. Lacks vigor in dry soil. Space 2 ft. apart.

PLANTING: Plant divisions in spring, acclimatized potted plants at any time during growing season. Sow seed indoors or out at 55 to 75°F, barely covered. Prefers reduced nighttime temperatures; germinates in 21 to 30 days.

CARE: Apply 2 handfuls rotted manure to each clump in fall. Divide every other year in spring. Remove running roots where plants are not wanted. Transplant seedlings when crowded. Keep soil moist. Mulch. Pinch back tall types in early to midsummer for bushiness. Deadhead.

HARVESTING AND CONDITIONING: Cut when lower flowers on stem have opened, in morning or evening. Spikes look awkward after lower flowers go to seed. Stand in deep water for several hours.

USES: Linear material.

PIERIS
ANDROMEDA
P. japonica

DESCRIPTION: Shrub or small tree. Broadleaf evergreen with slender, pointed leaves. Flowers prolifically for about 6 weeks in spring. Small, bell-shaped greenish white, cream, or pink flowers in branched, drooping racemes. New leaves are bronze or reddish, then glossy green; some cultivars, such as 'Mountain Fire', intensely and lastingly red; also some types are green with white variegation. Plants bushy, 4 to 12 ft. tall. Flowers, leaves, and racemes of unopened buds (available from late summer to the next spring) stay fresh more than 7 days in vase.

HARDINESS: Zones 5 to 8.

GROWING CONDITIONS: Prefers rich, loamy, acidic, well-drained soil; average moisture; partial shade. Space 8 ft. apart.

PLANTING: Set out acclimatized plants in spring. If possible, purchase and plant while in bloom. Take cuttings of semi-ripened, new growth in summer.

CARE: Mulch with compost, pine needles, pine bark, chopped leaves, or other acidic mulch. Use acidic fertilizer such as is used for hollies and rhododendrons. Prune after flowering. Deadhead. Water if soil becomes dry. Protect from scale, lace bug, and leaf spot.

HARVESTING AND CONDITIONING: Cut foliage and unopened flower buds any time of year. Cut flowers when the clusters are halfway opened. Slit stem ends. Stand in deep water for several hours.

USES: Flowers, leaves, and buds all as background, filler, or focal elements.

PLATYCODON
BALLOON FLOWER
P. grandiflorus

DESCRIPTION: Perennial. Large, inflated buds suddenly open to wide, star-shaped flowers with five points. Doubles are formed by two star-shaped corollas layered together trimly. Several flowers at ends of branched stems. Mainly rich violet-blue; also white, lilac, or pink; blooms for several weeks from mid to late summer. Plant height from 10 in. to 3 ft.; taller types best for cutting. Leaves whitened, pointed, oval to lance-shaped. Cut flowers last 5 to 7 days.

HARDINESS: Zones 3 to 9.

GROWING CONDITIONS: Prefers full sun, average moisture, and light, well-drained soil of average richness. Does well in sandy soil near seashore. Space 15 to 24 in. apart.

PLANTING: Set out divisions in early spring, acclimatized potted plants preferably in late spring. Sow seed indoors in spring or summer at 70°F on surface of moist medium; prefers light for germination in 2 to 4 weeks. Flowers second year.

CARE: Apply 1 handful manure or compost to each established clump in fall or early spring. Do not disturb plants once established; however, division in early spring is possible if plants are dug without harming carrotlike roots. Deadhead.

HARVESTING AND CONDITIONING: Cut when several flowers on stem have opened, in early morning or evening. Dip stem ends in boiling water and stand in warm water for several hours.

USES: Focal or accent element.

POLEMONIUM
JACOB'S LADDER
P. caeruleum, P. carneum,
P. reptans

DESCRIPTION: Perennial. Clusters of small five-petaled, bell-shaped flowers on tidy, clump-forming plants. *P. caeruleum* and *P. reptans*, blue or white. *P. carneum*, pink or salmon; withstands a little more sun and heat. Each plant produces many floral spikes about 1½ ft. tall for over a month in spring, starting while daffodils bloom. Multiplies rapidly. Handsome, brittle, fernlike leaves, 1 to 3 ft. tall, feature paired leaflets, forming the "ladder" in common name. Foliage may die back in hot, dry summer weather; regrows in fall. Cut flowers last more than 1 week.

HARDINESS: Zones 4 to 8.

GROWING CONDITIONS: Prefers rich, loamy soil with average moisture, good drainage, and partial shade. Plant 12 to 18 in. apart.

PLANTING: Set out divisions in early spring, acclimatized potted plants during weather that is not excessively cold or hot. Sow seed ⅛ in. deep either indoors in spring or outdoors in summer; often germinates in 3 weeks; likes reduced temperatures at night. Self-sown plants are of good quality.

CARE: Divide in early spring every third year if crowded. Transplant volunteers in spring or fall, but do not disturb during hot or dry weather. Mulch. Deadhead.

HARVESTING AND CONDITIONING: Cut stems when sprays of flowers begin to open, in morning or evening. Stand in deep, cool water for several hours.

USES: Filler or massed element.

POLIANTHES
TUBEROSE
P. tuberosa

DESCRIPTION: Tuberous, tender perennial. Many intensely sweet-smelling, single or double, waxy white tubular flowers on each long spire. Singles have stronger scent; doubles are showier. Plants 2 to 3 ft. tall; leaves slender, straplike, upright. Blooms for several weeks in summer or fall. Lasts 7 to 14 days in vase.

HARDINESS: Zones 8 to 11; farther north with protection. Killed by frost. Needs a long warm season.

GROWING CONDITIONS: Prefers loamy, light, fertile soil; excellent drainage; average moisture; full sun. Set bulbs 3 in. deep, 6 in. apart.

PLANTING: In zone 8 and above, plant tubers indoors in pots in early spring; transplant to outdoor beds after danger of frost. In zones 9 to 11, plant tubers directly outdoors when received—best in fall or winter.

CARE: Apply liquid fertilizer every 2 weeks throughout growth. Stake if necessary. Deadhead. In zone 8, mulch deeply in winter. In zones 7 and above, dig in fall, let dry with soil attached, and store through winter in a paper bag containing peat moss, in temperatures around 60°F. Where hardy, thin or divide in winter or spring.

HARVESTING AND CONDITIONING: Cut when half of flowers on stem have opened, before lower flowers have withered. Split stem bases. Stand in deep, cool water. Best to recut stems every other day after arranging.

USES: Linear or scented accent.

POLYGONATUM
SOLOMON'S SEAL
P. commutatum, P. hirtum,
P. multiflorum

DESCRIPTION: Perennial. Slender stems bear paired, dangling green-and-white bell flowers at nodes of trimly alternating oblong leaves. Most types have green foliage, some variegated green and white. Plants, 2 to 5 ft. tall, bloom for several weeks in late spring. Leaves last well into summer. Underground rhizomes spread into sizable clumps. Cut flowers and foliage last about 5 days.

HARDINESS: Zones 4 to 9.

GROWING CONDITIONS: Prefers rich, deep, loamy soil in full to partial shade; moist but well-drained conditions. Excellent woodland plant. Space clumps 2½ ft. apart.

PLANTING: Plant divisions in late summer. Set out acclimatized potted plants at any time during growing season. Sow seed ⅛ in. deep in shaded beds in fall for germination in spring, or indoors after prechill-ing for 6 weeks. Germination takes from 1 month to 1½ years.

CARE: Apply 1 in. layer of compost to beds in fall. Divide plants in late summer after leaves die, to propagate or if crowded. Leave new plants alone for several years to become established. Thin or transplant seedlings if crowded. Mulch. Protect from sawfly.

HARVESTING AND CONDITIONING: Cut stems when flowers have opened in early morning, or when foliage has matured in late spring. Harvest sparingly to keep plants healthy. Stand in cool water for several hours.

USES: Linear element.

PRIMULA
PRIMROSE, POLYANTHUS, COWSLIP
P. species and hybrids

DESCRIPTION: Perennial (most species). Sometimes grown as annual or biennial. Tubular blossoms, usually with wide, flat, lobed faces, arranged in circular, globular, or elongated clusters, usually on short, slender stems. There are hundreds of species, in all colors. Hardy garden perennials are *P. vulgaris*, with low clusters of large flowers, all shades; *P. japonica*, red, white, or pink, pointed spires; *P. denticulata*, 2-in. globes of white or blue flowers on 1-ft. stems; many more. All have basal rosettes of oval leaves, and most bloom in spring. Cut flowers last 3 to 7 days.

HARDINESS: Those listed, zones 4 to 8. Some others are tender.

GROWING CONDITIONS: Most species prefer partial shade and moist but well drained, loamy, fertile soil. *P. japonica* prefers wet soil; grows well near streams. Space plants 8 to 12 in. apart.

PLANTING: Plant in spring or fall. For hardy types, prechill 3 weeks; sow seed indoors in winter on soil surface at 60°F. Germinates in about 3 weeks.

CARE: Divide in early spring or late summer. Set out seedlings when large enough to handle, during cool, moist weather. Mulch. Fertilize lightly throughout growing season. Water if necessary. Protect from slugs.

HARVESTING AND CONDITIONING: Cut when half of flowers on stem have opened. Stand in deep water, cool but not too cold, for several hours.

USES: Focal or accent element.

PRUNUS
FLOWERING CHERRY, PLUM, APRICOT, PEACH
P. species and hybrids

DESCRIPTION: Tree or shrub. Profuse, showy, single or double 1- to 2-in. white, red, violet, or pink flowers on graceful branches for several weeks in spring. Deciduous leaves are rich, glossy dark green or bronze; summer fruits, if any, may be purple, red, orange, yellow, or green, $1/4$ in. to over 2 in. wide. Hundreds of species and cultivars, spreading, upright, or weeping, 15 to 50 ft. tall. Flowering cherries are deservedly popular. Blossoms of fruiting peach, plum, and apricot are highly ornamental. Lasts more than 7 days in vase.

HARDINESS: Most, zones 5 to 8, with species for zones 3 to 9.

GROWING CONDITIONS: Prefers rich, loamy, well-drained soil; average moisture; full sun to partial shade. Space 12 or more ft. apart.

PLANTING: Set out acclimatized plants in spring. If possible, purchase in bloom. Can be grown from seed planted outdoors in fall for spring germination; takes many years to flower.

CARE: Fertilize in spring and summer. Prune in early to midspring. Water if soil becomes dry. Remove limbs affected by fireblight. Protect from aphids, scale, and leaf spot.

HARVESTING AND CONDITIONING: Cut flowers when buds have begun to open, or earlier to force indoors. Slit and peel bark of stem ends. Stand in deep water for several hours.

USES: Flowers, leaves, and fruit as background, filler, or massed elements.

PULMONARIA
LUNGWORT, BETHLEHEM SAGE
P. angustifolia, P. saccharata

DESCRIPTION: Perennial. Funnel-shaped, lobed, ruffled pinkish flowers 1 in. long. Blooms appear on low stalks in late winter or early spring. Stalks stretch to 1 ft. tall as warmer weather arrives, flowers turning blue-violet as they age. Small, semievergreen leaves in basal rosette grow, too, and last all summer and fall. Small hairs on the leaves give them a silvery appearance. *P. angustifolia* has 9-in. green, linear leaves and blue, pink, or white flowers; the blues are very intense. *P. saccharata* has wider, pointed 12-in. leaves and pink and blue flowers. Silver spots mark leaves of favorite cultivars 'Mrs. Moon' and 'Margery Fish'. Lasts about 4 days in vase.

HARDINESS: Zones 4 to 8.

GROWING CONDITIONS: Prefers rich, moist, loamy soil; partial to deep shade in summer, brighter light in winter—place under deciduous trees. Space 1 to 2 ft. apart.

PLANTING: Plant divisions in fall or spring, acclimatized potted plants at any time during growing season.

CARE: Apply 1 handful rotted manure and compost to each clump in fall. Divide in spring or fall, preferably fall to prevent spoiling blooms. Keep soil moist. Mulch. Cut off flower stalks after bloom ends.

HARVESTING AND CONDITIONING: Cut when first few flowers on stem have opened, in morning or evening. Stand in deep water for several hours.

USES: Filler or massed material.

RANUNCULUS
PERSIAN BUTTERCUP
R. asiaticus

DESCRIPTION: Tuber. Round flowers with overlapped layers of waxy, oval petals in bright shades of yellow, orange, red, pink, peach, and white. Blooms several weeks, late spring to early summer, 1 to 4 in. wide, up to four flowers per stem; $1\frac{1}{2}$ to 2 ft. tall. Stout stems; divided, palmate, ferny leaves. Cut flowers last 5 to 7 days.

HARDINESS: Zones 8 to 11; all zones if kept from freezing. Dislikes high heat, does best between 50 and 80°F.

GROWING CONDITIONS: Prefers rich, sandy loam soil with average moisture, full sun to partial shade, and flawless drainage. Improve drainage with a layer of gravel below soil in bed. Plant 1 in. deep, 1 ft. apart. Good pot plant.

PLANTING: Presoak dormant, dried, claw-shaped tubers overnight in cool water before planting; plant pointed ends down. Treat with fungicide and plant outdoors in midspring or indoors in late winter.

CARE: Fertilize throughout growth. Mulch. Keep moderately moist during its 6 months' growth. After flowering, where ground freezes in winter, dig, dry, and store roots in a dry, airy place. Protect from mealybugs, aphids, and red spider mites.

HARVESTING AND CONDITIONING: Cut flowers before they have opened fully. Split stem ends and dip in boiling water. Stand in deep water for several hours.

USES: Focal element, accent, or single specimen.

RESEDA
MIGNONETTE
R. odorata

DESCRIPTION: Annual. Broadly cone-shaped, greenish yellow flower heads several inches long are grown for sweet, room-scenting fragrance, not for looks. Inconspicuous petals may be reddish, yellow, or white; anthers brownish. With many branches, plants are productive in summer and early fall. Leaves are green ovals, plants 1 to 2 ft. tall. Lasts about 5 days when cut.

HARDINESS: Zones 3 to 10. Tolerates light frost.

GROWING CONDITIONS: Prefers rich to average, sweet soil; average moisture; good drainage; light shade. Space 6 to 12 in. apart.

PLANTING: Set out bedding plants in spring near frost-free date. Sow seed 8 to 10 weeks earlier indoors for transplants, or directly outdoors as early as soil can be worked in spring, or in fall. Press seeds into surface of moist soil. Prefers light for germination, in 5 to 20 days. Dislikes disturbance of roots. Sow in fall and grow as biennial in zones 8 to 10.

CARE: Thin seedlings to correct spacing and desired sites when they are 4 in. tall or are crowded. Side-dress with flower fertilizer and compost during growth. Add lime if necessary. Mulch in hot or dry areas. Deadhead.

HARVESTING AND CONDITIONING: Cut when a fourth to a half of flowers on spike have opened, in evening. Strip off lower leaves. Stand in deep, warm water overnight.

USES: Filler element, for aroma.

RHODODENDRON
AZALEA
R. species and hybrids

DESCRIPTION: Shrub. Blooms en masse in spring or summer, some types covering bushes for several weeks. There are early, midseason, and late types among both azaleas and rhododendrons; countless species and cultivars. Small-leaved (1 to 2 in.) evergreen or deciduous types are usually called azaleas, while evergreen, large-leaved (to 8 in.) types are called rhododendrons. Lobed, flaring, tubular flowers are single or double, small or large (over 3 in.), in pink, white, peach, orange, yellow, magenta, or violet. Leaves oval, usually leathery; roots shallow. Mound-shaped plants from less than 2 to more than 30 ft. tall. Lasts about 7 days in vase.

HARDINESS: Most, zones 6 to 9. Some hardier, some more tender. Check locally.

GROWING CONDITIONS: Prefers partial shade and loamy, moderately acidic, moist but well-drained soil. Space about as far apart as the expected height. Young plants may be spaced closer, then moved when crowded.

PLANTING: Plant in spring. Take semiripe cuttings or layer plants in late summer or fall.

CARE: Fertilize throughout growing season with acidic or "holly" fertilizer. Mulch with pine needles, chopped leaves, compost, or bark chips. Prune after flowering. Deadhead. Treat for mildew, root rot, borers, and blight, if necessary.

HARVESTING AND CONDITIONING: Cut when half of the flowers are open. Slit stem ends. Cover stems and flowers with cool water for 2 hours before arranging.

USES: Focal or massed element.

ROSA
ROSE
R. species and hybrids

DESCRIPTION: Shrub. Blossoms, often scented, may be circular singles, elongated buds, or cabbage-layered doubles, from ½ in. to more than 4 in. wide, borne singly or in clusters. Colors are red and rose shades, white, yellow, orange, or violet. Some bloom in one overwhelming bash in June; others repeat bloom from spring to late fall. Leaves oval, serrated, deciduous; shape ground-hugging, upright bush, shrub, or climbing. Height from less than 1 ft. to more than 30 ft. Lasts 3 to 7 days in vase.

HARDINESS: Most, zones 4 to 10. Check locally.

GROWING CONDITIONS: Prefers full sun, plentiful moisture, excellent drainage, air circulation, and deep, rich soil. Rugosa roses tolerate infertile sand and salt spray. Space hybrid teas 4 ft. apart, climbers farther; spacing varies with type.

PLANTING: Plant in spring or fall. Take cuttings in summer or fall.

CARE: Fertilize throughout growing season. Prune tea roses and repeat bloomers hard in late winter, removing tops of long canes and any thin or crooked growth. Deadhead. Prune climbers lightly after bloom, removing thin, spindly growth and deadwood, but leaving strong and new canes. Train fat new shoots by tying to supports, for bloom next year. Treat for aphids, black spot, and mildew. Water if necessary.

HARVESTING AND CONDITIONING: Cut when buds have begun to open. Remove leaves below water level. Slit stem ends. Stand in deep water for several hours.

USES: Focal or massed element.

RUDBECKIA
GLORIOSA DAISY, BLACK-EYED SUSAN
R. fulgida, R. hirta

DESCRIPTION: Short-lived perennial, often grown as an annual. Stiff, branched stems bear brown-centered, gold, single or double daisies all summer. Leaves spear-shaped, covered with short hairs. Flat, basal rosettes in winter, bushy stalks in summer, 2 to 4 ft. tall. *R. fulgida*, single or double, small- or large-flowered, mainly gold-petaled. 'Goldsturm' is outstanding. *R. hirta* (gloriosa daisy), flowers up to 6 in. wide, gold, brown, orange, or rusty red bicolors. Lasts 7 to 14 days in vase.

HARDINESS: Zones 3 to 9. Withstands heat and cold.

GROWING CONDITIONS: Prefers full sun and average to rich, well-drained soil, average moisture. Space 1 to 3 ft. apart.

PLANTING: Set out divisions in early spring, acclimatized potted plants at any time during growing season. Sow seed indoors at anytime or outdoors around 75°F. Sown in winter, blooms the next summer; sown later blooms the following year. Plant ⅛ in. deep, 3 in. apart. In mild areas, sow in fall.

CARE: Transplant seedlings when crowded. Divide plants in early spring, to separate bunched rosettes. Protect from deer and rabbits. Deadhead, but let some go to seed for self-sown plants if desired—these produce nice variations for cutting. Cut off flower stems in late summer to promote development of basal rosettes.

HARVESTING AND CONDITIONING: Cut while flowers have tight centers. Remove lower foliage. Stand in cool water containing sugar for several hours.

USES: Focal or filler element.

RUTA
RUE
R. graveolens

DESCRIPTION: Perennial herb. Grown for evergreen, blue-green, finely lobed and divided foliage and clusters of small round golden flowers in early summer. 'Jackman's Blue' has strong blue color. Leaves and flowers are pungently aromatic if crushed, but the smell is not appreciated by everyone. Shrubby plants are 1½ to 3 ft. tall. Leaves and flowers last 1 week or longer when cut.

HARDINESS: Zones 5 to 9.

GROWING CONDITIONS: Prefers full sun, well-drained soil of poor to average fertility, and average to moist conditions. Space 1 ft. apart.

PLANTING: Plant divisions in early spring, acclimatized potted plants at any time during growing season. Sow seed indoors in individual pots in late winter or outdoors in summer at 70 to 80°F, ½ in. deep, 2 to 4 in. apart. Cuttings are difficult but may be taken in late summer.

CARE: Transplant seedlings when crowded. Divide plants in early spring, if crowded. Prune in spring to keep plants compact. Fertilize lightly each spring when new growth begins. Mulch if soil is hot and dry. Deadhead.

HARVESTING AND CONDITIONING: Cut fresh-looking leaves and flowers in morning or evening. Remove foliage below water line. Split stem ends. Stand in deep water for several hours.

USES: Flowers and leaves as accent or filler. Not edible. Do not use as garnish.

SALPIGLOSSIS
VELVET FLOWER
S. sinuata

DESCRIPTION: Annual. Broadly flaring trumpet-shaped flowers, 3 in. wide, on branched plants about 2 ft. tall. The blossoms, in rich colors such as royal blue, red, purple, rose, yellow, and brown, have a velvety sheen and are often veined with gold or silver. Toothed leaves, lance-shaped. Blooms in early summer until high heat burns plants. 'Splash' series faster growing, more weather-tolerant than species. Cut flowers last 3 to 7 days.

HARDINESS: All zones. Killed by frost and high heat.

GROWING CONDITIONS: Prefers full sun, rich soil, average to plentiful mois-ture, and good drainage. Plant 1 ft. apart.

PLANTING: Set out plants after danger of frost passes. Sow indoors by pressing seed into surface of soil of individual pots 8 weeks before last frost, at 70 to 80°F. Sow outdoors 2 in. apart after frost where summers are long and cool, or in fall in zones 10 to 11. Needs a cover or dark place to germinate; takes 4 to 12 days. Bring into light as soon as seedlings appear.

CARE: Thin or transplant seedlings to their correct spacing. Fertilize at planting time and throughout growth with low-nitrogen product. Do not let soil dry out. Mulch. Deadhead regularly. Protect from aphids. Subject to wilt diseases. Cut back if leggy.

HARVESTING AND CONDITIONING: Cut when flowers have begun to open, in evening. Stand in cool water up to base of flowerheads overnight.

USES: Focal element.

SALVIA
SAGE
S. species and cultivars

DESCRIPTION: Annual, biennial, or perennial. Salvias have tubular, hooded, two-lipped flowers. Among hundreds of species, few are hardy. Tender perennials grown as annuals blooming summer to frost are *S. farinacea* (mealy-cup sage), 1½ to 3 ft., slender spires of blue flowers, gray-green leaves; and *S. splendens* (scarlet sage), 1 ft. with spires of large, typically red flowers. *S. horminum* (clary sage), a hardy annual 2 ft. tall, has pink, purple, or white bracts in late summer. *S. nemerosa* (3 ft., slender spires of blue flowers) and *S. officinalis* (culinary sage, 1 to 3 ft., vio-let flowers, gray-green leaves) are sum-mer-blooming hardy perennials. Lasts 5 to 10 days in vase.

HARDINESS: *S. officinalis* and *S. nemerosa*, zones 5 to 9. Others, all zones, as annuals.

GROWING CONDITIONS: Prefers full sun and well-drained, rich to average garden soil. Space 1 to 3 ft. apart.

PLANTING: Set out bedding plants after frost. Sow seed of clary sage outdoors ¼ in. deep where it will grow in early spring. Sow tender perennials indoors in early spring. Sow hardy perennials indoors or out in spring or summer; prechill seed.

CARE: Transplant or thin seedlings if crowded. Divide hardy perennials in spring. Fertilize lightly throughout growth. Mulch. Deadhead.

HARVESTING AND CONDITIONING: Cut when lower flowers have opened. Stand in warm water for several hours.

USES: Linear element.

SANTOLINA
LAVENDER COTTON
S. chamaecyparissus

DESCRIPTION: Shrub. Pale silver foliage in numerous small, slender branchlets with divided leaves. Flowers are button-like, bright yellow; a cultivar, 'Bowles Variety,' has cream-colored flowers. Valued more for foliage. Plants are 2 to 3 ft. tall, somewhat wider; may be pruned to desired size. Blooms for about 1 month in summer; foliage attractive most or all of year. Foliage and flowers last more than 7 days in bouquets.

HARDINESS: Zones 6 to 9. Killed by harsh winters.

GROWING CONDITIONS: Prefers well-drained, average soil, not too rich (fertil-ize with bonemeal), and full sun. Gets leggy in shade. Space 3 ft. apart.

PLANTING: Set out acclimatized potted plants in spring or summer. Take cuttings of old wood in spring. Take cuttings of new growth in summer.

CARE: Side-dress established clumps with compost in fall or early spring. Prune for shape and to remove deadwood in spring. Older plants should be cut back fairly hard. Trim off flower heads and straggly shoots in autumn, but leave some excess foliage on for winter protection. Mulch lightly with pine boughs in winter in zone 6, where *Santolina* is only marginally hardy.

HARVESTING AND CONDITIONING: Cut in early morning or evening. Select fresh-looking stems; slit stem bases. Strip off leaves below water in vase. Stand in deep water for several hours.

USES: Leaves and flowers as filler or back-ground elements.

SCABIOSA
PINCUSHION FLOWER, SWEET SCABIOUS
S. atropurpurea, S. caucasica

DESCRIPTION: Annual or perennial. Lacy round flowerheads display pinlike pistils above whorls of florets. Bushy plants bloom summer and fall in white, pink, lilac, blue, burgundy, or purple. Basal leaves linear, light green; upper leaves divided. *S. atropurpurea*, annual, 18 to 36 in. *S. caucasica*, floriferous blue or white perennial, usually 2 ft. tall; dwarfs 1 ft. Lasts 4 to 8 days in vase.

HARDINESS: *S. purpurea*, all zones; *S. cau-casica*, zones 3 to 9. Dislikes heat.

GROWING CONDITIONS: Prefers full sun; well-drained, nonacidic sandy loam; plentiful moisture and fertility. Space 1 to 2 ft. apart.

PLANTING: Set out divisions in early spring, acclimatized potted plants after frost. Sow seed of annuals indoors 6 weeks before last frost, ⅛ in. deep, 2 to 4 in. apart, or outdoors just after last frost. In mild areas, sow in fall. Sow perennials in-doors or out at 70 to 80°F, same spacing.

CARE: Transplant seedlings when crowd-ed. Divide plants in early spring, if crowded. Support with branched sticks. Protect from slugs. Mulch if dry. Deadhead. In winter, cover perennials with airy 6-in. layer of salt hay; remove in spring.

HARVESTING AND CONDITIONING: Cut when most florets have opened in morn-ing or evening. Remove lower foliage. Split stem ends. Stand in cold water for several hours.

USES: Filler or focal element.

SCHIZANTHUS
BUTTERFLY FLOWER, POOR MAN'S ORCHID
S. pinnatus

DESCRIPTION: Annual. Orchidlike colors and markings. Numerous open-faced, 2-in. flowers in shades of pink, purple, white, and yellow, with contrasting throats and speckles or streaks, on bushy plants from less than 1 to more than 3 ft. tall. Plants of 15 in., such as 'Disco', are good for cutting, usually need no staking. Blooms summer to frost unless heat is excessive. Lasts 4 to 7 days when cut.

HARDINESS: All zones. Killed by frost and prolonged high temperatures.

GROWING CONDITIONS: Prefers full sun; rich, well-drained, loamy soil; average to moist conditions. Space 1 ft. apart.

PLANTING: Set out plants after danger of frost. Sow seed indoors in flats or individual pots in late winter at 60 to 70°F. Press lightly into soil to barely cover. Keep dark until germination starts in 7 to 14 days; then move to well-lit area. In cool greenhouse or frost-free areas, sow in fall.

CARE: Thin or transplant seedlings when crowded. Pinch back in spring to keep plants compact. Fertilize with flower fertilizer throughout growth. Mulch if soil is dry. Stake tall types. Use fungicide if necessary. Control leafhoppers, which transmit diseases. Deadhead.

HARVESTING AND CONDITIONING: Cut fresh-looking flowers in morning or evening. Remove foliage below water line. Split stem ends. Stand in deep water for several hours.

USES: Focal or accent material.

SCILLA
SQUILL, BLUEBELL
S. sibirica

DESCRIPTION: Bulb. Hordes of short spires, each carrying two to four bright blue bell-shaped flowers, very early in spring. Plants are 4 in. tall, flowers ½ in. wide. Leaves straplike; persist several weeks. Closely related *S. mischtschenkoana* has pale blue flowers, similar leaves. Both multiply rapidly. Cut flowers last 2 to 3 days.

HARDINESS: Zones 1 to 8. Needs chilling in winter. One of the hardiest of all perennials.

GROWING CONDITIONS: Prefers well-drained, average soil with average moisture and full sun in early spring, in places that will not be mowed before late spring. Grows well naturalized under deciduous trees and in grass. Plant 3 in. deep, 2 in. apart.

PLANTING: Plant bulbs in fall or immediately after dividing plants in late spring. Self-sows. Can be grown from seed sown ¼ in. deep outdoors in late spring. Husks turn tan and seeds turn black when fully ripened. Takes only 2 years from seed to flower—much faster than most bulbs.

CARE: Fertilize at planting time and in early spring. Keep moist during growth, drier during dormancy. Allow foliage to ripen; divide afterward every other year to propagate or if crowded.

HARVESTING AND CONDITIONING: Cut newly opened flowers in morning. Arrange immediately, or stand in cool water for several hours.

USES: Petite filler or massed element.

SEDUM
STONECROP
S. spectabile

DESCRIPTION: Perennial. Broad, flat-topped clusters of starry pink flowers in September, in clumps, with succulent stems and leaves; 2 ft. tall. Flowers continue to bloom throughout late summer and fall, changing from pink to wine red to rusty red-brown. Leaves are thick, pale gray-green, waxy ovals serrated on the edges. 'Autumn Joy' is a popular cultivar. Flowers last over 1 week in bouquets and may root in the vase.

HARDINESS: Zones 4 to 9.

GROWING CONDITIONS: Grows well in full sun or partial shade. Prefers well-drained, fertile soil with average moisture. Space clumps 1½ ft. apart.

PLANTING: Set out divisions in early spring, acclimatized potted plants at any time during growing season. Take tip or stem cuttings of new growth from late spring to summer. Take leaf cuttings in summer. Easily grown from seed planted indoors or in a cold frame in spring, at about 50°F. Sow on surface, keep moist. Germinates in 2 weeks and may bloom same year.

CARE: Divide every 2 or 3 years in early spring. Apply all-purpose fertilizer and compost throughout growth. Water during drought. Staking and deadheading not necessary. Cut down dead stems in late winter or early spring.

HARVESTING AND CONDITIONING: Cut flowers in morning or evening. Stand in deep water for several hours.

USES: Filler, accent, or focal element, fresh or dried.

SILENE
CATCHFLY, VISCARIA
S. armeria, S. coeli-rosa (syn. *Viscaria elegans*)

DESCRIPTION: Annual. *S. armeria* offers dense heads of tiny cherry-rose-colored flowers on stiff, 1-ft. stems, from decorative 3-in. rosettes of gray-green, pointed oval leaves. Blooms mid-spring until frost. *S. coeli-rosa*, often listed as *Viscaria*, has ½-in. pink, rose, violet, blue, and white flowers borne singly on branched stems 12 to 18 in. tall. Plants branched, linear leaves dark gray-green. Blooms in summer. Flowers last 4 days when cut.

HARDINESS: Zones 3 to 11. Tolerates frost and high heat if not prolonged.

GROWING CONDITIONS: Prefers rich to average soil, average moisture, good drainage, and full sun. Space 6 to 12 in. apart.

PLANTING: Set out acclimatized plants throughout growing season. Sow seed ⅛ in. deep, 1 to 3 in. apart. Sow indoors up to 12 weeks before last expected frost, outdoors in late spring or late summer, or in cold frame or in mild-winter areas in fall. Make successive sowings of *S. armeria*.

CARE: Thin or transplant seedlings when large enough to handle or crowded. Apply flower fertilizer and compost throughout growth. Mulch in hot or dry areas. Deadhead, or leave seedheads on for self-sown plants.

HARVESTING AND CONDITIONING: Cut when half of flowers on stem have opened, in morning or evening. Stand in deep, lukewarm water for several hours.

USES: Filler or massed element.

SOLIDAGO
GOLDENROD
S. canadensis

DESCRIPTION: Perennial. Arched, feathery sprays of tiny golden flowers on long, stiff stems. Flower heads 5 or 6 in. wide. Blooms late summer into fall. Prolific, common native meadow plant with an undeserved reputation for causing allergies and a deserved reputation for weediness. Leaves slender, deep green. Species and naturally occurring varieties are interbred and are unpredictable from seed. Garden types like 2-ft. 'Golden Baby' are suitable for border. Height ranges from 2 to 6 ft. When cut, stays fresh 7 to 10 days.

HARDINESS: Zones 3 to 9.

GROWING CONDITIONS: Prefers full sun, average moisture, and good drainage. Not particular about soil; grows in sand, clay, or loam. Grows rampantly in good garden soil. Space 2 ft. apart.

PLANTING: Set out divisions in spring, acclimatized plants in containers at any time during growing season. Sow seed indoors or outdoors at 50°F in spring or outdoors in fall for germination the next spring, barely covering.

CARE: Divide plants often to keep from crowding; can be divided every year in spring. Mulch in dry areas. Stake tall types. Cut stems to ground after bloom ends, unless self-sown plants are wanted. Fertilize in spring.

HARVESTING AND CONDITIONING: Cut when flowers have barely begun to open, in morning or evening. Stand in deep water for several hours.

USES: Filler or massed material, all sizes, fresh or dried.

SPIRAEA
BRIDAL WREATH, JAPANESE SPIRAEA
S. japonica, S. trilobata, S. × vanhouttei, others

DESCRIPTION: Shrub. Many species and cultivars. Japanese and similar types bloom at intervals throughout summer with pink, lilac, or red flowers in flat clusters; glossy green leaves. Bridal wreath types such as *S. × vanhouttei* have pure white blooms in April or May aligned on arching branches. Leaves are oval or lobed, blue-green in summer. Dwarf or tall plants from 2 to more than 8 ft. tall, varying with the species. Cut flowers last 5 to 8 days.

HARDINESS: Most, zones 4 to 8.

GROWING CONDITIONS: Prefers full sun to bright partial shade, well-drained soil of any type, average moisture and fertility. Space 4 to 8 ft. apart.

PLANTING: Set out acclimatized plants as soon as received. If possible, purchase plants in bloom because there is confusion about names. Take softwood cuttings in June or July. Make divisions by separating rooted suckers from main plant in early spring.

CARE: Prune and train for shape, especially bridal wreath types. Prune early bloomers (before May) after flowering. Prune summer and fall bloomers in early spring; they flower on new wood. Protect from aphids.

HARVESTING AND CONDITIONING: Cut when half of flowers on branch have opened, in morning or evening. Split stem ends. Remove lower foliage. Stand in deep water for several hours.

USES: Filler or massed element.

STOKESIA
STOKE'S ASTER
S. laevis

DESCRIPTION: Perennial. Branched, bushy plants produce numerous blue, lavender, or white 4-in. daisies midsummer to frost. Flowers are nearly double, stems strong. Evergreen leaves linear, hairy, silvery green. Plants 1½ ft. tall. Lasts 6 to 10 days in vase.

HARDINESS: Zones 5 to 9. Withstands prolonged heat.

GROWING CONDITIONS: Prefers full sun; rich, well-drained, sandy loam; average moisture. Withstands drought. Likes partial shade in hot areas. Does poorly if soil is wet in winter. Space 1½ ft. apart.

PLANTING: Set out divisions in early spring, acclimatized potted plants at any time during growing season. Sow seed indoors in February or March, ⅛ in. deep in small pots or cells. In cold frame or outdoors in areas with mild winters, sow in fall.

CARE: Thin or transplant seedlings when large enough to handle, if crowded. Divide plants in early spring, each year if crowded. Plants decline quickly in crowded conditions. Fertilize with aged manure or flower fertilizer throughout growth. Deadhead. Cut off tall stems after bloom to promote development of basal rosettes. Stake if necessary; if plants sprawl too much, replace with stronger cultivar.

HARVESTING AND CONDITIONING: Cut newly opened flowers in morning or evening. Remove lower foliage; split stem ends. Stand in lukewarm water containing sugar for several hours.

USES: Focal or massed element.

SYRINGA
LILAC
S. vulgaris

DESCRIPTION: Shrub or small tree. Dense, sweetly fragrant panicles of single or double tubular flowers in midspring. Purple, lilac, violet-blue, rose, magenta, or white flower clusters 4 to 8 in. long, on woody stems. Hundreds of named cultivars, most between 8 and 20 ft. tall, 6 to 12 ft. wide. Leaves heart-shaped, usually 5 in. long. Cut flowers last 5 days.

HARDINESS: Zones 4 to 7.

GROWING CONDITIONS: Prefers full sun; rich, loamy soil; pH slightly acid to neutral; average moisture. Requires good air circulation to prevent mildew. Space plants 8 to 20 ft. apart.

PLANTING: Set out bare-root plants in late winter, balled-and-burlapped or container-grown plants in spring. Suckers may be dug and transplanted while dormant in late winter.

CARE: Mulch beds with compost. Prune after flowering. Remove suckers from grafted plants. To rejuvenate an old, misshapen plant, prune hard or, if ungrafted, cut old, damaged trunks to the ground in spring and train new growth. Treat for mildew, leaf miner, lilac borer, and scale if necessary.

HARVESTING AND CONDITIONING: Cut when half of flowers in cluster have opened, in morning or evening. Remove lower foliage. Slit stem ends. Stand in deep water for several hours. Cool water prolongs freshness; warm water hastens forced branches.

USES: Versatile element used as focal point, as filler, or massed.

TAGETES
MARIGOLD
T. erecta, T. hybrids, T. patula

DESCRIPTION: Annual. Round, multi-petaled single or double flowers borne prolifically on branched plants. *T. erecta*, African marigold, comes in primrose yellow, lemon yellow, gold, or orange, double 3 in. flowers, plants to 3 ft. tall. *T. patula*, French marigold, 1 to 2 in. flowers, plants 8 in. to 1½ ft. tall, comes in same shades plus rusty red. Singles, doubles, and tufted forms. Hybrids between them combine attributes. Leaves are divided, with strong herbal scent. Unscented hybrids available. Blooms early summer to frost. Small types bloom earlier, tall types showier for cutting. Stays fresh 7 to 10 days and sometimes roots in vase.

HARDINESS: All zones. Killed by frost.

GROWING CONDITIONS: Prefers rich to average soil, average moisture, full sun. Space 8 to 18 in. apart.

PLANTING: Set out bedding plants in spring when the danger of frost ends. Sow seed 6 weeks earlier indoors or directly outdoors after danger of frost ends, ⅛ in. deep, 4 in. apart.

CARE: Thin seedlings to correct spacing and desired sites when they are 3 in. tall or are crowded. Side-dress plants lightly with flower fertilizer throughout growth. Mulch. Deadhead. Protect from slugs.

HARVESTING AND CONDITIONING: Cut flowers with tight centers in morning or evening. Strip off lower leaves. Stand in deep water for several hours.

USES: Focal or massed element.

TALINUM
JEWELS OF OPAR
T. paniculatum

DESCRIPTION: Tender perennial, grown as annual. Grown for airy sprays of glossy, round, beadlike red seedpods, which persist for many weeks in the garden in summer and fall—longer in mild-winter climates. These follow short-lived, tiny pink flowers on stalks 1 to 1½ ft. tall. Leaves are rosette-forming, oval, in a very pretty shade of apple green. When cut, pods stay fresh over 1 week.

HARDINESS: Zones 3 to 11. Tolerates light frost and heat. Killed by heavy frost.

GROWING CONDITIONS: Prefers loose, light soil; average fertility and moisture; good drainage; full sun. Easily grown. Space 1 ft. apart.

PLANTING: Sow seed outdoors, barely covered, 2 in. apart in spring or, in mild areas, autumn, in well-tilled, fertilized beds. Or start indoors in individual pots 6 weeks before outdoor planting time.

CARE: Water young plants until well established. Mulch in hot, dry areas. Water during drought; apply flower fertilizer in summer if soil is poor. Harvest or deadhead often to promote bloom, but allow a few flowers to set seed for self-sown plants, if wanted.

HARVESTING AND CONDITIONING: Cut when pods in each spray are ripe, well-formed and colorful. No conditioning required if they are used immediately; otherwise stand them in deep water until needed.

USES: Filler, accent, or massed material, fresh or dried.

THALICTRUM
MEADOW RUE
T. aquilegifolium, T. delavayi, T. flavum

DESCRIPTION: Perennial. Tall, graceful clumps bear fuzzy puffs of tiny pink, lilac, or white flowers in late spring, on 3- to 6-ft. stems. The many small, greenish white, lobed leaves on branched, wiry stems resemble those of columbine. *T. delavayi* blooms in summer. *T. flavum* has yellow flowers in late summer. Cut flowers and leaves last 4 to 6 days.

HARDINESS: Zones 5 to 8. *T. flavum*, zones 6 to 9.

GROWING CONDITIONS: Prefers average to rich, moist but well-drained, loamy soil in partial shade; full sun where summers are cool. Space clumps 3 ft. apart.

PLANTING: Set out divisions in early spring, acclimatized potted plants spring through fall. Sow seed indoors at 50 to 60°F in late winter, ⅛ in. deep, after prechilling for 3 weeks, or sow in cold frame in autumn for spring germination. Germination takes 2 to 3 weeks.

CARE: Apply 4 handfuls manure or compost to each established clump in fall. Let plants mature undisturbed for 5 or 6 years if possible. Divide in early spring if crowded or to propagate. Stake. Deadhead.

HARVESTING AND CONDITIONING: Cut flowers when half of cluster has opened, leaves when full size is reached, in early morning or evening. Stand in deep water for several hours.

USES: Flowers as filler or massed, leaves as filler, especially with columbine.

TITHONIA
MEXICAN SUNFLOWER
T. rotundifolia

DESCRIPTION: Annual. Round, single, 3-in. daisies in shades from gold to red-orange, with gold central discs, borne prolifically on robust, branched plants. Petals have a rich, velvety texture. Ray flowers large, flat, and neatly arranged. Oval leaves large, lobed, somewhat coarse-looking. Blooms August to frost on plants 2 to 6 ft. tall. Height controlled by planting short cultivars such as 'Goldfinger' (2 ft.) or sowing seed later than usual; decreasing day length triggers bloom regardless of height. Cut flowers stay fresh 7 days.

HARDINESS: Zones 4 to 11. Thrives in high heat; killed by frost.

GROWING CONDITIONS: Prefers rich soil, average moisture, good drainage, and full sun. Space 2 to 3 ft. apart.

PLANTING: Set out bedding plants in spring when danger of frost ends. Sow seed 6 weeks earlier indoors in individual 4-in. pots for transplants, or directly outdoors after danger of frost ends, ½ in. deep, 6 in. apart.

CARE: Thin seedlings to correct spacing and desired sites when they are 6 in. tall or are crowded. Side-dress plants with flower fertilizer throughout growth. Mulch in hot or dry areas. Stake if necessary. Harvest or deadhead regularly.

HARVESTING AND CONDITIONING: Cut nearly or fully opened flowers with tight centers in morning or evening. Strip off leaves and side branches. Stand in deep, warm water for several hours.

USES: Focal element.

TORENIA
WISHBONE FLOWER
T. fournieri

DESCRIPTION: Annual. Moderately flared, tubular flowers are about 2 in. long and 1 in. wide, borne from summer to frost on branched plants 1 ft. tall. Colors include blue, purple, rose, or white, touched with dots of yellow or orange. Leaves are toothed, narrowly heart-shaped, up to 3 in. long. Flowers on cut stems continue to open for more than 1 week; stems may sprout roots in vase.

HARDINESS: All zones. Killed by frost; thrives in heat.

GROWING CONDITIONS: Prefers partial shade, plentiful moisture, and fertile, well-drained, loamy soil. Space 8 to 12 in. apart.

PLANTING: Set out plants in warm weather, after all danger of frost. Sow seed indoors 8 weeks before last frost at 75°F in flats, small pots, or cells by pressing into moist growing medium, uncovered by soil. May self-sow outdoors in areas with mild winters. Root 3- to 5-in. tip cuttings in summer, in moist soil or water.

CARE: Thin or transplant seedlings if crowded. Apply flower fertilizer throughout growth. Water during drought or hot weather. Pinch or shear back for bushiness if necessary. Protect from caterpillars. Deadhead.

HARVESTING AND CONDITIONING: Cut stems bearing several newly opened flowers in morning or evening. Split stem ends and stand in deep, lukewarm water for several hours.

USES: Petite accent or filler.

TRACHYMENE
DIDISCUS, BLUE LACE FLOWER
T. coerulea

DESCRIPTION: Annual. Pale to deep blue florets densely fill lacy round umbels to 4 in. wide. Several flowers are borne on each branched 1- to 2-ft. plant in summer, earlier in frost-free climates. Leaves are feathery, divided, pale green. Cut flowers last up to 7 days.

HARDINESS: Zones 3 to 10. Cannot withstand frost or prolonged high heat.

GROWING CONDITIONS: Prefers fertile, sandy soil; average moisture; good drainage; and a sheltered position in full sun. Space 8 to 12 in. apart.

PLANTING: Set out bedding plants after danger of frost passes. Sow seed 8 weeks earlier indoors at 70°F or directly outdoors after danger of frost. Sow seeds 1/8 in. deep; prefers individual pots or wide spacing. Germinates in darkness in 2 to 4 weeks; cover until seedlings appear. Dislikes disturbance of roots. Sow in fall and grow as biennial in zones 9 to 10.

CARE: Thin or transplant seedlings to correct spacing and desired sites when they are 4 in. tall or are crowded. Side-dress with flower fertilizer and compost during growth. Mulch in hot or dry areas. Deadhead. Stake with slim sticks. Protect from high wind.

HARVESTING AND CONDITIONING: Cut when half of flowers on umbel have opened, in evening. Strip off lower leaves. Stand in deep, cool water overnight.

USES: Focal or massed element.

TROLLIUS
GLOBEFLOWER
T. europaeus, T. hybrids

DESCRIPTION: Perennial. Waxy double flowers 2 in. wide bloom on long stems for about 6 weeks in spring. Some types appear to stay closed, even when fully mature. Flowers may be cream, buttercup yellow, or orange. Dark green leaves are deeply divided and veined. Clump-forming, branched plants may be dwarf or tall; 2-ft. types best for cutting. Cut flowers last about 4 days.

HARDINESS: Zones 5 to 8. Dislikes hot summers.

GROWING CONDITIONS: Prefers rich, damp to wet, loamy soil enriched with compost and manure. Prefers part shade; grows in sun where soil is damp and heat moderate. Space 1½ ft. apart.

PLANTING: Plant divisions in fall, acclimatized potted plants at any time during growing season. Fresh seed germinates readily within a month. Prechill old seed for several weeks to break dormancy; may still take a year to germinate. Plant seeds 1/8 in. deep indoors or out at about 50°F.

CARE: Apply 2 handfuls rotted manure to each clump in fall. Divide in fall if necessary, very rarely. Keep soil moist at all times. Mulch. Deadhead, or let a few flowers go to seed for self-sown seedlings.

HARVESTING AND CONDITIONING: Flowers can be cut at mature bud stage or when partially open. Dip stem ends in boiling water, and stand in cool water for several hours.

USES: Focal or accent material.

TROPAEOLUM
NASTURTIUM
T. majus

DESCRIPTION: Annual. Long-spurred 2-in. flowers with six or more oval petals on low or climbing plants. Spicily scented; available in cream, gold, orange, peach, rose, and red. Leaves are smooth and circular, on fleshy stems. Types are tall (climbing or trailing), semitrailing, and dwarf (bushy). Blooms midsummer to frost on plants 6 in. to 6 ft. tall. Cut flowers and leaves stay fresh 3 to 5 days.

HARDINESS: Zones 2 to 11. Killed by frost.

GROWING CONDITIONS: Prefers average soil, not too rich; average moisture; good drainage; full sun. Space 10 to 24 in. apart.

PLANTING: Set out bedding plants in spring after danger of frost. Sow seed 4 to 6 weeks earlier indoors for transplants, or directly outdoors 2 weeks before danger of frost ends, ½ in. deep, 5 in. apart. Presoak seeds overnight to speed germination.

CARE: Thin seedlings to their correct spacing and desired sites when they have six leaves or are crowded. In poor soil, apply low-nitrogen flower fertilizer throughout growth. Mulch in hot or dry areas. Deadhead regularly. Protect from aphids and caterpillars. Provide support for climbers.

HARVESTING AND CONDITIONING: Cut newly opened flowers on long stems in morning or evening. Or cut tip sections of vines with several leaves and flowers attached. Stand in cool water for several hours.

USES: Massed in transparent vase to show off stems, or as filler.

TULIPA
TULIP
T. hybrids and species

DESCRIPTION: Bulb. Flowers for 2 weeks in spring in all colors but blue; types for early, middle, or late season. Many hybrids, most 2 ft. tall with smooth, upright, cup-shaped, six-petaled flowers. On sunny days petals spread 6 or 8 in. wide, change shape in vase. Stems strong, leaves linear, plants 6 in. to 3 ft. tall. Flowers classed single early, double early, triumph, Darwin hybrids, single late, lily-flowered, fringed, viridiflora, Rembrandt, parrot, double late, Kaufmanniana hybrids, Fosteriana hybrids, Greigii hybrids, and miscellaneous. Species and lily-flowered types more durable in garden than large hybrids. Cut flowers last 4 to 7 days.

HARDINESS: Zones 3 to 8.

GROWING CONDITIONS: Prefers full sun to light shade, average moisture, and fertile, well-drained soil. Space 4 to 6 in. apart and deep; the larger the bulb, the deeper it is planted.

PLANTING: Set out bulbs in fall. Seed impractical; takes many years for blooms. However, may be sown outdoors ⅛ in. deep in summer; germinates fall or spring.

CARE: Apply 1 in. rotted manure and compost over beds in fall. Allow foliage to ripen (turn yellow) before removing it in late spring. Divide every 3 years.

HARVESTING AND CONDITIONING: Cut flowers when color has begun to show on bud. Remove white portion from base of stem. Stand in cool water for several hours.

USES: Focal or massed element.

VERBENA
GARDEN VERBENA
V. hybrids

DESCRIPTION: Tender perennial, grown as annual. Rows of small, tubular, lobed florets form lacy round heads. Plants bloom from late spring until frost, in red, pink, blue, violet, or white, often with contrasting eyes. Plants are bushy, low, and spreading or trailing, 8 to 15 in. tall and somewhat wider. Stays fresh up to 7 days in vase.

HARDINESS: All zones. Killed by frost. May be short-lived perennial in frost-free areas.

GROWING CONDITIONS: Prefers rich to average, well-drained soil; average moisture; full sun. Space 1 to 2 ft. apart.

PLANTING: Set out bedding plants in late spring when the danger of frost ends. Sow seed 12 weeks earlier indoors, ⅛ in. deep, 4 in. apart. Prefers darkness until irregular germination occurs, in about 1 month. Also grown in greenhouse from cuttings taken in spring or fall.

CARE: Shift seedlings to larger pots when crowded, until time to set outdoors. Apply flower fertilizer throughout growth. Water often to keep soil from drying out. Mulch. Deadhead. Pinch back for bushiness. Protect from thrips and whiteflies.

HARVESTING AND CONDITIONING: Cut flowers when the outer two rings of florets have opened, in morning or evening. Split stem ends. Condition for about 8 hours, starting with warm water to which sugar has been added.

USES: Filler, focal, or massed element.

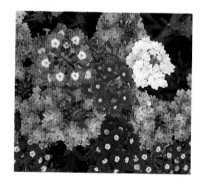

VERONICA
SPEEDWELL
V. austriaca subsp. *teucrium,*
V. spicata, V. virginica

DESCRIPTION: Perennial. Trim, shrublike plants bear numerous, pointed spikes of blue, white, lilac, or pink florets. Notable for blue shades. Species and cultivars vary in size, spike shape, and leaf color. Plants for cutting are 2 to 4 ft. tall, flower spikes up to 6 in. long. Threadlike anthers give flowers a fuzzy appearance. Leaves linear, green or silver, sometimes evergreen. Cut flowers last 4 to 6 days.

HARDINESS: Zones 4 to 8. Some strains less hardy. Dislikes hot weather.

GROWING CONDITIONS: Prefers average to rich, moist but well-drained, loamy soil in full sun to partial shade. Space 2 to 4 ft. apart.

PLANTING: Set out divisions in early spring or late fall, potted plants late spring. Take cuttings in summer. Sow seed indoors in late winter, ⅛ in. deep, after prechilling for 6 weeks, or sow in cold frame in autumn for spring germination. Prefers light for germination, which takes 1 to 3 months.

CARE: Apply 4 handfuls manure or compost to each established clump in fall or early spring. Divide in early spring if crowded, every 3 years. Stake tall types. Deadhead.

HARVESTING AND CONDITIONING: Cut when half of flowers on spike have opened, in early morning or evening. Remove lower leaves; split stem ends. Stand in deep water for several hours.

USES: Linear accent.

VIBURNUM
SNOWBALL
V. species and cultivars

DESCRIPTION: Shrub or tree. Over a hundred species, grown for spring or summer flowers, autumn berries, and handsome foliage. Clusters of white or pink flowers, sometimes tubular and fragrant. Bushy, rounded plants, usually deciduous, sometimes evergreen. Following recommendations are deciduous, hardy shrubs usually between 8 and 15 ft. tall: *V. carlesii,* pink flowers, heady fragrance, oval leaves; *V.* × *carlcephalum* (fragrant snowball), 6 ft. tall, 6-in. white flower clusters; *V. opulus* (highbush cranberry), white flowers, red fruits, lobed leaves; *V. plicatum* (Japanese snowball tree), white lacecap or domed flowerheads, double-file arrangement, oval leaves, red berries. Cut flowers last 5 to 7 days.

HARDINESS: Most, zones 5 to 9; *V. opulus,* zones 4 to 8; *V. carlesii,* zones 6 to 9.

GROWING CONDITIONS: Prefers rich, loamy, slightly acid soil; full sun or partial shade; average moisture. Recommended spacing equals expected height.

PLANTING: Plant bare-root plants in early spring, acclimatized potted plants at any time during growing season. Take softwood cuttings in summer.

CARE: Mulch and fertilize with chopped leaves, rotted manure, and compost. Prune after flowering. Do not let plants become too dense; cut off older shoots. Treat for mildew and leaf spot if necessary.

HARVESTING AND CONDITIONING: Cut as blooms begin to open. Scrape and slit woody stems; stand in deep water for several hours.

USES: Flowers as focal points, fruit and leaves as accent elements.

VINCA
PERIWINKLE, TRAILING MYRTLE
V. major, V. minor

DESCRIPTION: Perennial subshrub or vine. Tubular, lobed flowers ¾ to 1 in. wide bloom for 8 weeks in spring. Usually blue; also white or pink. Flowers scattered in small clusters along long stems of dense, mat-forming foliage. Dark green leaves are glossy, pointed ovals. *V. minor* has smaller leaves. *V. m.* 'La Grave' has unusually large, cobalt-blue flowers. *V. major* has larger leaves; *V. m. variegata* is widely grown in planters and window boxes for its showy green-and-white leaves. Cut foliage (with or without flowers) lasts more than 1 week.

HARDINESS: *V. major*, zones 7 to 9; *V. minor*, zones 5 to 8.

GROWING CONDITIONS: Prefers rich, moist, loamy soil in partial shade. Space rooted cuttings 6 in. apart.

PLANTING: Set out divisions or rooted cuttings in spring or fall. Take cuttings in early spring or late summer, during moist, mild weather.

CARE: Apply a 1-in. layer of compost and rotted manure to beds in fall. Divide in spring if necessary. Keep soil moist at all times. Mulch. Trim for neatness; trimmings may be used as cuttings to propagate more plants.

HARVESTING AND CONDITIONING: Cut long pieces of leafy stems, which can be used whether or not in flower. Harvest in morning or evening. Stand in lukewarm water for several hours.

USES: Trailing linear accent or as filler material.

VIOLA
PANSY
V. cornuta, V. × wittrockiana

DESCRIPTION: Biennial or perennial, often grown as annual. Flat, round-faced flowers with five petals, all colors. *V. × wittrockiana* (pansy) grown as annual or biennial. Prolific flowers 3 in. wide on slender stems. Branched plants have narrow, toothed leaves. Blooms late winter through spring. *V. cornuta* (garden viola) is similar, more reliably perennial, flowers 1 to 2½ in. wide; blooms early spring through fall. Grow pansies and violas in winter in low-frost climates. Lasts 3 to 6 days in vase.

HARDINESS: All zones. Prefers cool climates; unharmed in light frost. Grow as annual where temperatures exceed 92°F.

GROWING CONDITIONS: Prefers rich, loamy soil, steady moisture, full sun to part shade. Space 6 to 10 in. apart.

PLANTING: Set out bedding plants in early spring or as soon as available. Sow seed, ⅛ in. deep in moist soil, in cold frame late summer for winter and spring bloom, indoors in winter for spring and summer bloom. Take cuttings in spring or late summer.

CARE: Shift seedlings to larger pots if crowded, treat as bedding plants when flowers show. Apply flower fertilizer throughout growth. Mulch. Pinch back. Deadhead. Protect from slugs.

HARVESTING AND CONDITIONING: Cut newly opened flowers in morning or evening. Submerge flowers and stems in cold water for 1 hour; stand in cool water for several hours.

USES: Focal or massed element.

ZANTEDESCHIA
CALLA LILY
Z. aethiopica, Z. elliottiana, Z. rehmanni

DESCRIPTION: Rhizome. Funnel-shaped flowers, one per stem. Waxy, tapering spathe, white, green, yellow, peach, or pink, surrounds a prominent, yellow spadix. Large basal leaves are glossy, deep green, arrow- to heart-shaped. Height from 1 to 3 ft; flowers 3 to 6 in. long. *Z. aethiopica* is white; *Z. a.* 'Green Goddess' has huge green flowers mottled with white. *Z. elliottiana* has yellow flowers, spotted leaves. *Z. rehmanni* comes in peach and rose and is 16 in. tall. Blooms for several weeks in spring or summer. Cut flowers last 5 to 7 days.

HARDINESS: Zones 9 to 11; all zones if kept from freezing.

GROWING CONDITIONS: Prefers rich, sandy loam soil with average moisture, full sun to partial shade (hot areas), and good drainage. Plant 2 to 3 in. deep, 1 to 3 ft. apart. Grows in tubs.

PLANTING: Treat rhizomes with fungicide and plant outdoors after danger of frost or indoors in late winter. Discard rhizomes with soft, rotted areas.

CARE: Fertilize throughout growth. Mulch. Keep moderately moist during growth, nearly dry during dormancy. Where ground freezes, store indoors. Divide rhizomes in late winter. Protect from mealybugs and red spider mites.

HARVESTING AND CONDITIONING: Cut unopened but developed flowers, and cut well-formed leaves. Stand flowers in deep water; immerse leaves for several hours.

USES: Flowers as focal element or single specimen; leaves as accent.

ZINNIA
Z. elegans

DESCRIPTION: Annual. Masses of round, multipetaled flowers bloom on branched plants, in every shade but blue. Flower widths from 1 to 6 in. Ray flowers short or long, single or double, flat or quilled. May be listed in catalogs as dahlia form, cactus form, or miniature. Disc flowers gold. Oval leaves slightly downy. Blooms midsummer to frost on plants 6 in. to 4 ft. tall; tall types best for cutting. Cut flowers stay fresh 5 to 10 days.

HARDINESS: Zones 2 to 11. Thrives in high heat; killed by frost.

GROWING CONDITIONS: Prefers rich to average soil, average moisture, full sun. Needs extra water in hot weather. Space 10 to 20 in. apart.

PLANTING: Set out bedding plants in spring after danger of frost. Or sow seed 8 weeks earlier indoors for transplants, or directly outdoors after danger of frost, ¼ in. deep, 5 in. apart.

CARE: Thin seedlings to correct spacing and desired sites when they are 3 in. tall or are crowded. Pinch back tips for bushiness. Side-dress plants with flower fertilizer throughout growth. Mulch in hot or dry areas. Stake if necessary. Harvest or deadhead regularly.

HARVESTING AND CONDITIONING: Cut long-stemmed flowers with tight centers in morning or evening. Strip off leaves and side branches. Scald stem ends. Stand in deep water for several hours. Wire heavy heads.

USES: Focal or accent element.

BIBLIOGRAPHY

Bailey, L. H., Staff, Liberty Hyde Bailey Hortorium, Cornell University, *Hortus Third*, Macmillan, New York, 1976.

Bailey, Lee, *Lee Bailey's Small Bouquets*, Clarkson & Potter, New York, 1990.

Balfour, A. P., *Annual and Biennial Flowers*, Geoffrey Bles, London, 1963.

Bond, Rick, and Paterson, Allen, *Successful Flower Gardening*, Ortho Books, San Ramon, CA, 1990.

Brickell, Christopher, Editor, *The American Horticultural Society Encyclopedia of Garden Plants*, Macmillan, New York, 1990.

Christopher, Everett P., *The Pruning Manual*, Macmillan, New York, 1954.

de Bray, Lys, *Manual of Old-Fashioned Flowers*, The Oxford Illustrated Press, Somerset, England, 1984.

Dirr, Michael, *Manual of Woody Landscape Plants*, Stipes Publishing Company, Champaign, IL, 1990.

Embertson, Jane, *Pods: Wildflowers and Weeds in Their Final Beauty*, Charles Scribner's Sons, New York, 1979.

Everett, T. H., *Gardening Handbook*, Fawcett Publications, Inc., Greenwich, CT, 1970.

Fell, Derek, *Annuals: How to Select, Grow, and Enjoy*, HP Books, Tucson, AZ, 1983.

Fell, Derek, *The Easiest Flowers to Grow*, Ortho Books, San Ramon, CA, 1990.

Gattrell, Anthony, *Dictionary of Floristry and Flower Arranging*, B. T. Batsford, Ltd., London, 1988.

Halpin, Anne Moyer, *The Year-Round Flower Gardener*, Summit Books, New York, 1989.

Halpin, Anne Moyer, *Foolproof Planting*, Rodale Press, Emmaus, PA, 1990.

Haring, Elda, *The Complete Book of Growing Plants from Seed*, Hawthorn Books, New York, 1967.

Harper, Pamela, and McGourty, Frederick, *Perennials: How to Select, Grow, and Enjoy*, HP Books, Los Angeles, 1985.

Hill, Lewis, *Secrets of Plant Propagation*, Storey Communications, Pownal, VT, 1985.

Hillier, Malcolm, *Flower Arranging*, Reader's Digest Association, Pleasantville, NY, 1990.

Horton, Alvin, *Arranging Cut Flowers*, Ortho Books, San Ramon, CA, 1985.

Kieft Bloemzaden B.V., Staff, *Kieft's Growing Manual*, Blokker, Holland, 1989.

Mackey, Betty, et al., *The Gardener's Home Companion*, Macmillan, New York, 1991.

Nehrling, Arno, and Nehrling, Irene, *Gardening for Flower Arrangement*, Dover Publications, New York, 1976.

Newdick, Jane, *A Cascade of Flowers*, Salamander Books, Ltd., London, 1990.

Thompson & Morgan, Staff, *Successful Seed Raising*, Suffolk, England, 1991. (Pamphlet.)

Verey, Rosemary, *The Flower Arranger's Garden*, Little, Brown and Company, Boston, 1989.

SUPPLIERS

Bluestone Perennials, 7211 Middle Ridge Road, Madison, OH 44057

Burpee, 300 Park Avenue, Warminster, PA 18974

Lee Bristol Nursery, R.R. 1, Box 148, Gaylordsville, CT 06755

Carroll Gardens, P.O. Box 310, Westminster, MD 21157

The Country Garden, P.O. Box 3539, Oakland, CA 94609

Dutch Gardens, Inc., P.O. Box 588, Farmingdale, NJ 07727

The Fragrant Path, P.O. Box 328, Ft. Calhoun, NE 68023

Joseph Harris Company, Inc., 3670 Buffalo Road, Rochester, NY 14624

Ed Hume Seeds, Inc., P.O. Box 1450, Kent, WA 98032

Johnny's Selected Seeds, Foss Hill Road, Albion, ME 04910

Kinsman Company, River Road, Point Pleasant, PA 18950

Klehm Nursery, Route 5, 197 Penny Road, South Barrington, IL 60010

Logee's Greenhouses, 55 North Street, Danielson, CT 06239

McClure & Zimmerman, 1422 West Thorndale, Chicago, IL 60660

Mellinger's Inc., 2310 West South Range, North Lima, OH 44452-9731

Milaeger's Gardens, 4838 Douglas Avenue, Racine, WI 53402

Necessary Trading Company, 1 Nature's Way, New Castle, VA 24127

Park Seed, Cokesbury Road, Greenwood, SC 29647-0001

Clyde Robin Seed Co., 25670 Nickel Place, Hayward, CA 94545

Roses of Yesterday and Today, 802 Brown's Valley Road, Watsonville, CA 95076

Seeds Blüm, Idaho City Stage, Boise, ID 83706

Seeds West, 1 Las Colonias Road, P.O. Box 2817, Taos, NM 87571

Shepherd's Garden Seeds, 6116 Highway 9, Felton, CA 95018

R. H. Shumway, Seedsmen, P.O. Box 1, Rockford, IL 61101

Smith & Hawken, 25 Corte Madera, Mill Valley, CA 94941

Thompson & Morgan, Inc., Box 1308, Jackson, NJ 08527

Van Bourgondien & Sons, Inc., Box A, Route 109, Babylon, NY 11702

Andre Viette Farm and Nursery, Route 1, Box 16, Fisherville, VA 22939

Wayside Gardens, Hodges, SC 29695

White Flower Farm, Litchfield, CT 06759

Gilbert H. Wild & Son, 1112 Joplin Street, Sarcoxie, MO 64862

INDEX

USDA HARDINESS ZONE MAP

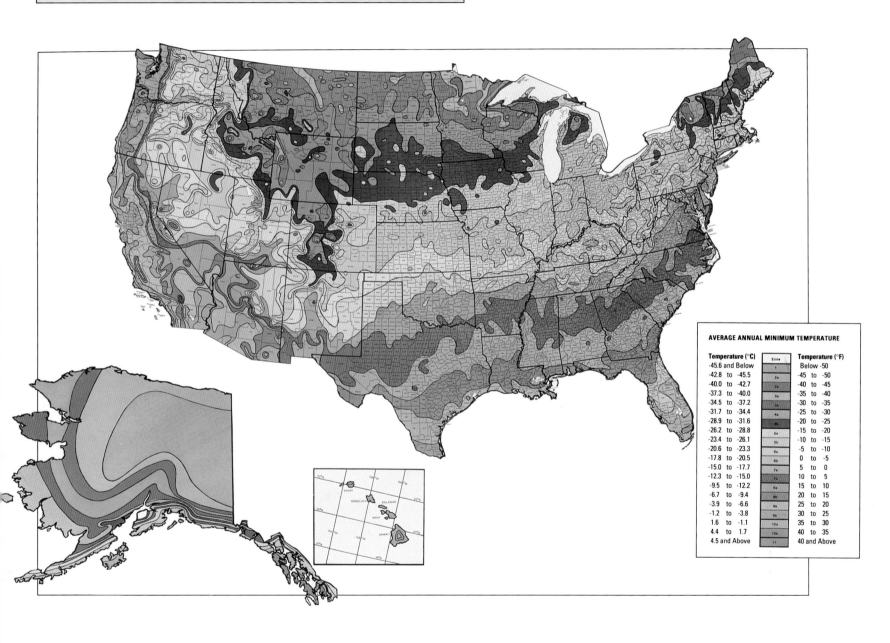

AVERAGE ANNUAL MINIMUM TEMPERATURE

Temperature (°C)	Zone	Temperature (°F)
-45.6 and Below	1	Below -50
-42.8 to -45.5	2a	-45 to -50
-40.0 to -42.7	2b	-40 to -45
-37.3 to -40.0	3a	-35 to -40
-34.5 to -37.2	3b	-30 to -35
-31.7 to -34.4	4a	-25 to -30
-28.9 to -31.6	4b	-20 to -25
-26.2 to -28.8	5a	-15 to -20
-23.4 to -26.1	5b	-10 to -15
-20.6 to -23.3	6a	-5 to -10
-17.8 to -20.5	6b	0 to -5
-15.0 to -17.7	7a	5 to 0
-12.3 to -15.0	7b	10 to 5
-9.5 to -12.2	8a	15 to 10
-6.7 to -9.4	8b	20 to 15
-3.9 to -6.6	9a	25 to 20
-1.2 to -3.8	9b	30 to 25
1.6 to -1.1	10a	35 to 30
4.4 to 1.7	10b	40 to 35
4.5 and Above	11	40 and Above